JN213258

Japan: Then and Now

英語で語る

日本事情 2020

江口裕之
CEL英語ソリューションズ Chief Education Officer

ダニエル・ドゥーマス
CEL英語ソリューションズ Chief Instructor

Eguchi Hiroyuki & Daniel Dumas

the japan times 出版

音声のご利用案内

本書の音声は、スマートフォン（アプリ）やパソコンを通じてMP3音声をダウンロードし、ご利用いただけます。

 ## スマートフォン

1. ジャパンタイムズ出版の音声アプリ「**OTO Navi**」をインストール

2. **OTO Navi** で本書を検索
3. **OTO Navi** で音声をダウンロードし、再生

   3秒早送り・早戻し、繰り返し再生などの便利機能つき。学習にお役立てください。

 ## パソコン

1. ブラウザからオーディオブックサービス「**audiobook.jp**」にアクセス

   https://audiobook.jp/exchange/japantimes

   ※初めてご利用の方は「会員登録」が必要です。

2. 本書のシリアルコード【**16698**】を入力
3. 「ライブラリ」にある音声をダウンロードし、iTunes などに取り込んで再生

   ※音声は zip ファイルを展開（解凍）してご利用ください。
   ※技術的な問題は audiobook.jp へお問い合わせください。

audiobook.jp

audiobook.jp FAQ（よくある質問・ヘルプ）

https://otobankhelp.zendesk.com/hc/ja

＊本書は、『英語で語る日本事情 2020　Japan: Then and Now』（CDつき）の音声ダウンロード版です。本文の内容や音声に変更はありません。

✳ ❀ ✳ はしがき

　このたび、2度の全面改訂を経て、『英語で語る日本事情2020』をお届けすることになりました。前回、全面改訂を行い、書名を『英語で語る日本事情』から『新・英語で語る日本事情』に改めたのが6年前の2011年でした。それ以降、時計の針が急に速度を上げたかのような感覚があります。

　この6年間の日本のキーワードは「防災」と「観光」であった気がします。『新・英語で語る日本事情』の初版が発行された2011年3月5日の6日後の3月11日、東日本大震災が起こりました。この未曽有の大災害は、日本人に自然と向き合う態度をあらためて考え直させ、人々の絆の大切さを再確認させる出来事となりました。

　その一方で、日本を訪れる観光客は激増し、世界的な日本旅行ブームが盛り上がる中、2013年には、東京が2020年のオリンピック・パラリンピック競技大会の開催地として選ばれました。拡大し続ける日本の国際観光業とともに、この国際大会に向けたインフラや関連法の整備などが急がれ、日本は、防災国家と観光国家の両立へ向けて大きく変化してきています。

　このような背景から、本書も内容を更新させていただく運びとなりました。改訂新版においては、2020年の東京大会を念頭に、巻末に「Tokyo: Japan's Heartbeat（東京：日本の中枢）」という新しい章を設けました。外国人観光客を英語で東京案内される方々に、お役に立てていただければと思います。

　思えば、私が日本文化を英語で説明することを自分のライフワークにしようという志を立てたのは、国家資格「通訳案内士」の合格証書を手にした1988年のことでした。

　20代の私は、アメリカのカントリー音楽の歌手・演奏家として大半を過ごしましたが、活動の舞台で特に多かったのが在日米軍キャンプでした。米国の軍人を相手にカントリー音楽を披露するとなれば、アメリカ文化の理解が欠かせず、そのため英語学習に没頭し、図らずも、英語通訳・翻訳家へと転身することになりました。

ミュージシャンや通訳・翻訳の仕事を通じて痛感したのは、「ネイティブは超えられない」ということでした。カントリー音楽にせよ英語にせよ、それらのネイティブとして生まれ育った人でなければ理解できないものがある、という考えが大きな壁となり、英語に対する探究心は低下し、職業として通訳・翻訳を続ける不安につながっていきました。通訳案内士という国家資格に出会ったのはそんなときです。

　通訳案内士試験には、日本の歴史・地理・一般常識という日本語の試験があります。理系出身の私にとって、最も欠けている分野と思われ、これらの試験をクリアできれば、何かが変わるのではと思ったのが受験動機でした。学習の甲斐あり、初めての受験で合格しましたが、大きな発見がありました。それは、私がカントリー音楽や英語に対して、ネイティブでなければ理解できないものがあると感じたのと同様、日本文化に対しても、この日本に生まれ育った、日本の文化を愛する日本人にしか伝えられないこと、あるいは、そのような日本人が伝えなければ意味のないことがある、ということでした。

　例えば、「みそ」は、どの辞書を見ても fermented soybean paste と書いてあります。しかし、「発酵した大豆の練り物」では、それが日本人にとってどのような食べ物か、日本文化においてどのような意義を持っているのかなどは伝わりません。それは、みそとともに生きてきた人にしかわかりませんし、そのような人が伝えなければ意味がないことです。

　私の人生後半のライフワークはここで決まりました。「自分が生まれ育った国や文化を、自分の体験・視点から、自分の言葉で説明すること」です。そこに、ネイティブを超える日本人の英語がある、と確信を持ちました。

以後、13年にわたって、予備校の英語講師を続けつつ、日本全国に足を運び、日本の文化を体験し、学び、またそれらを英語で記述していき、一部は雑誌などで紹介されました。ジャパンタイムズさんから、出版の話をいただいたのはそのころです。そして、このような私の思いを、同じ予備校で長年一緒に働いていたDaniel Dumas氏とつづり、2001年5月に『英語で語る日本事情』として出版しました。

　同じころ、東京・新宿にCEL英語ソリューションズという英語学校を立ち上げ、通訳案内士の育成に力を入れることになりましたが、本の出版からさらに輪が広がり、2009年から2013年の4年間は、日本文化を英語で説明することを学ぶ、NHK Eテレの語学番組「トラッドジャパン」の講師を担当させていただきました。同番組の制作と出演は、私の集大成ともいえる仕事となりました。
　一方で、書籍のほうは、最初の出版から改訂新版『新・英語で語る日本事情』まで、通算24回も版を重ねてきました。このように長年にわたりご愛読いただける書となったことに感慨を覚えるとともに、読者の皆様には感謝の気持ちで一杯です。
　今後も、私と同じように、日本文化を自分の言葉で発信したいと思われる方々に本書を読んでいただき、自分ならではの英語を発見していただければ、それに勝る幸せはございません。

　最後になりましたが、本書の全面改訂にあたりまして多大なご協力とご指導をいただいた、ジャパンタイムズ出版・教育事業担当の伊藤秀樹執行役員、英語出版編集部の西田由香さんに、この場を借りて、御礼申し上げます。

執筆者を代表して　江口裕之

Contents ◆ 目次

編集協力	松本靜子
英文校閲	ロゴポート
カバーデザイン	大森裕二
本文デザイン	(有) ディーイーピー
本文イラスト	名渡山彩子
DTP組版	朝日メディアインターナショナル (株)
ナレーション	Chris Koprowski、Edith Kayumi、水月優希
録音・編集	ELEC録音スタジオ
MP3音声収録時間	約3時間15分

◆ 本書の構成と使い方 ◆

　本書では、日本の「過去」と「現在」について、20の分野に分けて紹介しています。各章は、Introduction（概説）、Key Words（キーワード）、Related Key Words（関連キーワード）、Related Vocabulary（関連語彙）、Dialogue（対話）などで構成されています。また、巻末には、東京案内に特化した「Tokyo: Japan's Heartbeat（東京：日本の中枢）」というセクションを設けています。

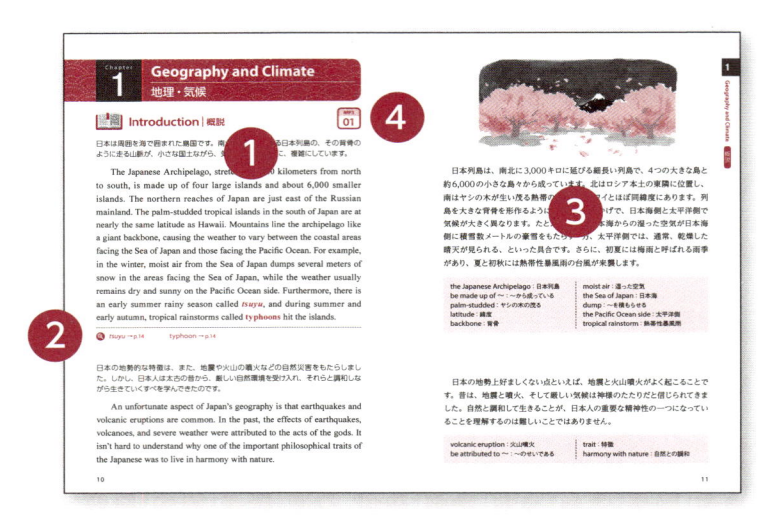

❶ Introduction（概説）
章全体についての解説です。文中に赤太字で表示している用語は、Key Words 欄で詳しく説明しています。

❷参照ページ
Key Words の説明が参照できるページを示しています。

❸和訳
英文の対訳になります。英文読解に必要な語注も掲載していますので、意味がわからない単語は確認するようにしましょう。

❹ MP3 音声
MP3形式の音声データをご用意しています。トラック番号のついた英文が収録されていますので、リスニングやスピーキングの練習にご活用ください。音声のご利用方法については2ページをご覧ください。

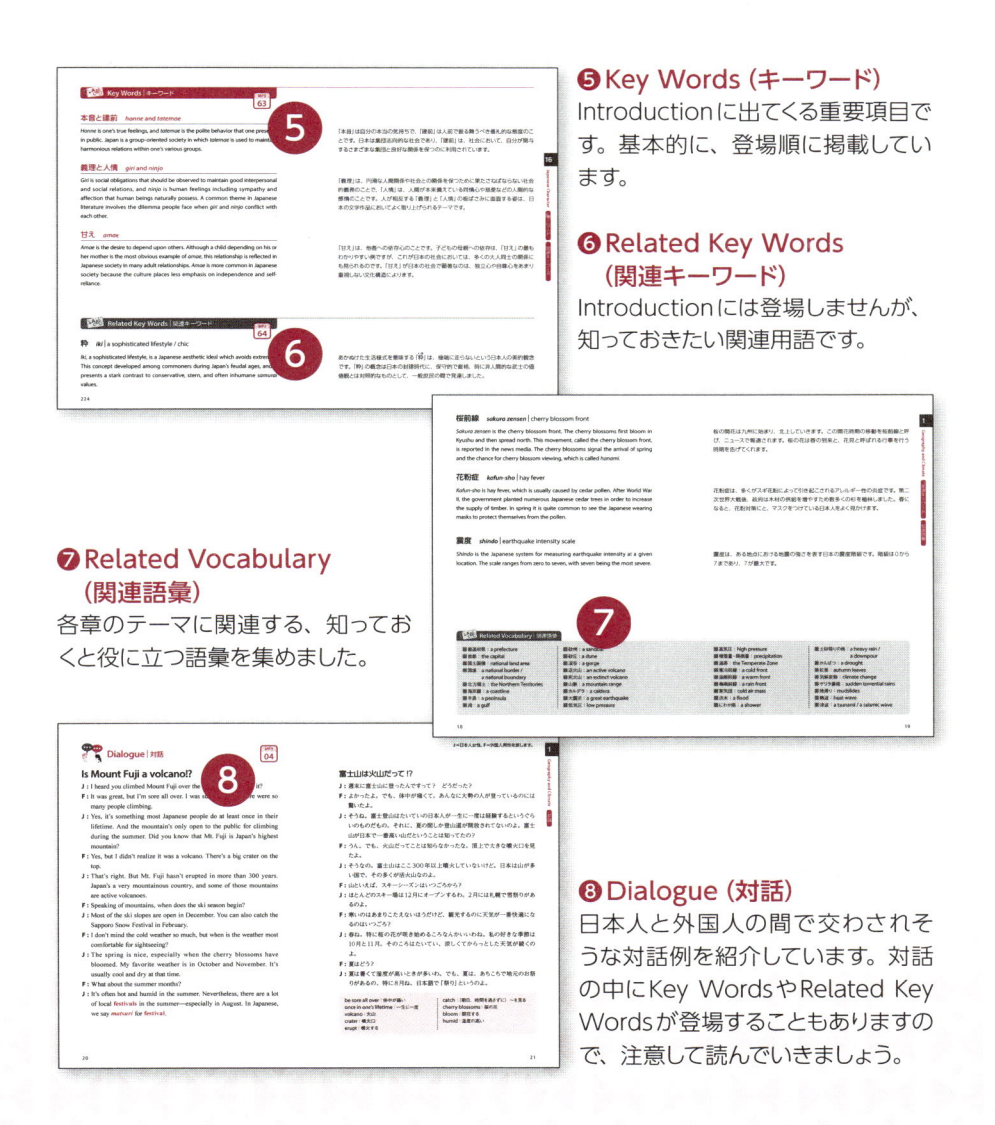

❺ Key Words（キーワード）
Introductionに出てくる重要項目です。基本的に、登場順に掲載しています。

❻ Related Key Words（関連キーワード）
Introductionには登場しませんが、知っておきたい関連用語です。

❼ Related Vocabulary（関連語彙）
各章のテーマに関連する、知っておくと役に立つ語彙を集めました。

❽ Dialogue（対話）
日本人と外国人の間で交わされそうな対話例を紹介しています。対話の中にKey WordsやRelated Key Wordsが登場することもありますので、注意して読んでいきましょう。

Tokyo: Japan's Heartbeat（東京：日本の中枢）
日本の首都・東京について、さまざまな切り口で紹介しています。英語で東京案内をする際にぜひ活用してください。

Geography and Climate
地理・気候

 Introduction | 概説

日本は周囲を海で囲まれた島国です。南北に細長く延びる日本列島の、その背骨の
ように走る山脈が、小さな国土ながら、気候と地勢を豊かに、複雑にしています。

The Japanese Archipelago, stretching 3,000 kilometers from north to south, is made up of four large islands and about 6,000 smaller islands. The northern reaches of Japan are just east of the Russian mainland. The palm-studded tropical islands in the south of Japan are at nearly the same latitude as Hawaii. Mountains line the archipelago like a giant backbone, causing the weather to vary between the coastal areas facing the Sea of Japan and those facing the Pacific Ocean. For example, in the winter, moist air from the Sea of Japan dumps several meters of snow in the areas facing the Sea of Japan, while the weather usually remains dry and sunny on the Pacific Ocean side. Furthermore, there is an early summer rainy season called *tsuyu*, and during summer and early autumn, tropical rainstorms called **typhoons** hit the islands.

🔍 *tsuyu* → p.14   typhoon → p.14

日本の地勢的な特徴は、また、地震や火山の噴火などの自然災害をもたらしまし
た。しかし、日本人は太古の昔から、厳しい自然環境を受け入れ、それらと調和しな
がら生きていくすべを学んできたのです。

An unfortunate aspect of Japan's geography is that earthquakes and volcanic eruptions are common. In the past, the effects of earthquakes, volcanoes, and severe weather were attributed to the acts of the gods. It isn't hard to understand why one of the important philosophical traits of the Japanese was to live in harmony with nature.

　日本列島は、南北に3,000キロに延びる細長い列島で、4つの大きな島と約6,000の小さな島々から成っています。北はロシア本土の東隣に位置し、南はヤシの木が生い茂る熱帯の島々で、ハワイとほぼ同緯度にあります。列島を大きな背骨を形作るように走る山脈のおかげで、日本海側と太平洋側で気候が大きく異なります。たとえば、冬、日本海からの湿った空気が日本海側に積雪数メートルの豪雪をもたらす一方、太平洋側では、通常、乾燥した晴天が見られる、といった具合です。さらに、初夏には梅雨と呼ばれる雨季があり、夏と初秋には熱帯性暴風雨の台風が来襲します。

the Japanese Archipelago：日本列島	moist air：湿った空気
be made up of 〜：〜から成っている	the Sea of Japan：日本海
palm-studded：ヤシの木の茂る	dump：〜を積もらせる
latitude：緯度	the Pacific Ocean side：太平洋側
backbone：背骨	tropical rainstorm：熱帯性暴風雨

　日本の地勢上好ましくない点といえば、地震と火山噴火がよく起こることです。昔は、地震と噴火、そして厳しい気候は神様のたたりだと信じられてきました。自然と調和して生きることが、日本人の重要な精神性の一つになっていることを理解するのは難しいことではありません。

volcanic eruption：火山噴火	trait：特徴
be attributed to 〜：〜のせいである	harmony with nature：自然との調和

日本の戦後の経済成長は、その一方でひどい環境破壊を引き起こしました。しかし、浄化力の強い日本の国土が、問題の克服に大きな役割を果たしました。日本は今、昔の日本人が実践していた「持続可能な社会」の再現方法を模索していますが、そのヒントが里山にあるかもしれません。

During Japan's rapid economic growth in the last half of the 20th century, severe environmental damage occurred. Fortunately, heavy precipitation, and short rivers that rapidly flow out into the ocean, have enhanced the land's capacity to cleanse itself and restore nature. Japan has overcome environmental problems to some extent because of the unique topographical conditions as well as government regulation. When looking at the Japanese way of life in olden times, we see a society that strived to live in harmony with nature, both spiritually and practically.

An interesting example is the Japanese *satoyama*. *Satoyama* is the semi-natural border areas managed by humans. They provide human beings with timber, firewood, and edible wild plants, while providing food and habitats for non-human life. Unfortunately, the number of *satoyama* areas has decreased during the past half century. The primary causes are modern lifestyles, depopulation, and land development. However, the environmental benefits of *satoyama* are receiving renewed attention. In fact, the Japanese government has been implementing measures to protect *satoyama* areas, for example, by designating them as cultural landscapes and natural parks. In the future, Japan may once again live in harmony with nature based on the sustainable concepts of *satoyama*.

---

 satoyama → p.14

　20世紀後半の日本の急速な経済発展は、ひどい環境破壊を引き起こしました。幸いにも、大量の降水と急流の短い河川が四方の海へと注いでいることで、土地の自浄が進み、自然環境の回復が促進されました。政府の規制だけでなく、こうした独特の地勢的条件のおかげもあって、日本はある程度まで環境問題を克服してきたのです。昔の日本人の生活様式を振り返ると、精神面でも実際の生活面でも、自然との調和を図りながら生きる社会が形成されていたことがわかります。

　その興味深い例に、日本の里山があります。里山は、人間が管理する、半自然的な境界地域です。人間は里山で、木材、薪、山菜などを得る一方、動物はそこで食料や生息環境を得ます。不幸にも、ここ半世紀の間に、里山地域の数は減少してきました。その主な理由は、生活様式の近代化、過疎化、土地の開発などです。しかし、里山が環境にもたらす恩恵が新たな注目を浴びてきています。事実、日本政府は、里山を文化的景観や自然公園に指定するなどして、里山を保護する政策を実施するようになってきています。将来的に日本は、里山における持続可能性という概念に基づいて、再び自然と調和して生きる国になるかもしれません。

precipitation：降水量
enhance：～を高める
cleanse：～を浄化する
to some extent：ある程度まで
topographical：地勢的な
olden：古い（文語）
strive to *do*：～しようと努める
the semi- ～：半～
timber：木材

edible：食用の
habitat：生息環境、住むための場所
depopulation：過疎化
implement：～を実施する
cultural landscape：文化的景観
sustainable：
　持続可能な（「環境を破壊しない、環境にやさしい」の意）

梅雨　*tsuyu* | rainy season

Tsuyu is the Japanese rainy season. A rain front settles over the middle to the western part of Japan. Usually this occurs from mid-June to mid-July.

台風　*taifu* | typhoon

Taifu are violent tropical rainstorms in the Pacific Ocean. Called typhoons in English, they are most likely to hit Japan during the July through September period.

里山　*satoyama*

Satoyama is the semi-natural border area where human beings and nature coexist for mutual benefit. Although modernization and rural depopulation have degraded the existence of the *satoyama* areas, organizations interested in environmental protection are promoting this traditional method of land management.

津波　**tsunami**

Tsunami is a seismic sea wave or series of waves that are generated by an earthquake or undersea volcanic eruption.

梅雨は日本の雨季にあたります。通常6月中旬から7月中旬にかけて、梅雨前線（ばいう）が日本の中部から西部に停滞するのです。

台風は太平洋上の熱帯性暴風雨のことです。英語ではタイフーンと呼ばれ、7月から9月にかけて、日本に上陸する可能性が高くなります。

里山は、人間と自然が相互的な恩恵を得るために共存するための、半自然的な境界地域です。近代化と田舎の過疎化によって、里山地域の状態が悪化してきましたが、環境保護に関心のある組織は、里山に見られる伝統的な土地運用方法を推進しています。

津波は、地震や海底火山の噴火によって生じる波です。

東日本大震災

Higashi-Nihon daishinsai | Great East Japan Earthquake

Higashi-Nihon daishinsai refers to the disasters caused by the Great East Japan Earthquake, which struck northern Honshu on March 11, 2011. Among the 15,000 victims, more than 90% were killed by the tsunami following the earthquake. In addition, the loss of electrical power caused three nuclear reactors to melt down in Fukushima Prefecture. Approximately 150,000 people were evacuated. The effort to safely decommission the reactors is expected to be a long and expensive process.

阪神淡路大震災

Hanshin-Awaji daishinsai | Great Hanshin-Awaji Earthquake

Hanshin-Awaji daishinsai is the Great Hanshin-Awaji Earthquake, which struck the city of Kobe and surrounding areas on January 17, 1995. With a magnitude of 7.2, it killed more than 6,000 people. This incident revealed Japan's insufficient emergency control capability and taught the government and the nation the importance of preparation for possible disasters in an earthquake-prone country.

関東大震災

Kanto daishinsai | Great Kanto Earthquake

Kanto daishinsai is the Great Kanto Earthquake, which struck the Kanto area, including the city of Tokyo, on September 1, 1923. More than 140 thousand people were reportedly killed in the quake and the fires that followed. The quake devastated the Kanto area's infrastructure and the nation's entire economic system.

東日本大震災は、2011年3月11日に本州北部を襲った大地震による災害です。1万5,000人以上の犠牲者のうち、9割以上が地震の後に起こった津波によって亡くなりました。加えて、福島県では、電源喪失により3基の原子炉がメルトダウンを起こし、約15万人が避難する結果となりました。これらの原子炉の廃炉作業は、長期にわたり、多額の費用がかかると推測されています。

阪神淡路大震災は、1995年1月17日に神戸とその周辺地域を襲った大地震による災害です。マグニチュード7.2を記録し、6,000人以上の死者を出しました。この災害によって、日本の危機管理能力が不十分なことが明らかになり、政府も国民も、地震が多い日本における防災対策の重要性を認識させられました。

関東大震災は、1923年9月1日に、東京を含む関東一円を襲った大地震による災害です。地震と直後の火災で、14万人を上回る死者が出たといわれています。この地震で、関東地域の社会基盤が崩壊し、当時の日本経済全体が機能しなくなりました。

桜前線　*sakura zensen* | cherry blossom front

Sakura zensen is the cherry blossom front. The cherry blossoms first bloom in Kyushu and then spread north. This movement, called the cherry blossom front, is reported in the news media. The cherry blossoms signal the arrival of spring and the chance for cherry blossom viewing, which is called *hanami*.

花粉症　*kafun-sho* | hay fever

Kafun-sho is hay fever, which is usually caused by cedar pollen. After World War II, the government planted numerous Japanese cedar trees in order to increase the supply of timber. In spring it is quite common to see the Japanese wearing masks to protect themselves from the pollen.

震度　*shindo* | earthquake intensity scale

Shindo is the Japanese system for measuring earthquake intensity at a given location. The scale ranges from zero to seven, with seven being the most severe.

Related Vocabulary | 関連語彙

- 都道府県：a prefecture
- 首都：the capital
- 国土面積：national land area
- 国境：a national border / a national boundary
- 北方領土：the Northern Territories
- 海岸線：a coastline
- 半島：a peninsula
- 湾：a gulf
- 砂州：a sandbar
- 砂丘：a dune
- 渓谷：a gorge
- 活火山：an active volcano
- 死火山：an extinct volcano
- 山脈：a mountain range
- カルデラ：a caldera
- 大震災：a great earthquake
- 低気圧：low pressure

桜の開花は九州に始まり、北上していきます。この開花時期の移動を桜前線と呼び、ニュースで報道されます。桜の花は春の到来と、花見と呼ばれる行事を行う時期を告げてくれます。

花粉症は、多くがスギ花粉によって引き起こされるアレルギー性の炎症です。第二次世界大戦後、政府は木材の供給を増やすため数多くの杉を植林しました。春になると、花粉対策にと、マスクをつけている日本人をよく見かけます。

震度は、ある地点における地震の強さを表す日本の震度階級です。階級は０から７まであり、７が最大です。

■高気圧：high pressure
■積雪量・降雨量：precipitation
■温帯：the Temperate Zone
■寒冷前線：a cold front
■温暖前線：a warm front
■梅雨前線：a rain front
■寒気団：cold air mass
■洪水：a flood
■にわか雨：a shower

■土砂降りの雨：a heavy rain /
　　　　　a downpour
■かんばつ：a drought
■紅葉：autumn leaves
■気候変動：climate change
■ゲリラ豪雨：sudden torrential rains
■地滑り：mudslides
■熱波：heat wave
■津波：a tsunami / a seismic wave

 **Dialogue** | 対話

Is Mount Fuji a volcano!?

J : I heard you climbed Mount Fuji over the weekend. How was it?

F : It was great, but I'm sore all over. I was surprised that there were so many people climbing.

J : Yes, it's something most Japanese people do at least once in their lifetime. And the mountain's only open to the public for climbing during the summer. Did you know that Mt. Fuji is Japan's highest mountain?

F : Yes, but I didn't realize it was a volcano. There's a big crater on the top.

J : That's right. But Mt. Fuji hasn't erupted in more than 300 years. Japan's a very mountainous country, and some of those mountains are active volcanoes.

F : Speaking of mountains, when does the ski season begin?

J : Most of the ski slopes are open in December. You can also catch the Sapporo Snow Festival in February.

F : I don't mind the cold weather so much, but when is the weather most comfortable for sightseeing?

J : The spring is nice, especially when the cherry blossoms have bloomed. My favorite weather is in October and November. It's usually cool and dry at that time.

F : What about the summer months?

J : It's often hot and humid in the summer. Nevertheless, there are a lot of local **festivals** in the summer—especially in August. In Japanese, we say *matsuri* for **festival**.

富士山は火山だって!?

J：週末に富士山に登ったんですって？　どうだった？

F：よかったよ。でも、体中が痛くて。あんなに大勢の人が登っているのには驚いたよ。

J：そうね。富士登山はたいていの日本人が一生に一度は経験するというぐらいのものだもの。それに、夏の間しか登山道が開放されてないのよ。富士山が日本で一番高い山だということは知ってたの？

F：うん。でも、火山だってことは知らなかったな。頂上で大きな噴火口を見たよ。

J：そうなの。富士山はここ300年以上噴火していないけど。日本は山が多い国で、その多くが活火山なのよ。

F：山といえば、スキーシーズンはいつごろから？

J：ほとんどのスキー場は12月にオープンするわ。2月には札幌で雪祭りがあるのよ。

F：寒いのはあまりこたえないほうだけど、観光するのに天気が一番快適になるのはいつごろ？

J：春ね。特に桜の花が咲き始めるころなんかいいわね。私の好きな季節は10月と11月。そのころはたいてい、涼しくてからっとした天気が続くのよ。

F：夏はどう？

J：夏は暑くて湿度が高いときが多いわ。でも、夏は、あちこちで地元のお祭りがあるの、特に8月ね。日本語で「祭り」というのよ。

be sore all over：体中が痛い	catch：（期日、時間を逃さずに）〜を見る
once in *one's* lifetime：一生に一度	cherry blossoms：桜の花
volcano：火山	bloom：開花する
crater：噴火口	humid：湿度の高い
erupt：噴火する	

History 1
歴史 1

 **Introduction** | 概説

MP3
05

一国の歴史を簡略に語り尽くすことは、たやすいことではありません。日本史の黎明<small>れいめい</small>は4世紀ごろ。まず、各地の豪族を統一し、中央集権国家を築いていった大和朝廷の紹介から始めるのが妥当でしょう。

It is estimated that various warring countries in Japan were united around the 4th century. At that time, the ancestors of the current Imperial Family established a central government called *Yamato Chotei*. Nevertheless, the periods during which the emperors, called **tenno** in Japanese, wielded political power were brief. Believed to be divine, the emperors transcended worldly politics. Most of the time, the real political powers were delegated by the emperor to the strongest political leader of the time.

🔍 *tenno* → p.26

平安遷都から鎌倉、そして戦国時代を経て、権力の中心が現在の東京、江戸へと移っていくまでを、武士の台頭を中心に説明します。

The Heian Period (794–1192) saw the Japanese capital move from **Nara** to **Kyoto**, which used to be called *Heian-Kyo*. During this period the Imperial Court ruled Japan. It was also a time when much of the culture took on a distinctive Japanese flavor. Paintings, literature, and a variety of Buddhist art were created during this time. Toward the end of the Heian Period, the warriors, or **samurai**, became increasingly powerful and eventually took control of the country.

　国内の多くの豪族が統一されたのは、4世紀ごろだと考えられています。その当時、現在の天皇家の祖先が、大和朝廷と呼ばれる中央政府を確立しました。しかしながら、天皇が政治的権力を実際に握ったのはわずかな期間でした。天皇は神格化され、世俗的な政治を超越した存在だったのです。たいてい、実権は、天皇から与えられる形で、その時代の最も強力な政治的指導者が握ったのです。

ancestor：祖先	worldly：世俗的な
the Imperial Family：皇室	be delegated by A to B：
wield political power：権力を振るう	AによってBに委任される

　平安時代（794 〜 1192）には、都が奈良から、かつて平安京と呼ばれた京都に移されましたが、この間は朝廷が日本を支配し、また、多くの文化が日本独特の特徴を備えるようになった時期でもありました。絵画、文学作品、さまざまな仏教美術がこの時期につくり出されました。平安時代も終わりに近づくにつれ、侍と呼ばれる武人が次第に力を蓄えていき、ついには全国を統治する権力を手中にすることになりました。

Beginning with the Kamakura Period (1192–1333) and ending with the **Edo Period** (1603–1867), Japan was primarily ruled by military governments, or *bakufu*, each with a *shogun* at its head. The 14th, 15th, and 16th centuries were characterized by political instability, anarchy, and civil war. In the mid-16th century, Europeans introduced firearms and Christianity to Japan. In the late 16th century, the country gradually reunited under the leadership of Oda Nobunaga and Toyotomi Hideyoshi.

Nara → p.48   Kyoto → p.48   *samurai* → p.26
Edo Period → p.26   *bakufu* → p.26   *shogun* → p.28

近代以前の日本にはどのような文化が花開いたのでしょうか。中世には禅の影響を受けた武家文化が栄え、さらに江戸時代になると、鎖国政策によって、独特な発展を遂げました。

During the period of military rule, culture increasingly centered around the *samurai*. *Zen* and *noh* flourished. **Flower arrangement** and the **tea ceremony** developed. Great **temples**, **shrines**, and castles, called *shiro*, were built.

The **Edo Period** is the time during which the Tokugawa Shogunate ruled from the city of Edo, which was renamed **Tokyo** in 1868. This period was characterized by a national seclusion policy called *sakoku*. Japanese culture and character evolved with little influence from outside the country. It was during this period that *kabuki*, *ukiyo-e*, and *sumo* developed.

noh → p.186   flower arrangement → p.172
tea ceremony → p.172   temples → p.144   shrines → p.144
shiro → p.28   Tokyo → p.48   *sakoku* → p.28
kabuki → p.186   *ukiyo-e* → p.172   *sumo* → p.160

　鎌倉時代（1192 ～ 1333）から江戸時代（1603 ～ 1867）は、日本は主に、将軍が率いる幕府と呼ばれる軍事政権が支配した時代でした。14、15、16世紀は、政治が安定せず、下剋上の内乱に彩られた時代です。16世紀半ばには、ヨーロッパから鉄砲とキリスト教がもたらされました。16世紀後半には、織田信長と豊臣秀吉によって、国は再び統一へと向かいました。

distinctive：独特の	anarchy：無秩序
take control of ～：～の主導権を握る	civil war：内戦、内乱
instability：不安定	firearms：火器

　武士が支配する時代には、文化は武家社会を中心に栄えました。禅と能が繁栄し、生け花や茶の湯も発展しました。大きな寺社や、城郭も建てられました。

　江戸時代は、江戸（1868年に東京と改称）を本拠地とした徳川幕府の治世です。この時代は、鎖国と呼ばれる孤立政策によって特徴づけられます。日本独特の文化が外国の影響をほとんど受けずに発展したのです。歌舞伎や浮世絵、相撲が盛んになったのもこの時代でした。

flourish：栄える	seclusion：隔絶
develop：発展する	evolve：進化する

天皇　*tenno* | Emperor of Japan

Tenno is the Japanese term for emperor. For most of Japan's history, the emperor's power has only been symbolic. The emperor was also considered the leader of *Shinto*—Japan's indigenous religion. The postwar Constitution defines the role of the emperor as a symbol of Japan.

侍　*samurai* | warriors

Samurai refers to premodern Japanese warriors. *Samurai* were originally servicemen working for the court nobles, who later took on security roles. In the 12th century, the *samurai* class came to power and formed its own military government called *bakufu*.

江戸時代　*Edo Jidai* | Edo Period

Edo Jidai, the Edo Period, is the time during which the Edo *Bakufu* ruled. The period is probably the most familiar to foreigners and Japanese alike as the time representing traditional Japan. The period is often described in TV programs as "*jidaigeki*."

幕府　*bakufu* | shogunate

Bakufu, or shogunate, refers to the military government that existed in Japan. Although the functions and structure differed according to the time in history, the *bakufu* basically controlled the feudal lords nationwide by assigning them fiefs and requiring loyalty to the *shogun* in return.

天皇は皇帝を意味する日本語。日本の歴史を通じて、天皇の権力は象徴的なものである場合がほとんどでした。天皇はまた、日本固有の宗教である神道の最高権威とも考えられていました。戦後の日本国憲法では、天皇の役割を日本国の象徴と規定しています。

侍とは、近代以前の日本の武人のことをいいます。もともと貴族に仕える役人でしたが、のちに警護する役回りに変化したものです。12世紀になると侍（武士）階級が権力を握り、幕府と呼ばれる軍事政権を樹立するに至りました。

江戸時代は江戸幕府の治世を指します。伝統的な日本を代表する時代として、おそらく日本人にも外国人にも最もよく知られている時代です。テレビ番組の「時代劇」によく登場するのもこの時代です。

幕府とは、日本に存在した軍事政権のことをいいます。その機能と機構は時代によって異なりますが、基本的には、領地を与え、見返りに将軍への忠誠を求めることで、全国の大名（封建領主）を支配していました。

将軍　*shogun*

Shogun was a position granted by the emperor to the leader of the *samurai*, although in later years the position became hereditary. The position allowed the *shogun* to establish a military government called *bakufu* to govern the nation. In the Edo Period, the *shogun* was the de facto leader of the country. The last *shogun* resigned in 1867, and the *samurai* class itself was abolished soon after the Meiji Restoration started in 1868.

城　*shiro* | Japanese castle

Shiro are the Japanese castles originally built before the 18th century by feudal lords. They are characterized by multi-layered tiled roofs, stone walls, moats, and a donjon at the top. Some castles, such as Osaka Castle, are replicas.

鎖国　*sakoku*

Sakoku was the national isolation policy of the Edo Period. The aim of the policy was to expel Christianity from Japan and put foreign trade under the dominance of the Edo *Bakufu*, or Tokugawa military government. Though Japan was late to modernize due to the policy, it allowed a distinctive Japanese culture to develop.

 **Related Key Words** | 関連キーワード

MP3 07

武士道　*bushido*

Bushido is the ethical code of the *samurai* warriors. It emphasized not only martial spirit and weaponry skills, but also loyalty, honor, and courage.

切腹　*seppuku (hara-kiri)*

Seppuku is ritual suicide by self-disembowelment. It was practiced mostly in the Edo Period as a means of punishing wrongdoers among *samurai* classes without tarnishing their honor and self-respect.

将軍は、武士の指導者に天皇が与える地位ですが、のちには世襲的なものとなりました。この地位によって将軍は、幕府と呼ばれる軍事政権を置くことができたのです。江戸時代には、将軍が事実上の日本の統治者でした。最後の将軍は1867年にその地位を降り、武士階級も1868年に始まった明治維新のすぐ後に廃止されました。

城は18世紀より前に各地の封建領主によって建てられた日本の城郭。何層にもわたる瓦屋根と、石塀、掘割と天守閣を備えているのが特徴です。大坂城など、再建されたものもあります。

江戸時代に取られた対外孤立政策。キリスト教の追放と、徳川家による軍事政府であった江戸幕府が、対外貿易を独占することを目的としていました。これによって日本の近代化が遅れることになりましたが、日本固有の文化の繁栄をもたらすことにもなりました。

武士道は、侍が持つ倫理規定を意味します。武士道は、武道の精神や武術の技能だけでなく、忠誠心、面目、勇敢さなども重視しています。

切腹（腹切り）は、腹部を自ら切開する儀式的な要素を持った自殺です。切腹は、主に江戸時代に、武士階級の者が犯した犯罪に対して、面目や自尊心を汚すことなく処罰するための手段として行われていました。

 # Dialogue｜対話

MP3
08

The way of the warrior

J : How was your trip to **Kyoto** and **Nara**?

F : It was fantastic. I especially enjoyed **Nara**. The giant statue of Buddha at Todaiji Temple was incredible. I also went to Horyuji Temple. The guide told us that it was the world's oldest wooden building.

J : That's true. It was built at the end of the 7th century.

F : One day when we were in **Kyoto**, we saw some actors dressed up like *maiko* and *samurai*. I'd like to learn more about the *samurai*.

J : Well, the *samurai* were at the top of the social hierarchy, which included farmers, craftsmen, and merchants. There were periods of civil war in Japan, but during the **Edo Period**, Japan was mostly at peace. If you see a movie or drama about *samurai*, you might think that they were always fighting, but it's a bit of an exaggeration. You might be surprised, but many *samurai* devoted themselves to intellectual or cultural pursuits. There were quite a few notable *samurai* painters, for example.

F : You're right. I can't imagine *samurai* warriors painting. By the way, what is *bushido*?

J : *Bushido* translates as "the way of the warrior." It's basically the ethical code of the *samurai*. This included loyalty, self-discipline, honor, and courage. Of course it also refers to military skills.

F : Why did they do *hara-kiri*?

J : *Seppuku* was performed after defeat in battle. It was considered a more honorable way of dying than execution. Also, *seppuku* was a punishment for *samurai* who committed serious crimes.

F : It sounds painful. Let's change the subject.

武士道とは

J：京都、奈良への旅はどうだった？

F：実に良かったよ。特に奈良が楽しかった。東大寺の大仏は信じられないくらいすごかったよ。法隆寺にも行ったよ。ガイドの人が世界最古の木造建築だと言ってたな。

J：そのとおりよ。法隆寺は7世紀末に建立されたの。

F：京都に行ったときに、舞妓さんや侍のような格好をした役者を見かけたんだ。侍についてもう少し教えてくれないかな。

J：そうね。侍は、農民、職人、商人を含む社会階級の最上級に位置していたの。日本には内乱の時期があったけど、江戸時代になって平和な時代がやってきた。テレビや映画の時代劇を観ると、侍がいつも戦っていたみたいに思えるけど、それは誇張ね。驚くかもしれないけど、侍の多くは知的なことや文化活動に専念していたのよ。たとえば、有名な侍の画家もけっこういたわ。

F：なるほど、侍が絵に打ち込むなんて、なんだかミスマッチな感じだね。で、武士道ってどんなものなの？

J：武士道は、「武士のあるべき道」ということ。侍が持つべき一種の倫理規範のようなものね。つまり忠誠心、自己鍛錬、名誉、勇気といったものよ。もちろん戦いの技術も入るけど。

F：彼らはどうして腹切りをしたんだろう。

J：切腹は戦に負けた後にしたのよ。処刑されるより名誉ある死に方だと考えられていたのね。また別に、重罪を犯した侍の処罰の方法でもあったんだけど。

F：痛そうだな。話題を変えようよ。

incredible：信じられない、すごい
hierarchy：階級、階層
devote *oneself* to ～：～に専念する
pursuit：追求
ethical code：倫理規範

loyalty：忠誠心
self-discipline：自己鍛錬
refer to ～：～を指す
execution：処刑

 **Introduction** | 概説

MP3
09

日本の近代は、19世紀半ば、浦賀沖に突如現れた米国の「黒船」艦隊、その圧力の前に、幕府が開国を余儀なくされたことに端を発します。そして明治維新。日本は近代国家に向けて一気に走り出します。

In the middle of the 19th century, Japan was increasingly pressured by foreign countries to open the country to trade. In 1853, U.S. Admiral Matthew Perry and his fleet of "black ships" visited Japan. The next year, a treaty of amity was signed, effectively ending Japan's isolation. In 1868, a new, modern government was formed with the Emperor Meiji at its head. This is called the **Meiji Restoration**.

 Meiji Restoration → p.36

明治政府の急激な近代化政策、さらに日清戦争・日露戦争を経て日本は軍事強国へと変貌していきます。しかし、それも太平洋戦争での敗戦によって水泡に帰し、日本の戦後はマイナスからのスタートとなりました。そして連合国の占領下時代を経て、今度は経済の分野で見事に世界第2位の力を持つまでになりました。

During the Meiji Period (1868–1912), Japan implemented a policy of rapid modernization—mostly with the intent of protecting itself from the more powerful Western countries. The transformation was so dramatic that by the end of the Meiji Period, Japan had defeated its two largest neighbors in war. Both the **Sino-Japanese War** (1894–1895) and the **Russo-Japanese War** (1904–1905) ended with Japanese victories. These military accomplishments boosted national pride and significantly increased the political power of the military. A second war with China began in 1937 and escalated into the **Pacific War** when

　19世紀も半ばになると、交易のために開国を求める諸外国の圧力がますます強くなりました。1853年には米国のペリー提督率いる「黒船」艦隊が来訪しました。翌年、和親条約が結ばれ、日本の鎖国政策に事実上、終止符が打たれました。1868年には、明治天皇を元首に戴いて新しい近代的な政府が成立しました。これが明治維新です。

pressure：〜に圧力をかける　　　　　fleet：艦隊

　明治時代（1868 〜 1912）に日本は急速な近代化政策を推し進めましたが、そのねらいは主に、西洋列強から日本を守ることにありました。近代化の勢いはすさまじく、明治末期になると、日本は近隣の2大国を戦争で破りました。日清戦争（1894 〜 1895）と日露戦争（1904 〜 1905）は、いずれも日本の勝利に終わったのです。これらの軍事的成功によって日本国民の自尊心は高揚し、軍部の政治発言力は強大になっていきました。1937年に勃発した、2度目の中国との戦争は、1941年の真珠湾攻撃とともに太平洋戦争へと拡大していきました。戦争は、1945年に広島と長崎に原子爆弾が落とされた後、壊滅状態の日本が無条件降伏をのみ、終結しました。

Japan bombed Pearl Harbor in 1941. The war ended in 1945 after **atomic bombs** were detonated over Hiroshima and Nagasaki, resulting in a devastated Japan offering an unconditional surrender.

The initial postwar period saw Japan occupied by the United States and its allies. Numerous reforms were implemented, most of which had the intent of making Japan a democratic nation. In 1952, Japan regained its autonomy, and by 1968 it was the world's second largest economy.

🔍 Sino-Japanese War → p.36   Russo-Japanese War → p.36
   Pacific War → p.36   atomic bomb → p.38

2011年3月11日に日本を襲った東日本大震災は、地震、津波、原子炉のメルトダウンという三重の災害を引き起こしました。政府は、将来的な地震災害について、さまざまな対策を講じていますが、自然の力はなかなか予測できません。

Beginning on March 11, 2011, Japan suffered a triple disaster. A powerful earthquake measuring 9.0 on the Richter scale struck off the Pacific coast of the Tohoku region. It was followed by a massive **tsunami** that destroyed many coastal communities. At the Fukushima Daiichi Nuclear Power Station the overflowing water caused a loss of power. Eventually, three of the reactors suffered meltdowns and spread radiation into the surrounding areas.

Over 15,000 people lost their lives and hundreds of thousands of people were displaced. It is expected to take many years and many trillions of yen to properly shut down the damaged nuclear power plant.

Earthquakes of a similar scale are rare, but have occurred in the past. The country has worked hard to understand the science of earthquakes and make all possible preparations. Nevertheless, the power of nature is unpredictable.

🔍 tsunami → p.14

戦後まもなくは、日本は米国と連合軍の占領下にありました。数多くの改革が実施されましたが、その多くは日本を民主主義国家へと変革することにねらいがありました。1952年に、日本は独立を果たし、1968年までには世界第2位の経済大国となっていました。

implement：〜を実施する
the intent of 〜：〜を意図すること
transformation：変遷
military accomplishment：戦果
detonate：（爆弾）を爆発させる

devastated：荒廃した
unconditional surrender：無条件降伏
occupy：〜を占領する
autonomy：独立

　2011年3月11日を初めに3つの災害が日本を襲いました。まずは、マグニチュード9.0という大地震が東北地方の太平洋沖に起こったのです。続いて、巨大な津波が襲い、沿岸地域の多くが破壊されました。福島第一原子力発電所は、押し寄せる海水に飲み込まれ、電源を喪失しました。最終的に、3つの原子炉がメルトダウンを引き起こし、周辺地域に放射能を拡散させました。

　1万5,000人以上が亡くなり、何十万という人たちが避難を余儀なくされました。破損した原子力発電所を確実に廃炉にするには、この先、長い年月と、何十兆円もの費用がかかると予期されています。

　同じ規模の地震が起こることはめったにありませんが、過去には実際に起こっています。日本は地震に関する科学を理解し、可能な限りの策を講じることに力を尽くしています。それでも、自然の力は予測できないのが現状です。

the Richter scale：リヒタースケール
⇒地震の規模を示すマグニチュードのこと。
　英語圏では考案者の名にちなんだthe
　Richter scaleの名称が一般的。

massive：巨大な
displace：（人を）追い出す
unpredictable：予測できない

明治維新　*Meiji Ishin* | Meiji Restoration

Meiji Ishin, or the Meiji Restoration, refers to the 1868 political change that ended the *bakufu* system and the period of rapid modernization that immediately followed. The period saw the establishment of a new government, which later developed into a constitutional monarchy with the Emperor Meiji at its head.

日清戦争　*Nisshin-senso* | Sino-Japanese War

Nisshin-senso refers to the Sino-Japanese War. In this war the Qing Dynasty of China was defeated by Japan. The war was fought over the control of the Korean Peninsula. The resulting peace accord, called the Shimonoseki Treaty, gave Japan control over some Korean and Chinese territories.

日露戦争　*Nichiro-senso* | Russo-Japanese War

Nichiro-senso refers to the Russo-Japanese War. This war between Russia and Japan was a result of friction caused by the two countries' desire to control Korea and Manchuria. Japan's victory marked the first time in modern history that an Asian power had defeated a European power.

太平洋戦争　*Taiheiyo-senso* | Pacific War

Taiheiyo-senso is the Pacific War. Japan's occupation of parts of China caused tension between Japan and some Western countries, including the United States. In 1941, Japan attacked Pearl Harbor, Hawaii, and British Malay, bringing Japan and the United States into the conflict known as World War II. Japan offered an unconditional surrender after atomic bombs were dropped on the cities of Hiroshima and Nagasaki in 1945.

明治維新は、1868年の幕府制度を終結させた変革、およびその直後の急速な近代化の時期をいいます。この時期に新政府が発足し、のちに明治天皇を元首とする立憲君主制が成立しました。

日清戦争は清国と日本の間で起きた戦争で、清国が日本に敗れました。この戦争は朝鮮半島の支配権をめぐって争われました。下関条約と呼ばれる講和条約の締結によって、日本は中国と朝鮮半島の一部を支配することになりました。

日露戦争はロシアと日本の間に勃発した戦争です。この戦争は朝鮮および満州支配をめぐる2国間の軋轢（あつれき）から起こりました。この戦争における日本の勝利は、近代では、アジアの国がヨーロッパの国に勝った最初の例となりました。

日本が中国の一部を占領していたことから、日本と、米国をはじめとする西洋諸国との間の緊張が高まりました。1941年に日本はハワイの真珠湾と英国領のマレーを攻撃し、日本と米国は第二次世界大戦に参戦することになりました。1945年に広島と長崎に原子爆弾が投下された後、日本は無条件降伏を申し出ました。

原爆　*genbaku*｜atomic bomb

Genbaku is an atomic bomb. On August 6, 1945 the first atomic bomb to be used in warfare was detonated over Hiroshima. Another bomb was dropped on Nagasaki three days later. More than 200 thousand people were killed in the attacks. Some survivors are still suffering from the after-effects of radiation poisoning.

 **Related Key Words**｜関連キーワード

 MP3 11

日の丸　*Hinomaru*

Hinomaru is Japan's national flag. It has a large red circle, which represents the rising sun, and a white background.

君が代　*Kimigayo*

Kimigayo is Japan's national anthem. The theme is to wish for the everlasting rule of the emperor.

Related Vocabulary｜関連語彙

- ■元号：an era name
- ■古墳：a burial mound
- ■埴輪：a clay doll (buried with the dead)
- ■銅鏡：a copper mirror
- ■記紀神話：mythology
- ■儒教：Confucianism
- ■仏教：Buddhism
- ■皇位につく：ascend to the throne
- ■大名：a *daimyo* / a feudal lord
- ■封建制：the feudal system
- ■（大名の）領地：a fief
- ■戦国大名：a warlord
- ■近代化：modernization

1945年8月6日に、戦争史上初の原子爆弾が広島上空で炸裂しました。その3日後に、もう一つの原子爆弾が長崎に投下されました。これらの攻撃により20万人以上の人が犠牲となりました。今でも放射性物質による後遺症に苦しんでいる生存者がいます。

日の丸は日本の国旗です。白地に、日が昇る姿を表す、大きな赤い円が描いてあります。

君が代は日本の国歌です。歌詞の主旨は、天皇の治世が永遠に続くことを願ったものです。

■産業革命：the industrial revolution
■世界大恐慌：the Great Depression
■第一次世界大戦：World War I / the first World War
■第二次世界大戦：World War II / the second World War
■宣戦布告：a declaration of war

■（広島・長崎の）被爆者：an A-bomb victim
■占領軍：occupational forces
■独立：independence
■高度経済成長：rapid economic growth
■経済復興：economic recovery

 **Dialogue** | 对话

How long has Japan had an emperor?

F : Have you ever seen the **Emperor**?

J : Only on TV. But there are two opportunities a year for anyone to see the **Emperor**—on January 2 and on the **Emperor's birthday**. On those days the grounds of the Imperial Palace are opened to the public and the entire Imperial Family greets the visitors from their balcony.

F : Oh, really? That sounds interesting. I don't hear much about the Japanese Imperial Family in the news. Why is that?

J : Well, that's a good question, and I'm not sure I know the answer completely. At one time the **emperor** was considered divine, but after the war the new **Constitution** stipulated that the **emperor** is a symbol of the state. The Imperial Family performs many official functions, but otherwise they keep a low profile.

F : How long has Japan had an **emperor**?

J : Oh, more than 1,500 years. At one time they ruled the country, but eventually the *samurai* became very powerful and a *shogun* was appointed. Somehow the two managed to coexist for hundreds of years. In fact, before Japan modernized, the **emperor** lived in **Kyoto**, while the *shogun* ruled the country from Edo.

F : That was convenient. But I thought the **Emperor** lived here in **Tokyo**?

J : Yes, the Imperial Family lives in **Tokyo** now. In 1867, the *shogun*'s power was transferred to the **emperor**. At that time the Emperor Meiji was only sixteen years old. The properties of the *shogun* were transferred to the Imperial Family and the Emperor Meiji moved to **Tokyo**.

日本にはいつごろから天皇がいるの？

F： 天皇陛下にお会いしたことはある？

J： テレビでならね。でも、誰でも天皇陛下にお会いできる機会が年に２回あるのよ。１月２日と天皇誕生日。どちらの日も皇居内に入ることが許されて、皇室ご一家がバルコニーから参賀者にご挨拶されるの。

F： ほんと？　面白そうだね。皇室に関する話題はあまりニュースでは報道されないように思うけど、どうして？

J： うーん、難しい質問ね。うまく答えられるかどうか自信がないわ。天皇は神様と考えられていた時期があったんだけど、戦後の新憲法で国の象徴と規定されたわけ。天皇ご一家は多くの公式行事をこなしていらっしゃるけど、それ以外のときは、あまり目立たないようにされているようね。

F： 日本にはいつごろから天皇がいるの？

J： 1,500年以上前からよ。日本を統治した時期もあったけど、そのうち武士が台頭してきて将軍が任命されたの。天皇と将軍は数百年の間いろいろ工夫して共存したのよ。事実、日本が近代化する前は、天皇は京都にいて、将軍は江戸から日本を統治する形を取っていたわ。

F： 都合がいい仕組みだったんだね！　でも天皇は、ここ東京に住んでいたと思ってたけど？

J： そう、今では皇室は東京にお住まいよ。1867年に将軍の大権が天皇に奉還されたの。当時の明治天皇はまだ16歳でいらしたのよ。将軍家の地所は皇室のものとなって、明治天皇は東京に移られたの。

※「天皇」の英語での表記方法は文書によって異なります。本書では、歴史上これまでに複数存在した天皇を意味する場合はan emperor、emperors、日本の元首としてその地位を意味する場合はthe emperor（南北朝時代を除き、常に天皇は一人なのでtheが付く）としています。今上天皇の意味では、固有名詞としてthe Emperor（theを付けてEを大文字）と表記します。なお、天皇に名称を加える場合、実名であれば、Emperor Hirohito（Eは大文字でtheは付かない）、諡号であれば、the Emperor Showa（Eは大文字でtheが付く）のように区別しています。

F : Only sixteen! That must have been scary for him. Did the ***shogun*** have a **castle** in **Tokyo**?

J : Yes, but the main structure doesn't exist anymore. There are twelve original **castles** that remain from the premodern days. If you get a chance, I recommend that you visit some of them.

F : I want to. I was reading about Himeji Castle in Hyogo Prefecture. Have you been there?

J : Yes, but a long time ago. Last year I went to Matsumoto Castle. It's also worth a visit.

F : What was it like?

F： 16歳の若さでかい！　天皇にとってはおっかない話だったろうね。将軍は東京に城を持っていたのかい？

J： ええ、でも中心の建物はもうないわ。近代以前の城で現存しているのは12あるわね。もし機会があったら、どれか訪れてみたら？

F： 行きたいとも。兵庫県の姫路城について読んだことがあるよ。行ったことがあるかい？

J： ええ、でもずいぶん前にね。去年は松本城に行ったわ。ここも行く価値があるわよ。

F： どんな城だったかい？

the Imperial Palace：皇居	coexist：共存する
the Imperial Family：皇室	be transferred to ～：～に移される
divine：神聖な	property：地所、不動産
stipulate：～と規定する	premodern：
keep a low profile：	近代以前の（日本史では「明治時代より前
目立たないようにしておく	の時代の」の意）

Chapter 4

Travel Japan
日本観光

 **Introduction** | 概説

四季があり自然にも恵まれた日本には、京都、奈良、鎌倉といった定番スポットはもちろん、北は北海道から南は沖縄まで、魅力的な観光スポットが数多くあります。温泉も外国人に非常に人気があります。

Japan is a wonderful country to travel in. Those interested in religion and history can find many places of interest. Just three ancient capitals—**Kyoto**, **Nara**, and **Kamakura**—could keep a traveler busy for a long time. The current capital, **Tokyo**, also has historic sites as well as a vibrant nightlife, a wide variety of cuisine to sample, and shopping opportunities that are out of this world. Winter sports enthusiasts will find numerous ski slopes—some less than two hours from **Tokyo**. If that sounds chilly, Okinawa and the other tropical islands in the south will warm up any visitor. Since 70% of the country is mountainous, it's easy to find beautiful views, great hiking trails, and lots of nature. If all that sightseeing gets tiring, an evening spent soaking in an **outdoor hot spring** at a *ryokan* in a quiet, rustic town is the perfect way to relax.

Kyoto → p.48   Nara → p.48
Kamakura → p.48   Tokyo → p.48
outdoor hot spring → p.48   *ryokan* → p.50

外国人の間では「日本の国内旅行は高い」という見方もあるようですが、民宿に泊まったり、地元の居酒屋などで食事をしたり、公共交通機関を上手に利用すれば、米国やヨーロッパ並みに安く、快適な旅ができることを紹介しましょう。

There are various ways to enjoy traveling in Japan depending on your budget. An inexpensive holiday in Japan might entail staying at family-run inns called *minshuku*, eating Japanese food at discount

　日本はすばらしい観光国です。宗教や歴史に興味のある方は、京都、奈良、鎌倉という３つの古都を訪れれば、時が経つのも忘れて堪能できるでしょう。日本の現在の首都、東京にも史跡はありますが、ほかにも活気のあるナイトライフ、ありとあらゆる食べ物、魅力的な買い物スポットなどが盛りだくさんです。ウインタースポーツ愛好者のためには、東京から２時間もかからないところにたくさんのスキー場があります。ちょっと寒そうに聞こえたでしょうか。それなら沖縄など南の島々が旅人を温めてくれるでしょう。日本は国土の70パーセントが山なので、美しい景色、すばらしいハイキングコース、豊かな自然を簡単に見つけることができます。もしこれらの観光に飽きたら、夕方、静かな田舎旅館の露天風呂につかりましょう。最高にリラックスできます。

place of interest：史跡・名勝	chilly：寒い
ancient：古代の	mountainous：山岳の
capital：首都	soak in 〜：〜につかる
historic site：史跡	rustic：田舎の
vibrant：活気のある	

　日本の観光は、予算次第でさまざまな楽しみ方ができます。民宿と呼ばれる家族経営の宿に泊まり、回転寿司と呼ばれる安い寿司屋で食事をとり、居酒屋と呼ばれる昔ながらの日本の飲食店に飲みに行けば、安く休暇を過ごす

sushi bars called ***kaiten-zushi***, and having some nights out at traditional Japanese taverns called ***izakaya***. The trains and subways would be great for getting around in the cities, and of course riding the ***shinkansen*** is a comfortable way to travel between distant destinations.

🔍 *minshuku* → p.50   *sushi* → p.80   *kaiten-zushi* → p.82
   izakaya → p.82   *shinkansen* → p.50

日本は観光立国を目指し、2003年に「ビジット・ジャパン」キャンペーンを発足させ、2008年には観光庁も設置されました。さらに、2013年には東京が2020年夏季オリンピック・パラリンピック大会の開催地に選ばれ、訪日外国人数は急増しています。

In 2003, the government launched the "Visit Japan" campaign aimed at promoting tourism to Japan, and in 2008, the Japan Tourism Agency was newly founded. The government has been cooperating with the private sector to promote travel to Japan by developing new travel services and expanding multi-lingual information services.

The campaign has paid off well, greatly increasing the number of foreign visitors, especially from Japan's Asian neighbors such as China, Taiwan, and South Korea. Moreover, in 2013 the International Olympic Committee elected **Tokyo** as the host city of the 2020 Summer Olympic and Paralympic Games, which is further spurring the Japan travel boom. A challenge for Japan's tourism industry now is how to better respond to the new demands of visitors who have different languages and cultures.

ことができます。電車や地下鉄は都市を回るのに便利ですし、もちろん新幹線を利用すれば、遠いところへも快適に行くことができます。

entail：〜を伴う	tavern：飲み屋、居酒屋

　政府は、日本旅行を振興する目的で、2003年に「ビジット・ジャパン」キャンペーンを開始し、2008年には観光庁も新設されました。政府は民間セクターと協力して、新たな旅行商品を開発し、外国語による情報サービスを充実させることで、日本旅行を促進しています。

　キャンペーンの効果が表れ、特に中国、台湾、韓国などのアジアの近隣諸国からの訪問客が飛躍的に増加しました。さらに、2013年、国際オリンピック委員会は2020年の夏季オリンピック・パラリンピック大会開催地として東京を選出し、日本旅行ブームにますます拍車がかかっています。今後の日本の観光業の課題としては、言葉や文化が異なる訪問者の新たな要求に、どのようにうまく応えていくかということが挙げられます。

multi-lingual：多言語の pay off：成果を上げる	spur：〜に拍車をかける challenge：課題

京都　Kyoto

Kyoto was the capital of Japan for over 1,000 years, until Tokyo was designated as the capital in 1869. The area has a vast number of cultural assets, including temple and shrine buildings, Buddhist statues, religious items, and paintings. Many are designated as National Treasures.

奈良　Nara

Nara was the capital of Japan in the 8th century. Along with nearby Kyoto, the area is quite famous for its numerous cultural assets. Some of the popular tourist spots include Todaiji Temple, which has an immense statue of Buddha, and Horyuji Temple, both of which are on the World Heritage List.

鎌倉　Kamakura

Kamakura is located south of Tokyo and was the government seat for the Kamakura *Bakufu* between the 12th and 14th centuries. The area has a number of cultural treasures, including the large statue of Buddha at Kotokuin Temple.

東京　Tokyo

Tokyo is the capital of Japan and Japan's largest city, with over 13 million people. Before becoming the capital, Tokyo was the seat of the Edo *Bakufu* for nearly 300 years. Some of the popular sightseeing spots include Asakusa (Sensoji Temple), Tokyo Tower, Tokyo Sky Tree, the Imperial Palace grounds, Ueno Park (Tokyo National Museum), and the large shopping districts of Ginza, Shibuya, Harajuku, Shinjuku, and Akihabara.

露天風呂　*rotenburo* | outdoor hot spring

Rotenburo are outdoor baths—usually hot springs. Since Japan has many hot springs, the lodgings in sightseeing spots often have outdoor hot spring baths.

京都は、1869年に東京が首都と定められるまでの1,000年以上もの間、日本の都でした。京都には寺院・神社建築、仏像、法具、絵画などを含む膨大な数の文化財があり、その多くが国宝に指定されています。

奈良は8世紀に日本の都だった地です。奈良は近くの京都と並んで、数多くの文化財があることでよく知られています。人気のある観光地としては、大仏のある東大寺、法隆寺などがあり、いずれも世界遺産リストに登録されています。

鎌倉は東京の南方に位置し、12世紀から14世紀の間、鎌倉幕府が置かれた地です。鎌倉には、高徳院の大仏を含め数多くの文化財があります。

東京は日本の首都で1,300万人以上が住む日本最大の都市です。東京は、首都になる前、江戸幕府が300年間にわたって置かれていた地です。人気のある観光地としては、浅草寺のある浅草、東京タワー、東京スカイツリー、皇居前広場、東京国立博物館のある上野公園と、銀座、渋谷、原宿、新宿、秋葉原などの大規模商業エリアなどがあります。

露天風呂とは野外にあるお風呂のこと。たいていは温泉です。日本には温泉がたくさんあるので、観光地の宿には、しばしば露天風呂がついています。

旅館　*ryokan* | Japanese-style inn

Ryokan are Japanese-style inns. The guest rooms are *tatami*-matted and guests use *futon* for bedding. The cost of a stay usually includes two meals, which are served in the guest rooms or in a large hall. Most *ryokan* have large baths, which add to the pleasure of staying at *ryokan*.

民宿　*minshuku* | family-run inn

Minshuku are family-run Japanese-style inns. Since *minshuku* are ordinary private houses remodeled to accommodate visitors, their rates are usually cheaper than *ryokan*. Although the service is usually rather limited, each *minshuku* has its own selling point, which might be a good meal, a hot spring, or a rustic atmosphere.

新幹線　*shinkansen* | super-express train

Shinkansen, or bullet trains, are super-express trains that can travel at more than 200 kilometers per hour. *Shinkansen* tickets can be purchased at the so-called "green windows" in train stations.

 **Related Key Words** | 関連キーワード

MP3
15

ペンション　*penshon* | pension

Penshon are Western-style inns, usually located near sightseeing areas, ski resorts, and hot spas. Although their facilities are not as good as those at hotels, the charges are reasonable and usually include two meals.

ビジネスホテル　*bijinesu hoteru* | business hotel

Bijinesu hoteru are lodgings designed mainly for business travelers. The service and facilities are simple, and the rates are usually reasonable. Since they are located near train stations in urban centers, they are convenient for tourists.

旅館は和式の宿です。客室には畳が敷いてあり、宿泊客は夜具として布団を使います。宿泊料金にはたいてい2食が含まれており、食事は客室あるいは大宴会場で出されます。ほとんどの旅館は複数の大浴場を備えており、旅館での宿泊をいっそう楽しくしてくれます。

民宿は家族で経営される和式の宿です。民宿は一般の個人住宅を宿泊設備として改造したものですから、料金は旅館より低く設定してあるのが普通です。サービスが限られてはいますが、それぞれの民宿が、おいしい食事、温泉、あるいは田舎の雰囲気を楽しめるなど、独特のセールスポイントを持っています。

英語でbullet train（弾丸列車）に相当する新幹線は、時速200キロ以上で走る超特急列車です。新幹線の切符は、駅構内の「みどりの窓口」で購入できます。

ペンションは洋式の宿泊施設で、主に観光地、スキー・リゾートや温泉地などの近くにあります。ペンションの設備はホテルほど良くありませんが、料金は安めで、通常、2食が含まれています。

ビジネスホテルは、主に出張旅行者のための宿泊施設です。ビジネスホテルのサービスや設備は最小限にしてあるため、通常は手ごろな料金設定にしてあります。ビジネスホテルは都心部の駅近くにあるので、旅行者にとっても便利な施設です。

宿坊　*shukubo* | accommodations at temples

Shukubo are accommodations offered by temples. They are basically designed for followers, but many offer accommodations for tourists too. Some may require visitors to follow the temple's religious practices, but staying at *shukubo* may be a good chance for travelers to learn about Buddhism.

日光　Nikko

Nikko is located north of Tokyo and is famous for Toshogu Shrine. The shrine was built in the 17th century and is well known for its extravagantly designed exterior. Nearby, one can visit Kegon waterfalls and beautiful cedar forests. Nikko attracts tourists throughout the year.

Related Vocabulary | 関連語彙

- 交通：traffic
- 交通網：the transportation system
- 各駅停車：a local train
- 特急列車：an express train
- 回送列車：a train out of service
- 予約席：a reserved seat
- 自由席：a non-reserved seat
- 乗り換え：transfer
- 時刻表：a timetable
- 運賃精算：fare adjustment
- 乗車券販売機：a ticket vending machine
- 周遊券：an excursion ticket
- 定期券：a commuter pass / a commuter ticket
- 往復乗車券：a round-trip ticket
- 1日乗車券：a one-day pass
- 国内線：a domestic flight
- 国際線：an international flight
- 欠航便：a cancelled flight

宿坊は寺が用意している宿泊施設です。元来、その寺の信徒のためのものですが、多くは観光客も宿泊できます。なかには、その寺で行われている宗教習慣に従うように宿泊客に求める宿坊もありますが、宿坊に宿泊するのは仏教について学ぶ良い機会となるはずです。

日光は東京の北方にある地で、東照宮があることで知られています。東照宮は17世紀に建てられ、その豪奢な外装でよく知られています。旅行者は近くにある華厳の滝や美しい杉並木に立ち寄ることもできます。日光は1年中観光客が絶えることがありません。

■安売りチケット：a discounted ticket
■宿泊施設：accommodations
■民泊：paid accommodations in private homes
■温泉：a hot spring / a hot spa
■史跡：a place of historical interest
■名勝：a place of scenic beauty
■天然記念物：a natural monument
■国宝：a national treasure
■重要文化財：important cultural assets

■重要有形文化財：important tangible cultural assets
■重要無形文化財：important intangible cultural assets
■世界遺産：World Heritage
■公共物破壊行為：vandalism
■入場料：entrance fee

Dialogue 1 | 対話

How come the trains don't run all night?

F : How do you get to work?

J : By train. It takes about 90 minutes door to door. I only have to transfer once.

F : Ninety minutes! That's awful. How can you stand it?

J : It's not so bad. I do a lot of reading on the train. And if I'm lucky enough to get a seat, I take a little nap.

F : Speaking of trains, I notice some people just swipe a card over the front of the gate when they enter and exit. What is that?

J : Those are prepaid cards. They have IC chips, and the train fare is automatically deducted from the card. You really should get one. You can use them on almost any train, subway, or bus in the **Tokyo** area. You can also use them in some stores and shops.

F : How do I get one?

J : You can get one from some ticket machines at larger train stations. They have instructions in English, so you won't have any problem.

F : That's great. There is one other thing that I'm curious about. Why is it that the trains don't run all night?

J : I'm not sure. I suppose noise is a big factor. People living near the tracks wouldn't be happy if the trains ran all night.

どうして夜どおし走る電車がないの？

F： 通勤には何を利用してるの？

J： 電車だよ。ドアツードアで約90分。乗り換えは1度だけ。

F： 90分ですって！ それはすごいわ。よく我慢できるわねえ。

J： いや、それほどでもないよ。電車の中で本もたくさん読めるし。それにうまく座れれば一眠りもできるよ。

F： 電車といえば、改札を出入りするときに、ゲートの手前でカードをかざしているだけの人がいたわ。あのカードは何？

J： あれはプリペイドカード。なかにICチップが入っていて、自動的に運賃をカードから引いてくれるんだよ。君もぜひ手に入れてみたら？ 東京のほとんどすべての電車、地下鉄、バスに使えるし、お店での買い物でも使うことができるよ。

F： どうやって手に入れるの？

J： 大きな駅の券売機から入手できるよ。英語の説明があるから、心配ご無用さ。

F： いいわね。もう一つ興味深いことがあるの。日本ではなぜ電車を一晩中走らせないの？

J： よくわからないな。主に騒音のせいかもしれないね。もし終夜運転をしたら、沿線の人はいやがると思うよ。

---

transfer：（電車を）乗り換える
awful：ひどい
stand it：耐える
take a nap：居眠りをする

swipe：（カードなど）を読み取り機に通す
be deducted from 〜：
　〜から差し引かれる
factor：要素

 **Dialogue 2** | 対話

Don't jump in the bath!

F : I'm going to a hot spring this weekend. It'll be my first time staying at a *ryokan*. What's it like?

J : They're really nice. They serve both dinner and breakfast—you can expect typical Japanese fare such as fish and *miso* soup.

F : That sounds yummy. As long as I don't have to eat *natto*.

J : Everything will be Japanese style, so make sure you know the rules. Try not to make any faux pas.

F : What rules? What do you mean?

J : Hmm, let's see. Take your shoes off in the entryway—that's the *genkan*. Also, there is a schedule for the meals and the bath, so try to find out the times.

F : Ah, the bath. Wash before I jump in, right?

J : Umm, right. And please don't "jump" in. Oh, and the staff will usually come to your room to lay out your *futon* while you're in the bath. I'm sure you'll have a great time.

お風呂にとび込んじゃだめ！

F：この週末、温泉に行くつもりなんだけど、旅館に泊まるのは初めてなんだ。どんなところ？

J：とてもいいわよ。夕食と朝食を出してくれるのよ。魚とかみそ汁なんていう日本らしい食事が楽しめるわ。

F：おいしそうだな。でも「納豆」は、食べられないんだけど。

J：何もかも日本式だから、日本の流儀をちゃんと覚えておいてね。ミスしちゃだめよ。

F：流儀って？　どんな？

J：えーと、そう、入り口、つまり玄関では、靴を脱ぐこと、食事とお風呂の時間が決まっているから、ちゃんと確認してね。

F：あ、お風呂ね、湯船にとび込む前に体を洗うってことでしょ？

J：まあ、そのとおりよ。でもお願いだから、とび込んだりしないでね。ああ、それから、たいていお風呂に入っている間に、仲居さんが部屋にやってきて布団を敷いてくれるのよ。きっと、うんと楽しめるわよ。

---

typical：典型的な
fare：食事、食べ物
yummy：おいしそうな

faux pas：エチケット違反
entryway：（建物の）入り口

Clothing and Housing
衣類・住居

MP3
18

📖 Introduction | 概説

日本人はみな木の家に住み、毎日着物を着て生活している、などというステレオタイプのイメージを抱いている外国人がまだいるとしたら、現在の日本の変貌ぶりにきっと驚くことでしょう。

What visitors to Japan expect to see, and what they actually see, can be quite different. Instead of people wearing *kimono*, they'll find people wearing mostly Western-style clothing. And instead of seeing the traditional-style wooden homes and shops depicted in a *samurai* movie, they'll see modern and sometimes futuristic-looking buildings. Finding the traditional aspects of Japan isn't always easy.

 kimono → p.62　　　*samurai* → p.26

現代の日本で、着物を生活着として利用している人を探すのは難しいですが、結婚式などのイベントでは、女性を華やかに彩る衣装としての「着物」が生きていることを説明しましょう。

Kimono actually translates as "clothing," yet most Japanese people wear traditional *kimono* only for special events. The most beautiful silk *kimono* are worn by brides on their wedding day. As *kimono* cost millions of yen, most modern women are content to rent their wedding *kimono*. Other times when people, usually women, wear *kimono* are university commencement ceremonies, **festivals**, fireworks displays, and the ceremony for **Coming-of-Age Day**.

Although the popularity of the traditional *kimono* declined throughout most of the 20th century, there has recently been an uptick in sales and creativity. Some famous Japanese fashion designers have

　日本に行けばこんな光景が見られるだろうと思っていたのに、日本で実際に目にするものは全く違っていた、ということがあるかもしれません。着物を着ている人たちをイメージしていたのに、見かけるのはもっぱら洋服を着た人たちばかり。それに、時代劇に登場するような伝統的な木造の家屋や商店の代わりに、近代的で、なかには未来的ともいえそうな建物を見かけるはずです。日本の伝統文化を発見するのは、そう簡単ではないのです。

futuristic-looking：未来的な見かけの

　着物は、直訳すると「着るもの」ですが、たいていの人は特別な行事のときにしか着ません。最も豪華な絹の着物は、結婚式のときに花嫁が着ます。ただし、数百万円もするので、現代の女性は結婚式の着物はレンタルで済ませるのが普通です。それ以外に、たいていは女性ですが、大学の卒業式や、祭り、花火大会、成人式などでも着物を着ます。

　20世紀の大半を通じて、伝統的な着物の人気は下がる一方でしたが、このところの着物の売上げは伸び、その創造性が見直されつつあります。なかには国際的なファッションショーで着物を用いる有名な日本人デザイナーもいます。また以前よりも安価な生地が輸入されるようになったおかげで、着物の価格は下がってきています。

used *kimono* in their international shows. Also, cheaper imported fabrics have brought down *kimono* prices in Japan.

🔍 festivals → p.114　　　　Coming-of-Age Day → p.98

身近な「着物」として、若い世代にはゆかたが流行してきました。今まで考えられなかった「新しい」ゆかたも出現しています。

Light, cotton *kimono*, called *yukata*, are especially popular now with young people. While attending summer **festivals** or fireworks displays, a *yukata* is a popular choice for fashion-conscious women and sometimes men.

🔍 *yukata* → p.62

住宅についても、都会では伝統的な日本家屋はめったに見られません。かといって、純粋な西洋式住宅とも違っているのが日本式流儀です。現代の日本の住宅には、日本人にとって捨てがたい伝統がさまざまな形で息づいているのです。

Traditional Japanese housing design has also become less common in Japan. Many Japanese live in high-rise condominiums called *manshon*. Further from the city center, there are many single-family homes in the Japanese version of urban sprawl. Despite having a Western appearance, there are many traditional Japanese designs incorporated into these buildings. You can still find some modern homes with a traditional *tatami* room, which likely includes a traditional *tokonoma* alcove. The Japanese may have adopted many Western ways out of convenience, but it's clear that some traditional aspects of Japanese culture are still embraced by the Japanese people.

🔍 *manshon* → p.62　　　　*tatami* → p.62　　　　*tokonoma* → p.64

bride：新婦、花嫁
commencement ceremony：卒業式
fireworks display：花火大会

decline：衰退する
uptick：上向き

　ゆかたと呼ばれる簡素な綿の着物が、若い人たちの間で人気が出てきています。夏祭りや花火大会に出かけるときには、ゆかたが、ファッションに敏感な女性や一部の男性には魅力のようです。

fashion-conscious：流行に目がない

　昔ながらの日本家屋もあまり見かけなくなってきています。多くの日本人はマンションと呼ばれる高層分譲住宅に住んでいます。日本でも、市街地から離れるほど、郊外には住宅地が広がるという現象が見られますが、そこには多くの一戸建て住宅が並んでいます。外見は洋風であっても、伝統的な日本家屋の設計が数多く組み込まれています。今でも、モダンな造りの住宅に、「床の間」の付いた畳の部屋が見られることがあります。日本人は西洋の生活様式の便利さをさまざまに取り入れてきましたが、日本の伝統がなおも受け継がれていることは明らかでしょう。

high-rise condominium：高層分譲住宅
urban sprawl：
　都市のスプロール（郊外への拡大化）現象
incorporated into 〜：〜に組み込まれて

alcove：（床の間のような）部屋のくぼみ
out of convenience：便利さから
embrace：〜を受け入れる

着物   *kimono*

Kimono is traditional Japanese clothing. A typical *kimono* is a long robe folded in front and fastened in back at the waistline with a thick sash called an *obi*. There are different types of *kimono* for different occasions and even for women of different generations. For example, young single women would wear *furisode*, which are usually more colorful and have sleeves hanging almost to the floor. *Kimono* are usually made of silk or cotton fabrics.

ゆかた   *yukata*

Yukata is an informal *kimono* usually made of cotton. It is used as nightwear or casual summer wear. Today, *yukata* are usually provided at lodgings for use by guests or worn at summer festivals and fireworks displays.

マンション   *manshon*

The term *manshon* comes from the English word mansion. In Japan it refers to multistoried apartments and condominiums that are made of concrete. An *apaato* is smaller than a *manshon* and is only available for rent. These are usually made of wood or mortar.

畳   *tatami*

Tatami mats are the traditional flooring in a Japanese room. They have a rice straw base and are covered with tightly woven soft rush. *Tatami* come in standard, rectangular sizes. The number of *tatami* used in a room also indicates the size of the room.

着物は日本の伝統的な衣類です。典型的な着物は、長い裾を前で合わせ、帯と呼ばれる厚い帯状の布で、腰の高さで後ろで締めて着ます。着物は、着ていく行事によって、あるいは着る女性の年代によって、さまざまな種類があります。たとえば、若い独身女性は、地面に届くほど長い袖がある華やかな色の「振袖」を着ます。着物はたいてい、絹か綿の生地でできています。

ゆかたは略式の着物で、たいてい生地は綿です。夜着や夏の普段着として用いられています。今日では、ゆかたは、旅館などで客の着替え用として用意されていたり、夏祭りや花火大会で着用されています。

マンションという語は英語のmansionに由来します。日本では、コンクリート製で多層構造を持つアパートや分譲住宅を指します。アパートはマンションよりも小型の賃貸住宅をいい、たいていは木造かモルタル造りです。

畳は、和室の床に用いられる伝統的な床材です。ワラでできた芯があり、硬く編んだイグサで覆われています。畳は長方形で大きさが決まっており、部屋に敷かれる畳の数で部屋の大きさを示すこともできます。

床の間　*tokonoma*

Tokonoma is a decorative alcove found in a Japanese-style room that adds an element of formality and grace to a rather simple interior. A hanging scroll is usually hung on the back wall, and a flower arrangement or other piece of art is placed within.

Related Key Words | 関連キーワード

MP3 20

羽織袴　*haori* and *hakama*

Haori is a jacket worn over a *kimono*. *Hakama* are pleated, loose-fitting trousers. *Haori* and *hakama* are usually worn by men at traditional wedding ceremonies and other occasions.

風呂敷　*furoshiki*

Furoshiki is a decorative cloth that is used to wrap and carry clothes, gifts, or other goods. *Furoshiki* can be made of a variety of materials, including silk and cotton. They come in squares of various sizes. The colors and designs vary, often having flower motifs or geometrical patterns.

布団　*futon*

Futon is Japanese bedding. A set of *futon* is usually folded and stored inside the *oshiire* closet during the day, and is spread on the *tatami*-matted floor when used. A set of *futon* consists of a mattress and a quilt.

床の間は、和室にしつらえられた装飾的なくぼみで、比較的簡素な和室の内装に、格式と優雅さを感じさせてくれます。床の間の正面の壁には、たいてい掛け軸が掛けられたり、生け花やその他の飾りが置かれます。

羽織は着物の上から着用する上着で、袴はゆったりとした、ひだ付きのズボンです。羽織袴は主に男性用で、伝統的な様式で行う結婚式やその他の行事で着用されます。

風呂敷は、着物や贈り物などを包んで運ぶための、模様の美しい布です。風呂敷は、絹や綿など、いろいろな素材で作られています。風呂敷は正方形で、さまざまな大きさがあります。色や柄も多様で、草花の模様や幾何学模様などの柄があります。

布団は日本式の寝具。布団一式は普通、昼間は押入に収納しておき、使うときに畳の上に敷きます。敷布団と掛布団で布団一式です。

座布団　*zabuton*

Zabuton is a Japanese floor cushion. It is used on the *tatami*-matted floor of a Japanese room. Guests are offered a *zabuton* soon after they arrive at a Japanese home.

はっぴ　*happi*

Happi is a traditional Japanese workman's coat, usually bearing a family crest, shop name, or the name of a neighborhood association. They are often worn by workers, including carpenters and gardeners, or by participants in festivals.

下駄　*geta*

Geta are traditional Japanese clogs that are often worn with *kimono*. *Geta* have a thong, like a sandal, and some have a wooden platform with two cross supports on the bottom.

扇子　*sensu*

Sensu is a folding fan that functions both as a tool for cooling oneself and as a decorative object. Though folding fans are also seen in other countries, the *sensu* is a Japanese invention.

団扇　*uchiwa*

Uchiwa is a round paper fan. Made of bamboo, one end is the handle and the other is splayed into thin strips and covered with thick Japanese paper.

襖　*fusuma*

Fusuma are sliding doors which consist of a wooden frame covered with thick Japanese paper. A traditional Japanese structure is designed so that two or more rooms can be combined by removing the sliding doors.

座布団は和式の床用クッションで、和室の畳の上で使われます。日本の家を訪れた客は、まずこの座布団を勧められます。

はっぴは日本の伝統的な労働者用の上着で、家紋や屋号、または町内会の名称などが入っているのが普通です。大工や植木職人などの職人、あるいは祭りの参加者などが着ます。

下駄は日本の伝統的な木製の履き物で、しばしば着物を着るときに履きます。下駄には、サンダルと同様の鼻緒が付けてあり、木製の底板の裏に、横向きの支え板が2本取り付けてあるものもあります。

扇子は涼を取るために、また装飾品として用いられる折りたたみ式のファンです。扇子はほかの国にもありますが、日本で発明されたものです。

団扇は丸い形をしたファンです。竹製で、一方の端が持つところになっており、もう一方を扇状に広げ、放射状になった部分に厚手の和紙を貼って作ります。

襖は引き戸式の扉で、木製の枠に厚手の和紙を貼り付けたものです。伝統的な日本建築は、この襖を取り外して、2部屋またはそれ以上の部屋をつなぐことができるように造られています。

障子　*shoji*

Shoji is a sliding screen that separates traditional Japanese rooms from corridors. It consists of a thin wooden frame covered with thin Japanese paper so as to allow sunlight into the room.

Related Vocabulary | 関連語彙

- 振袖：a *kimono* with long hanging sleeves worn by unmarried women
- 紋：a crest
- 日本髪：Japanese coiffure
- 足袋：split-toe Japanese socks
- 草履：Japanese slippers
- 入り口：an entrance
- 出口：an exit

- 天井：a ceiling
- 廊下：a corridor
- 板の間：a wooden floor
- 屋根：a roof
- 屋根裏：a loft / an attic
- 瓦：a roof tile
- 居間：a living room
- 軒：eaves

障子（しょうじ）は、和室を廊下と仕切るための引き戸式の戸。日光が室内に入るように、木製の細い枠に薄い和紙を貼り付けたものです。

■縁側：a wooden veranda found in some traditionally designed houses
■アパート1室：an apartment / a flat
■アパート1棟：an apartment building
■メゾネット式アパート：a duplex apartment
■団地：public housing
■町内会：a neighborhood association

■ヒノキ：cypress
■たんす：a chest of drawers
■ちゃぶ台：a low dining table
■いろり：an open hearth
■屏風：a folding screen

Dialogue 1 | 対話

Where can I buy a *kimono*?

F : How come so few Japanese people wear *kimono*?

J : *Kimono* are expensive and a bit tricky to put on. Many Japanese put them aside for special occasions like weddings, commencement ceremonies, **Coming-of-Age Day**, and so on. These days an increasing number of people, especially women, use *kimono* as everyday clothes.

F : I was hoping to buy one to take back with me. How expensive are they?

J : A cheap silk *kimono* might cost over 100,000 yen, and high-quality *kimono* could easily cost several million yen. Why don't you get yourself a *yukata*? They're relatively inexpensive. You can probably find one for less than 10,000 yen.

F : Okay, but what's a *yukata*?

J : A *yukata* is an informal *kimono* made of cotton. People wear them to **festivals** and fireworks displays. They're also worn as nightwear— most *ryokan* provide *yukata* for their guests.

F : Great. But where can I buy one?

J : I'm sure you can find one at a department store. Most large department stores have a whole section of high-quality, traditional Japanese goods. You should be able to find some nice gifts and souvenirs there.

着物はどこで買えるの？

F： どうして、日本人はあまり着物を着ないの？

J： 着物は値段が高いし、着つけも簡単にはいかないからだよ。結婚式とか、卒業式や成人の日みたいなイベントでしか着ない人が多いね。ただ最近、特に女性は、普段着として着物を着る人が増えているけどね。

F： 1つ買って帰りたいと思っていたのよ。どのくらいするの？

J： 絹の着物なんて、安くて10万円、良い物だと数百万円もするんだよ。ゆかたにしたら？　それなら割と安いし、たぶん、1万円以下であるんじゃないかな。

F： わかったわ。でも、その、ゆかたってどういうの？

J： 綿の普段着の着物ってとこだね。お祭りとか花火大会に着ていくんだ。寝間着にもなって、旅館に泊まるとたいてい貸してくれるよ。

F： いいわね。でも、どこに行けば買えるの？

J： デパートに行けば必ずあるよ。大型店ならたいてい、質のいい日本の伝統品が揃っている売り場があるから、そこで、気の利いた贈り物やお土産品も買えるよ。

---

tricky：扱いにくい
put on 〜：〜を着る

Coming-of-Age Day：成人の日
souvenir：お土産

 **Dialogue 2** | 対話

Oh, wonderful! A regular toilet!

F : You have such a beautiful house. Is this a traditional Japanese home?

J : There are many traditional things here. As you can see, this room has *tatami* flooring, and these sliding doors are called *fusuma*. They're made of paper. And this is what we call a *butsudan*. We give offerings and pray to our ancestors here.

F : The whole place is beautiful. It has an elegant simplicity to it.

J : But this house is only ten years old, so we have many modern conveniences. You'll be happy to know we have a Western-style toilet.

F : Oh, good. A *ryokan* I stayed at had only a Japanese-style toilet. It was just a hole in the floor! I didn't know what to do.

J : You just face the hooded section, squat, and do your business. It's as simple as that.

F : Thanks. I'll remember that.

すばらしい！　いつものトイレだわ！

F : すばらしいお宅ですね。伝統的な日本家屋と言っていいんですか。

J : 伝統的なものがたくさんありますよ。ご覧のとおり、この部屋は畳敷きですし、この引き戸は襖。紙でできています。そしてこれが仏壇。ここで先祖の霊にお供えをして祈ります。

F : どこもすべて美しい。シンプルで実に優雅です。

J : でも、この家は築10年ほどで、現代の便利なものもたくさんありますよ。洋式トイレですから安心していいですよ。

F : それは良かった。旅館に泊まったときには和式のトイレしかなくて、床に穴が1つ空いているだけでした！　どう使っていいのやら……。

J : 覆いがあるほうを向いて、しゃがんで用を足します。それだけですよ。

F : ありがとう。覚えておきます。

offering：お供え物
pray：祈る
ancestor：先祖
elegant：優美な

simplicity：簡素さ
convenience：便利なもの
do *one's* business：用を足す

5
Clothing and Housing
対話

 **Introduction** | 概説

MP3
23

外国人が好む日本食の代表選手は、「すし」と「スキヤキ」でしょうか。このほかにも、日本には、庶民的な食事処で楽しめる日本食が、たくさんあることを紹介しましょう。

When a Westerner thinks of Japanese food, *sushi* and *sukiyaki* quickly spring to mind. But Japanese cuisine has so much more to offer. For example, *tempura* is a variety of deep-fried foods that are served piping hot and then dipped in a special sauce. If that sounds too fattening, one might try one of the many *udon* or *soba* noodle dishes. Another noodle dish, originally from China, is *ramen*. Other options are the inexpensive *sushi* restaurants called *kaiten-zushi* or Japanese-style taverns called *izakaya*, which serve both food and alcohol. Also, there are many restaurants that serve reasonably-priced combination meals called *teishoku*. And if one wishes to splurge, there's *kaiseki ryori*—a sophisticated Japanese cuisine that is accompanied by *sake*.

sushi → p.80   *sukiyaki* → p.80   *tempura* → p.80
udon, soba → p.80   *ramen* → p.80   *kaiten-zushi* → p.82
izakaya → p.82   *kaiseki ryori* → p.82   *sake* → p.82

また、日本食の特徴として、「目で食べる」料理も説明したいところです。見栄え良く、芸術的なまでに盛り付けられた一皿の料理に、日本人の美意識をも発見してほしいものです。

What is interesting to note about Japanese food preparation is that great care is taken to provide an appealing appearance. Foods are arranged carefully and matched with appropriately sized and colored dishes and bowls. The meal often looks too good to eat!

　西洋人にとって日本料理といえば、すしとスキヤキがすぐに頭に浮かぶでしょう。しかし、日本料理にはもっともっと種類があります。たとえば、てんぷらは、さまざまな材料を用いた揚げ物の料理で、揚げ立ての熱々を特別なつゆにつけて食べます。これではカロリーが高すぎると思う方は、うどんやそばといった麺料理を食べてみるとよいでしょう。また、これとは別に、中華料理から発達したラーメンと呼ばれる麺料理もあります。その他、回転寿司と呼ばれる安価な寿司屋や、酒食両方をまかなう居酒屋と呼ばれる和風の飲み屋を利用するのも楽しみです。また、定食と呼ばれる手ごろなセット料理を出す料理店も数多くありますし、逆に、美食三昧を望むときは、高級和風料理である懐石料理を日本酒と一緒に味わうのもよいでしょう。

spring to mind：頭に浮かぶ	fattening：太らせる、高カロリーの
cuisine：料理	tavern：飲み屋、居酒屋
deep-fry：〜を油で揚げる	splurge：美食三昧をする
piping hot：	sophisticated：高級の、通向けの
とても熱い、ジュージューいっている	be accompanied by 〜：
dip：〜を（…に）つける	〜とともに出される

　日本料理に関して特に興味深い点は、料理の見ためを魅力的に仕上げるのに細心の注意が払われることです。皿や鉢の大きさや色を料理に合わせて調え、ていねいに盛り付けます。まるで、食べてしまうのがもったいないと思えるほどです！

Traditional Japanese cuisine also reflects the seasons and is associated with traditional events. For these reasons, it has been added to UNESCO's Intangible Cultural Heritage List.

伝統的な日本の家庭料理は魚、野菜、ご飯、みそ汁で、味付けの基本はみそとしょうゆです。健康食として日本料理は理想的ともいえるものでしょう。

A traditional home-cooked Japanese meal consists of fish, rice, *miso* soup, and vegetables. Many Japanese dishes are seasoned with *miso*, which is made from soy beans, and *shoyu*—known as soy sauce in the West. The longevity and lack of obesity among the Japanese seem to indicate that this traditional diet is very healthy.

miso → p.82   *shoyu* → p.82

一方で、日本人の食生活も変化しています。ハンバーグやカレーは若い世代の定番メニューとなり、イタリアン、エスニック料理も人気です。外国の珍しい食材も手に入りやすくなっています。

Nevertheless, Japanese eating habits are rapidly changing. Hamburgers and curry rice are popular with children. In cities, there are an increasing number of restaurants serving non-Japanese cuisines, including Italian, Southeast Asian, and so on. At the supermarkets a wide range of imported items are available.

日本の伝統料理はまた、季節を映し出し、伝統行事と結び付いています。そのような理由から、日本料理はユネスコの無形文化遺産に登録されました。

| appearance：見ため | intangible：無形の |
| appropriately：適切に | |

　日本の伝統的な家庭料理は、魚、ご飯、みそ汁、野菜という組み合わせです。日本料理の多くは、大豆から造られたみそや、西洋ではソイソースとしておなじみのしょうゆで味付けされています。日本人の長寿や肥満率の低さは、日本の伝統食が健康にとても良いためのようです。

| longevity：長寿 | obesity：肥満 |

　それでも、日本人の食生活も急速に変化してきています。ハンバーグやカレーライスは子どもに人気がありますし、都会では、イタリア料理、東南アジア料理を含む和食以外を扱う料理店がどんどん増えています。スーパーマーケットでも、ありとあらゆる輸入食材が売られています。

| a wide range of 〜：幅広い種類の〜 |

最後に、日本人の食文化の変化への懸念をひとこと。肉食の普及や手軽なインスタント食品、レトルト食品などに押されて、理想の健康食を誇った日本人の食生活も崩れつつあります。

　Dietary changes certainly aren't new to Japan. Until the late 19th century, most Japanese people avoided animal meat for religious reasons. Today, a vegetarian would be hard-pressed to find a meatless meal. It's also important to note that some of the changes are unhealthy. Increased consumption of red meat adds fat to the diet, and instant foods often have many chemicals added. But people are becoming more aware of this and are demanding more healthy choices. As a result, many of the prepared meals found at supermarkets and convenience stores are relatively fresh and often include vegetables and seafood.

日本人の食生活の変化は、つい最近の出来事ではありません。19世紀後半まで、ほとんどの日本人は、宗教的な理由から獣肉を食することはありませんでした。菜食主義者の人が、現代の日本で肉が入っていない料理を見つけるのは一苦労でしょう。忘れてはならないのは、食生活の変化には不健康なものもあるということです。赤肉の消費が増えたことで、日ごろの食事の脂肪分が増え、即席食品には多くの添加物が含まれています。しかし、この事実に対する意識も高まり、もっと健康的な食べ物を求める人も増えています。その結果、スーパーやコンビニで見られる多くの調理済み食品は、比較的新鮮で、野菜や魚なども多く含んでいます。

vegetarian：菜食主義者
be hard-pressed to *do*：
　　〜するのに苦労する

red meat：赤肉、赤身肉
⇒牛肉や羊肉などの赤色の濃い肉。red meatに対し、鶏肉や豚肉など、赤色のあまり濃くない肉はwhite meatと呼ばれる。
chemicals：化学製品、添加物

すし   *sushi*

Sushi is a dish of cooked rice flavored with vinegar and sugar. The most common *sushi* is *nigirizushi*, where small oblong balls of hand-rolled rice are topped with various ingredients—usually raw fish. A bit of grated horseradish, called *wasabi*, is usually added as a condiment.

スキヤキ   *sukiyaki*

Sukiyaki is a dish of thinly-sliced beef cooked in a special pan with spring onions, *tofu*, *shiitake* mushrooms, and other ingredients. The dish is cooked at the table in a broth of soy sauce, a sweet *sake* called *mirin*, and sugar. The cooked items are dipped in raw egg before eating.

てんぷら   *tempura*

Tempura is a dish of deep-fried foods including fresh fish, prawns, and selected vegetables. On the side is a dish of sauce, called *tsuyu*, and grated radish. The radish is added to the sauce by the diner. The *tempura* is eaten after being dipped in this sauce.

そばとうどん   *soba* and *udon*

Soba and *udon* are both noodle dishes. *Soba* noodles are made from buckwheat flour and *udon* noodles are made from wheat flour. They can be served in a hot broth, or chilled with a dipping sauce on the side.

ラーメン   *ramen*

Ramen is a dish of Chinese noodles served in hot broth. Spring onions and bean sprouts are usually served on top. There are a wide variety of *ramen* dishes available depending on the restaurant and region. *Ramen* sold in a disposable cup is a popular instant food in Japan and overseas.

すしは、酢と砂糖で味付けをしたご飯料理。最もよく知られているのは握り寿司で、手で握った小さな俵型のご飯に、主に生魚などの食材をのせます。少量のすりおろしたワサビを香料として加えます。

スキヤキは薄切りの牛肉を、長ねぎ、豆腐、しいたけなどと特製の鍋で煮込んだ料理。しょうゆ、みりんと呼ばれる甘い酒、砂糖で作っただしを用い、食卓で料理されるものです。煮えたら生卵につけて食べます。

てんぷらは、生魚、海老、野菜などの食材を油で揚げた料理。てんぷらには、つゆと、おろし大根が添えられます。おろし大根は食べる人が自分でつゆに加えます。てんぷらは、そのつゆにつけて食べます。

そばとうどんは麺料理です。そばの麺はそば粉から、うどんの麺は小麦粉から作られます。いずれも、つゆにひたして温かくして出したり、冷たくして、つけ汁を添えて出したりします。

温かいスープの中に入っている中国風の麺のこと。通常、長ねぎ、もやしなどがのっています。店や地方ごとに、さまざまなラーメンがあります。使い捨ての容器に入って売られているラーメン（カップラーメン）は、インスタント食品として日本、そして海外で人気です。

回転寿司 *kaiten-zushi*

Kaiten-zushi are inexpensive *sushi* restaurants where plates of *sushi* rest on a circular conveyer belt. The chefs are in the middle and the customers sit on the outside of the circle. Customers can take any plate that is available or they can ask the chefs to prepare something different.

居酒屋 *izakaya* | Japanese tavern

Izakaya are Japanese taverns that serve a wide variety of dishes and drinks. Most *izakaya* automatically provide a small side dish called *tsukidashi* which is added to the bill, but generally each item on the menu is reasonably priced.

懐石料理 *kaiseki ryori*

Kaiseki ryori originally refers to a multi-course meal served at a tea ceremony. Today, it is regarded as the highest art of Japanese food preparation.

酒 *sake*

Sake is a fermented alcoholic drink made from rice, which can be served either warm or cold. *Sake* has been consumed for many centuries in Japan and is served at many different religious and social functions.

みそとしょうゆ *miso* and *shoyu* (soy sauce)

Miso is fermented soybean paste, and *shoyu*, or soy sauce, is a seasoning sauce made from fermented soybeans. Both are indispensable ingredients in Japanese dishes and are used as the base or seasoning for various dishes.

すしをのせた皿がベルトコンベアの上に置いてある値段の安い寿司屋のこと。料理人がベルトコンベアの内側にいて、外側には客が座ります。客はすでに出ているすしのお皿を取ることも、あるいは、料理人に注文して違うものを作ってもらうこともできます。

居酒屋とは、いろいろな食べ物や飲み物を出す日本式のタベルナ（飲み屋）のこと。ほとんどの居酒屋では、付きだしと呼ばれる小皿の料理が、注文せずとも出されて勘定に加えられますが、全体的に、メニューに載っている一品一品は安価です。

懐石料理は、もともと茶会で出されるフルコース料理を指します。今日では、日本料理の最高峰とされています。

酒は米から造られる醸造酒で、温めても冷やしても飲むことができます。酒は古くから日本で飲まれており、さまざまな宗教的・社会的行事の際に供されます。

みそは大豆を醗酵させたペースト状のもの、しょうゆはソイソースとも呼ばれ、醗酵させた大豆から造られる調味料。どちらも日本料理には欠かせないもので、さまざまな料理でベースの味付けや調味料として用いられます。

しゃぶしゃぶ *shabu shabu*

Shabu shabu is a dish of thinly-sliced, marbled beef cooked by dipping the meat into a pot of simmering, kelp-flavored broth. On the side is a sesame-flavored sauce or a citrus-flavored sauce. Other ingredients, such as *tofu*, Chinese cabbage, chrysanthemum leaves, or *shiitake* mushrooms are often cooked in the broth as well.

精進料理 *shojin ryori*

Shojin ryori is a vegetarian meal containing no meat or fish. It was originally eaten by *Zen* Buddhist monks because of the Buddhist prohibition of taking any life. Today, *shojin ryori* is still served at some Buddhist temples. It can also be found at restaurants that specialize in the cuisine.

お茶 *ocha* | green tea (leaves)

Ocha, or *ryokucha*, refers to green tea leaves or the tea made with them. Black and green tea are made from the same plant, but black tea has gone through a fermentation process. Typically, green tea is brewed. This type of tea is also sold in bottles. In the tea ceremonies, the tea is made by mixing hot water and powdered green tea called *matcha.*

焼酎 *shochu*

Shochu is a distilled alcoholic drink made from rice, potatoes, barley, buckwheat, or other materials. *Shochu* is often served as a mixed drink.

おちょこと徳利 *ochoko and tokkuri*

Ochoko are small ceramic glasses that are used for drinking *sake. Tokkuri* are ceramic flasks which usually hold 180 ml or 360 ml of *sake.*

薄切りの霜降り肉を、沸騰した鍋一杯の昆布だしのスープにさっとひたして食べる料理。しゃぶしゃぶには、胡麻風味のたれやポン酢たれが添えられます。豆腐、白菜、春菊、しいたけなど、ほかの材料もこのスープで煮ます。

精進料理とは肉や魚を一切用いない野菜料理のこと。もともとは、禅僧のための料理でした。仏教では生類の殺生が禁じられているからです。今でも、精進料理を出す仏教寺院がありますし、精進料理を専門に扱う料理店もあります。

お茶、または、緑茶は、緑茶の茶葉、あるいは、その茶葉で入れたお茶を意味します。紅茶や緑茶は同じ茶の木から作られますが、紅茶は発酵過程を経ています。緑茶は普通、煎じて飲みますが、この種のお茶はボトル入りでも売られています。茶の湯では、抹茶と呼ばれる粉末にした茶葉とお湯を混ぜてお茶を点てます。

焼酎は、米、芋、麦、そば、その他さまざまな材料から造られる蒸留酒。焼酎は、よくほかの飲み物と混ぜて出されます。

おちょこは小さな焼物の器で、日本酒を飲むのに用いられます。徳利は焼物の酒瓶で、日本酒が180か360ミリリットル入るのが普通です。

やきとり　*yakitori*

Yakitori literally means "grilled fowl," and the ingredients are usually chicken—meat, liver, or skin—and various vegetables, such as spring onion. Bite-size pieces are grilled on bamboo skewers. Often, *yakitori* is basted with a special sweet soy-based sauce called *tare*.

ファミリーレストラン　*family restaurant*

Family restaurants are franchised restaurants that cater to a wide variety of customers, especially families, at reasonable prices. They are often located along large roads, making them easily accessible by car. Although some specialize in a particular cuisine, many offer a wide range of dishes.

のれん　*noren*

Noren is a slit curtain that is hung in the doorway of a restaurant when it is open. If the *noren* is tucked inside the door, the establishment is not open for business.

丼物　*donburimono*

Donburimono is a dish that consists of a bowl of rice topped with various cooked foods. Some of the most popular *donburimono* are *tendon*, with a topping of deep-fried seafood and vegetables; *katsudon*, with a topping of pork cutlet; *oyakodon* with a topping of chicken and egg; and *gyudon*, which has a topping of sliced beef and onions.

海藻　*kaiso* | seaweed

Kaiso are various types of edible seaweed. *Nori* is a sheet of dried laver, which is typically used for wrapping *onigiri* rice balls and *sushi* rolls. *Wakame* is used for *miso* soup and salad. *Konbu* is dried kelp, used to make soup stock or as an ingredient of simmered dishes. *Hijiki* is usually cooked with deep-fried *tofu* and shredded carrots, seasoned with soy sauce and sugar. *Mozuku* is a type of seaweed found in Okinawa and is eaten as a vinegared dish. These various types of seaweed are very nutritious and an indispensable part of the Japanese diet.

やきとりは、直訳すると「火あぶりの鶏」という意味で、材料には、普通、鳥の肉、肝、皮のほか、ねぎなどいろいろな野菜も用います。一口サイズの材料を竹串に刺して焼きます。しばしば、たれと呼ばれる特製のしょうゆをベースにした甘いソースにつけます。

ファミリーレストランとは、特に家族連れを中心とした幅広い客層に安価な食事を提供するチェーンのレストランのこと。車で来やすいように、その多くは幹線道路沿いにあります。なかには、特定の料理を専門としているところもありますが、多くはいろいろな種類の料理を出します。

のれんとは、料理店が営業中に入り口にかける、切れ目が入ったカーテンのこと。のれんが入り口の内側にしまってあれば、その店は準備中です。

丼物は、どんぶりに盛ったご飯にさまざまな料理をのせた料理。最も人気がある丼物には、揚げた海の幸や野菜をのせた天丼、トンカツをのせたカツ丼、鶏肉と卵をのせた親子丼、薄切りの牛肉と玉ねぎをのせた牛丼などがあります。

海藻は、さまざまな種類の食用の海草です。海苔は、シート状にして、主に、おにぎりや巻き寿司を巻くのに使われます。ワカメは、みそ汁やサラダに使われます。昆布は、干物にして、だしを作ったり、煮物の具材として使ったりします。ヒジキは、油揚げや刻みにんじんと一緒に煮込み、しょうゆと砂糖で味付けするのが一般的です。モズクは、沖縄県に見られる海藻の一種で、酢の物にして食べます。こうした多様な海藻は栄養に富み、日本人の日々の食事に欠かせない存在となっています。

Types of tea｜お茶の種類

green tea	This tea is usually brewed using unfermented tea leaves, but can also be made by mixing powdered green tea with hot water to make tea.
tea or black tea	This tea is brewed using fermented tea leaves.
oolong-cha or oolong tea	This tea is brewed using half-fermented tea leaves.
sencha	As opposed to the tea made with powdered green tea, *sencha* refers to brewed tea. It also refers to the middle grade tea leaves for brewing. The leaves higher in grade than *sencha* are called *gyokuro*, and those lower in grade are called *bancha*.

Related Vocabulary｜関連語彙

- ■定食：a combo / a combination (meal)
- ■箸：chopsticks
- ■箸置き：a chopsticks holder
- ■爪楊枝：a toothpick
- ■材料：ingredients / materials
- ■あぶる：to grill / to roast
- ■焼く：to broil / to bake / to toast
- ■炒める：to fry
- ■揚げる：to deep-fry
- ■生姜：ginger
- ■豆腐：*tofu* / bean curd
- ■納豆：*natto* / fermented soy beans
- ■鰹節：dried bonito flakes
- ■里芋：taro
- ■れんこん：lotus root
- ■ごぼう：burdock
- ■しいたけ：*shiitake* mushroom
- ■まつたけ：*matsutake* mushroom
- ■漬物：Japanese pickles
- ■梅干：pickled Japanese apricot / pickled Japanese plum
- ■もち：a rice cake
- ■おにぎり：a rice ball
- ■おでん：a Japanese stew
- ■おせち料理：special dishes for the New Year celebration

緑茶	普通、発酵していない茶葉を煎じて入れるが、粉末にした茶葉にお湯を混ぜて入れることもある。
紅茶	発酵した茶葉を煎じて入れる。
ウーロン茶	半発酵茶を煎じて入れる。
煎茶	粉末にした抹茶に対する言葉で、煎じた茶を意味する。また、煎茶に使う茶葉で中等の品質のものも指す。煎茶より高級なものを玉露、品質が低いものを番茶という。

- ■雑煮：a special New Year's soup of rice cakes, vegetables, and meat
- ■せんべい：Japanese rice cracker
- ■和菓子：Japanese sweets
- ■甘酒：sweetened *sake*
- ■刺身：sliced raw fish
- ■ワサビ：Japanese horseradish
- ■ガリ：vinegared ginger
- ■コイ：carp
- ■サンマ：saury
- ■マグロ：tuna
- ■カツオ：bonito
- ■ブリ：yellowtail
- ■タイ：sea bream
- ■イワシ：sardine
- ■タコ：octopus
- ■イカ：squid / cuttlefish
- ■マグロのトロ：fatty tuna
- ■エビ：prawn / shrimp
- ■ウニ：sea urchin
- ■料亭：a Japanese restaurant
- ■屋台：a food stall / a food stand
- ■二日酔い：a hangover
- ■〜円で飲み放題：all-you-can-drink for 〜 yen
- ■〜円で食べ放題：all-you-can-eat for 〜 yen

 **Dialogue** | 対話

Food for a king

J : How would you like to have *sushi* tonight?

F : Sorry, I had *sushi* for lunch. I went to a place where the dishes of *sushi* were circulating on a conveyer belt. I've never been to a restaurant like that before.

J : Ah, that's what we call *kaiten-zushi*. Okay, I have another idea. I'm going to introduce you to one of my favorite Japanese B-*kyu* gourmet restaurants.

F : BQ? Do you mean barbeque?

J : No. B-*kyu* means B-grade food. There are a lot of really good and inexpensive foods that you can get in Japan. I know a really good restaurant that has *okonomi-yaki.* That is a really good pancake dish. It's not sweet, but savory, and has noodles, meat, and vegetables in it. This type of pancake is from Hiroshima, the western part of Honshu.

F : Sounds good to me.

J : Did you know that traditional Japanese cuisine is on UNESCO's Intangible Cultural Heritage List?

F : No, I didn't.

J : Japanese food is tasty and healthy. Many seasonal ingredients are used. And the chefs really put a lot of effort into presentation. If you get a chance to try *kaiseki ryori*, you'll understand why *washoku* has been placed on the Intangible Cultural Heritage List.

F : *Washoku*?

J : *Washoku* is translated as Japanese cuisine. We also say *yoshoku* for Western dishes that have been transformed by Japanese chefs.

F : You know, all this food conversation is making me hungry. Is that *okonomi-yaki* restaurant near here?

絶品の料理

J : 今夜は、おすしでもどう？

F : すまない、おすしは<u>昼</u>に食べたんだよ。すしの皿がベルトコンベアに乗って運ばれる店へ行ったんだ。あんな店は今まで行ったことがなかったよ。

J : ああ、私たちは回転寿司って呼んでるわ。わかった。じゃ別の案があるわよ。私の好きなB級グルメのお店を紹介してあげるわ。

F : BQ？　それって、バーベキューかい？

J : 違うわ。B級っていうのはBグレードの食べ物という意味。日本には、本当においしくて安い食べ物がたくさんあるんだから。お好み焼きが絶品のお店を知っているわ。とってもおいしいパンケーキみたいな料理よ。甘くはなくて、スパイシーに味付けしてあって、麺や肉や野菜が入っているの。この種類のお好み焼きは、日本の西寄りにある広島から伝わったのよ。

F : いいんじゃない。

J : 日本の伝統料理がユネスコの世界無形文化遺産だってこと知ってた？

F : いや、知らなかったよ。

J : 日本料理はおいしくて健康的。いろんな旬の食材を使うしね。それに板前さんが盛り付けにすごく手間をかけるのよ。懐石料理を食べる機会があったら、和食がなぜ無形文化遺産リストに掲載されたかわかるわよ。

F : 和食って？

J : 和食は日本料理のこと。洋食という言葉もあるわ。日本人の料理人が日本風にアレンジした西洋料理を意味するの。

F : ねえ、食べ物のことばかり話してたら、おなかが減ってきたよ。そのお好み焼きの店ってこの近くかい？

---

food (fit) for a king：
　（王様に適した料理という意味から）絶品
　の料理
conveyer belt：ベルトコンベア
gourmet：食通、グルメ

savory：薬味が効いた
seasonal ingredient：旬の食材
presentation：見栄え、盛り付け
be transformed：〜に変形させられる

National Holidays
祝日

Introduction | 概説

日本には、1年に祝日が何日あるかご存じでしょうか。加えて、振替休日や国民の休日などの規定で、それ以外の日が休日になることもあります。

There are 16 national holidays in Japan. Depending on the calendar, there may be other days that turn into holidays. If a national holiday falls on a Sunday, the nearest following workday, usually Monday, becomes a holiday. Also, when a day is sandwiched between two holidays, it also turns into a holiday. This periodically occurs between **Respect-for-the-Aged Day** and **Autumnal Equinox Day**.

🔍 Respect-for-the-Aged Day → p.102　　　Autumnal Equinox Day → p.100

日本の祝日を少し詳しく見てみると、皇室に関連する日が多いことに気づくでしょう。それぞれの祝日のいわれが年々薄れていき、ただの休日という意味しか持たなくなるのも時の流れでしょうか。

It is interesting to note that five of the national holidays are related to the Imperial Family. The current **Emperor's Birthday**, February 23, is a holiday for as long as he is on the throne. **National Foundation Day** falls on February 11, which according to legend was the day of the enthronement of Japan's first **emperor**—the Emperor Jimmu. **Showa Day**, April 29, was once celebrated as the Emperor Showa's birthday, and now the holiday commemorates the Showa Period (1926–1989). **Culture Day**, November 3, was once celebrated as the Emperor Meiji's birthday. **Labor Thanksgiving Day**, November 23, corresponds with an Imperial rite which features the **emperor** giving thanks for the new harvest.

In addition, the **Vernal** and **Autumnal Equinoxes** are national

　日本には16の法定祝日があります。暦によって、他の日も休日になることがあります。祝日が日曜日にあたる場合、その後の直近の平日（たいていは月曜日）が休日になります。また、祝日に挟まれた平日も休日になりますが、この状況は、敬老の日と秋分の日の間で周期的に発生します。

| turn into 〜：〜になる | periodically：定期的に、周期的に |
| fall on 〜：（日付・行事などが）〜にあたる | |

　注目すべきは、祝日のうち5日が皇室と関係があるという事実です。現在の天皇誕生日は2月23日で、御在位である限り祝日扱いになります。2月11日の建国記念の日は、伝説によると初代天皇の神武天皇が即位された日です。4月29日の昭和の日は、かつて昭和天皇の誕生日として祝われていましたが、今は昭和時代（1926 〜 1989）を記憶に刻むための祝日です。11月3日の文化の日は、かつて明治節（明治天皇の誕生日）として祝われていた日です。さらに、11月23日の勤労感謝の日は、天皇がその年の新たな収穫に感謝する皇室の儀式を行う日と同じ日です。

　加えて、秋分の日と春分の日が祝日になっています。1月の第2月曜日に祝われる成人の日は、成人に達した人たちを祝福する日です。7月の第3月曜日の海の日は海に感謝する日で、9月の第3月曜日の敬老の日は高齢者を敬う日です。体育の日は、1964年の東京オリンピックが開会された日に合わせて、

holidays. **Coming-of-Age Day**, the second Monday of January, honors those who have reached legal adulthood. **Marine Day**, the third Monday of July, is a day to thank the seas. **Respect-for-the-Aged Day**, the third Monday of September, honors the elderly. **Sports Day**, the second Monday of October, corresponds with the opening of the 1964 Tokyo Olympic Games. In 2016, a new holiday on August 11 called **Mountain Day** was added.

🔍 Emperor's Birthday → p.98   National Foundation Day → p.98
emperor → p.26   Showa Day → p.100
Culture Day → p.104   Labor Thanksgiving Day → p.104
Vernal Equinox Day → p.100   Coming-of-Age Day → p.98
Marine Day → p.102   Sports Day → p.102   Mountain Day → p.102

最後に、休日と日本の労働慣行に関しての一考察を。休暇を堂々と取るのが苦手な日本人が、家族サービスや帰省のために出かける旅行はまさに苦行。混雑覚悟でどうして一斉に移動しなければならないのか、外国人には理解できないかもしれません。

Work culture in Japan discourages people from taking long vacations, especially while other colleagues are still in the office. Therefore, most people make their travel plans during the holidays when all employees are off work. There are three periods when workers and students have several consecutive days off: The **New Year's holiday**, *Golden Week* (April 29–May 5), which includes **Showa Day**, **Constitution Memorial Day**, **Greenery Day**, and **Children's Day**, and lastly *obon* in mid-August. Because many people take their holidays during these periods, prices for travel and accommodation sky-rocket. There can also be terrible congestion at airports, on highways, and at popular travel destinations. The congestion that occurs at the end of a holiday period, when many people are making their way back home, has been labeled the U-turn rush.

🔍 New Year's holiday (New Year's Day) → p.98   *Golden Week* → p.102
Constitution Memorial Day → p.100   Greenery Day → p.100
Children's Day → p.100   *obon* → p.114

10月の第2月曜日に祝われます。2016年には、新しい祝日、8月11日の山の日が加わりました。

be related to 〜：〜と関連のある legend：伝説 enthronement：即位 commemorate：〜を記念する	correspond with 〜：〜に一致する give thanks for 〜：〜に感謝する harvest：収穫

　日本の労働慣行では、同僚が仕事をしているのに休みは取りづらいとする傾向があります。ですから、ほとんどの日本人は、全従業員が休暇を取る期間に旅行をすることになります。労働者も学生も、連続した休日が取れる期間が1年に3回あります。正月、昭和の日・憲法記念日・みどりの日・こどもの日を含むゴールデンウィーク（4月29〜5月5日）、それと8月中旬のお盆です。多くの日本人がこれらの期間に集中的に休暇を取るため、旅行や宿泊施設の料金は跳ね上がり、空港や高速道路や観光地はひどい混雑となってしまいます。これらの休暇期間の最終日に大勢の旅行者が帰途につくために引き起こされる混雑は、Uターンラッシュと呼ばれています。

colleague：（会社の）同僚 consecutive：連続する	accommodation：宿泊施設 sky-rocket：急騰する

National holidays in Japan | 日本の祝日

元日	New Year's Day
成人の日	Coming-of-Age Day
建国記念の日	National Foundation Day
天皇誕生日	Emperor's Birthday
春分の日	Vernal Equinox Day
昭和の日	Showa Day
憲法記念日	Constitution Memorial Day
みどりの日	Greenery Day
こどもの日	Children's Day
海の日	Marine Day
山の日	Mountain Day
敬老の日	Respect-for-the-Aged Day
秋分の日	Autumnal Equinox Day
体育の日	Sports Day
文化の日	Culture Day
勤労感謝の日	Labor Thanksgiving Day

1月1日	January 1
1月の第2月曜日	the second Monday of January
2月11日	February 11
2月23日	February 23
3月21日ごろ	around March 21
4月29日	April 29
5月3日	May 3
5月4日	May 4
5月5日	May 5
7月の第3月曜日	the third Monday of July
8月11日	August 11
9月の第3月曜日	the third Monday of September
9月23日ごろ	around September 23
10月の第2月曜日	the second Monday of October
11月3日	November 3
11月23日	November 23

1. 2019年は、「天皇の即位の日及び即位礼正殿の儀の行われる日を休日とする法律」に基づき、天皇の即位の日の5月1日及び即位礼正殿の儀が行われる日の10月22日は休日になります。
2. 2020年以降、「体育の日」は「スポーツの日」になります。
3. 国民の祝日に関する法律の特例によって、2020年に限り、「海の日」は7月23日に、「体育の日（スポーツの日）」は7月24日に、「山の日」は8月10日になります。
（内閣府HPより）

元日 *Ganjitsu* | New Year's Day

Ganjitsu is New Year's Day, which is Japan's most important holiday. It is customary to make the year's first visit to a temple or shrine. This is called *hatsumode*. There are many family reunions, where a traditional meal called *osechi* is eaten and a special sweet herb *sake* called *toso* is consumed. Children receive money gifts called *otoshidama*. Entryways are decorated with bamboo and pine branch arrangements called *kadomatsu* and a straw and paper decoration called *shimekazari.*

成人の日 *Seijin-no-hi* | Coming-of-Age Day

Seijin-no-hi is Coming-of-Age Day. Observed on the second Monday of January, this holiday celebrates adulthood for all those who will have turned twenty within the school year, which in Japan ends on April 1. Local municipal communities have ceremonies where the new adults are congratulated and invited to participate responsibly in the community.

建国記念の日
Kenkoku-kinen-no-hi | National Foundation Day

Kenkoku-kinen-no-hi is National Foundation Day. Observed on February 11, this holiday commemorates the legendary enthronement of the Emperor Jimmu, Japan's first emperor, in 660 B.C.

天皇誕生日 *Tenno-tanjobi* | Emperor's Birthday

Tenno-tanjobi is the current Emperor's Birthday. Observed on February 23, this holiday celebrates the birthday of Emperor Naruhito. The general public is allowed onto the Imperial Palace grounds on this day, and the Imperial Family greets the visitors.

元日は日本人にとって最も大切な祝日です。お寺や神社に新年最初の参詣をする
のが習慣になっており、これは「初詣」と呼ばれています。多くの家族が集まり、
「おせち」と呼ばれる伝統料理を食べ、「とそ」と呼ばれるハーブで香りを付けた特
別な甘い酒を飲みます。子どもたちは「お年玉」と呼ばれるお金の贈り物をもらい
ます。家の入り口は、「門松」と呼ばれる竹と松で作られた置物や、「しめ飾り」と呼
ばれるワラと紙で作られた飾り物で飾られます。

成人の日は1月の第2月曜日で、学齢において20歳に達したすべての人たちが成
人になったことを祝うための祝日です。地方自治体が行う式典では、新成人は祝
福されるとともに、地域社会への責任ある参加を促されます。

建国記念の日は2月11日で、日本の神話上の初代天皇である神武天皇が紀元前
660年に即位したことを記念する日です。

天皇誕生日は2月23日で、今上天皇であられる徳仁陛下の誕生日を祝う日です。
この日には、国民は皇居広場に入ることが許され、天皇ご一家が訪問者にご挨拶
をされます。

春分の日と秋分の日
Shunbun-no-hi and *Shubun-no-hi* | Vernal Equinox Day and Autumnal Equinox Day

Shunbun-no-hi is Vernal Equinox Day, and it usually falls on March 21. *Shubun-no-hi* is Autumnal Equinox Day, which usually falls on September 23. Both holidays have a focus on the Buddhist philosophy of respecting one's ancestors. Relatives gather to visit the graves of their ancestors and attend Buddhist services.

昭和の日 *Showa-no-hi* | Showa Day

Showa-no-hi, or Showa Day is observed on April 29. Its official definition is a day "to reflect on Japan's Showa Period when recovery was made after the turbulent war years, and to think of the country's future." The day used to be celebrated as the birthday of Emperor Hirohito, whose reign is called the Showa Period.

憲法記念日 *Kenpo-kinenbi* | Constitution Memorial Day

Kenpo-kinenbi is Constitution Memorial Day. Observed on May 3, this holiday commemorates the day when Japan's present Constitution went into effect in 1947.

みどりの日 *Midori-no-hi* | Greenery Day

Midori-no-hi is Greenery Day. Observed on May 4, this day used to be celebrated on April 29, the former Emperor Showa's birthday, to commemorate his interest in biology. When April 29 was redesignated as Showa Day, Greenery Day was moved to May 4.

こどもの日 *Kodomo-no-hi* | Children's Day

Kodomo-no-hi is Children's Day. Observed on May 5, this holiday is to give thanks for the health and happiness of Japan's children. Once celebrated as Boys' Day, the tradition of flying carp streamers on a pole to wish for the healthy growth of boys is still observed as part of the holiday.

春分の日は3月21日ごろに、秋分の日は9月23日ごろに祝われます。両日とも、先祖を敬う仏教思想に基づいています。親戚が集まり、先祖の墓を訪れ、法事に参列します。

昭和の日は4月29日です。昭和の日の法律上の定義は「激動の日々を経て、復興を遂げた昭和の時代を顧（かえり）み、国の将来に思いをいたす」日です。4月29日はかつて、昭和時代に即位していた昭和天皇の誕生日として祝われていました。

憲法記念日は5月3日で、現行の日本国憲法が1947年に施行された日を記念する祝日です。

みどりの日は5月4日で、かつての昭和天皇誕生日の4月29日に、昭和天皇の生物学に対するご興味の深さを記念する意図で祝われていました。4月29日が新たに昭和の日として制定されるとともに、みどりの日は5月4日に移動されました。

こどもの日は5月5日で、日本の子どもたちの健康と幸福に感謝する日です。この祝日は、かつて男児の日（端午の節句）として祝われていたもので、お祝いの一部として、こいのぼりを長い竿（さお）にたなびかせ、男児の健全な成長を願う伝統習慣が今でも行われています。

ゴールデンウィーク *Golden Week*

Golden Week is a series of holidays comprising Showa Day on April 29, Constitution Memorial Day on May 3, Greenery Day on May 4, and Children's Day on May 5. *Golden Week* is one of the three annual holiday seasons in Japan, along with *obon* in mid-August and the New Year's holiday. Many people travel during this period, so transportation systems and tourist spots can become crowded.

海の日 *Umi-no-hi* | Marine Day

Umi-no-hi is Marine Day. Observed on the third Monday of July, this holiday is for expressing gratitude for the benefits given by the sea and praying for the prosperity of Japan as a maritime nation.

山の日 *Yama-no-hi* | Mountain Day

Yama-no-hi is Mountain Day. Observed on August 11, this holiday is for the nation to have opportunities to feel affinity toward mountains and to appreciate the benefits brought about by mountains.

敬老の日 *Keiro-no-hi* | Respect-for-the-Aged Day

Keiro-no-hi is Respect-for-the-Aged Day. Observed on the third Monday of September, this holiday honors seniors and celebrates their longevity.

体育の日 *Taiiku-no-hi* | Sports Day

Taiiku-no-hi is Sports Day. Observed on the second Monday of October, this holiday is for promoting the good physical and mental health of the Japanese. The day was established as a commemoration of the Tokyo Olympic Games held in 1964.

ゴールデンウィークは、4月29日の昭和の日、5月3日の憲法記念日、5月4日のみどりの日、5月5日のこどもの日を含む連休です。ゴールデンウィークは、8月中旬のお盆、正月の休暇と並んで、日本における三大連休の一つです。多くの人がこの期間に旅行に出かけるため、交通機関や観光地は混み合います。

海の日は7月の第3月曜日で、海から与えられる恩恵に感謝の意を表し、海洋国家としての日本の繁栄を祈る日です。

山の日は8月11日で、国民が山に親しむ機会を得て、山の恩恵に感謝するための日です。

敬老の日は9月の第3月曜日で、高齢者に対して敬意を表し、長寿を祝うための日です。

体育の日は10月の第2月曜日で、日本国民の心身の健康を振興するための日です。この日は、1964年に開かれた東京オリンピックを記念して定められました。

文化の日　*Bunka-no-hi* | Culture Day

Bunka-no-hi is Culture Day. Observed on November 3, this day celebrates Japanese culture. Local governments organize various cultural events and the national government presents a prestigious award called *Bunka Kunsho* (Order of Culture) to those who have excelled in art, culture, or science. Originally, this holiday was celebrated as the Emperor Meiji's birthday, but also commemorates the announcement of Japan's current Constitution on November 3, 1946.

勤労感謝の日　*Kinrokansha-no-hi* | Labor Thanksgiving Day

Kinrokansha-no-hi is Labor Thanksgiving Day, and it is observed on November 23. This is a day to give thanks to the nation's labor force and to appreciate the products of their labor.

11月3日は日本の文化を祝う日です。地方自治体は文化に関するさまざまな行事を行いますし、政府は芸術、文化、科学の分野で優れた功績を残した人をたたえて文化勲章を授与します。11月3日はもともと明治節 (明治天皇の誕生日) として祝われていましたが、現在は1946年11月3日の日本国憲法発布を記念する日でもあります。

勤労感謝の日は11月23日で、日本の労働者と労働の賜物としての生産物に感謝を捧げる日です。

 **Dialogue** | 対話

How many holidays do you have in Japan?

F : What's the biggest holiday in Japan?

J : **New Year's Day** is the biggest. We have a special meal, and we often visit relatives. My kids love it because they get money from their relatives—we call these gifts *otoshidama*.

F : And do they get Christmas presents too?

J : We give our kids just one small gift for Christmas, and we have a small family party. It's not a holiday in Japan. One or two weeks after **New Year's Day**, we have **Coming-of-Age Day**. That would be a good chance for you to take pictures of women wearing *kimono*.

F : Oh? What happens on **Coming-of-Age Day**?

J : Those who've become adults attend a ceremony where a public official gives them a kind of pep talk.

F : That doesn't sound so interesting. Are young people required to attend?

J : No, it's not required. To be honest, a lot of these young adults find the ceremony boring. But it's a good chance for them to meet up with old friends. After the ceremony they typically go out together for a party. And of course those wearing *kimono* enjoy taking pictures of each other.

F : Ah, that sounds more interesting. How many holidays do you have in Japan?

J : I think it's about sixteen now. There have been a few new ones over the years. I think the government is trying to get people to work less and spend more money.

F : Well, that's good news. Which holiday is your favorite?

J : These days I like *Golden Week* the best. It's a series of holidays in the spring. It starts with **Showa Day**, which was once celebrated as the birthday of the Emperor Showa, and ends with **Children's Day**. It's a nice time to relax or make a short trip.

祝日はいくつあるの？

F：日本で最も大切な祝日というと？

J：元日が一番かしら。特別な料理を食べて、親戚の家に年始参りに行くの。私の子どもたちは、親戚からお金のプレゼントをもらえるから楽しみにしてるわ。それはお年玉というのよ。

F：子どもたちはクリスマスプレゼントももらえるのかい？

J：クリスマスには子どもたちにちょっとした贈り物をあげて、家族で小さなパーティーをやるのよ。クリスマスは祝日ではないの。元日から1～2週間たつと成人の日。成人の日は着物を着た女性の写真を撮るにはいい機会よ。

F：へー。成人の日って何をするの？

J：成人になった人たちが式典に出席して、自治体の役人が激励の言葉みたいなものを贈るの。

F：あまり面白そうじゃないね。若い人たちは出席しないといけないのかい？

J：義務付けられてはないわ。正直、若い人たちの多くは式典が退屈と思ってるわ。でも、旧友に会う良い機会なのよ。式の後に皆でパーティーに出かけるのが普通だしね。それに、着物を着ている人たちはお互いの写真を撮って楽しんでるわ。

F：ああ、そっちのほうが面白そうだね。日本には祝日がいくつあるの？

J：今は16日ね。このところ、新しい祝日がいくつか増えたの。政府は国民の労働時間を短くして、もっとお金を使うように仕向けているんだと思うわ。

F：ふーん、それはいいことじゃないか。ところで、祝日ではどれが一番好き？

J：このごろはゴールデンウィークが一番ね。春の連休よ。かつて昭和天皇誕生日だった昭和の日から、こどもの日までの休み。くつろいだり、ちょっとした旅行ができるってわけ。

7

National Holidays

対話

---

pep talk：激励の言葉
boring：退屈な

meet up with ～：～に会う
a series of ～：一連の～

Annual Events
年中行事

 Introduction | 概説

年中行事には、その国の国民性や生活習慣が反映されています。日本では、伝統的な習わしに加えて、外国からもさまざまな習慣を取り入れてきました。

Other than official holidays, there are numerous festivals, called *matsuri*, and other annual events held in Japan throughout the year. Some have existed in Japan for centuries, and others are recent imports. For example, the Gion Matsuri in **Kyoto** has been held yearly for over 1,000 years, while Christmas celebrations became popular only after World War II.

🔍 *matsuri* → p.114   Kyoto → p.48

お盆は1年に1度、家族や親族のもとに戻ってくるとされる先祖の霊を、心を尽くして迎え入れ、慰める仏教行事です。

One very important event is *obon*, or the *bon* festival, which is a time to honor the spirits of those who have passed away. During the summer, it is common to see lively *bon'odori*, or *bon* dances, where members of the community join in traditional dance. The dances and many other aspects of *obon* ceremonies are done to guide and entertain the spirits of the deceased, who are thought to visit their homes during this period.

🔍 *obon* → p.114

　日本では祝日以外に、祭りなどの年中行事が1年を通じて数多く行われています。何世紀も前から続いてきたものもありますが、近年になって外国からもたらされたものもあります。たとえば、京都の祇園祭は、1,000年以上も毎年行われてきましたが、クリスマスのお祝いが盛んになったのは戦後のことです。

numerous：無数の	import：輸入品

　日本人にとって非常に大切な行事に、故人の霊を供養するためのお盆があります。夏には、町内の人たちで集まって昔からの踊りを楽しむ、盆踊りをよく見かけます。お盆の期間には故人の霊が家に戻ってくると考えられていますが、盆踊りなどのお盆の儀式の多くは、故人の霊を供養するために行われるのです。

pass away：死ぬ、亡くなる	lively：にぎやかな

お盆が、地方によって7月に行われたり8月になったりする理由を説明します。昔ながらの暦にのっとって行われることがある、というのがその答えです。

Most regions observe *obon* in the middle of August, which was the seventh month according to the old lunisolar calendar. Some areas, such as **Tokyo**, celebrate *obon* in July. This is because when the lunisolar calendar was scrapped in 1873, the government insisted that *obon* continue to be celebrated on the same calendar dates—even though there was about a one-month difference in real time. Old traditions die hard—most of Japan resisted the government and to this day continues to celebrate *obon* during August.

 Tokyo → p.48

日本には子どもを中心にした面白い年中行事があります。節分では、子どもたちが家の邪気や災いを追い払う役目を担います。

Interesting annual events for children are *setsubun* and *shichigosan*. During *setsubun*, children can throw roasted beans about the house to ward off evil spirits and other misfortune. In some families, an adult might put on a demon's mask and approach the children. The demon is pelted with beans until it leaves.

Shichigosan is a time when girls of three and seven, and boys of three and five dress up, often in *kimono*, and visit a **shrine** with their parents to pray for the children's good health. This custom originated at a time when child mortality rates were much higher.

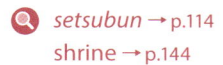 *setsubun* → p.114   *shichigosan* → p.114   *kimono* → p.62
shrine → p.144

お盆は、ほとんどの地域において、太陰太陽暦の7月にあたる、8月中旬に行われますが、東京など一部の地域では7月に行われます。これは、旧暦が1873年に廃止されたとき、新暦が旧暦とはおよそ1か月ずれていたにもかかわらず、政府が、お盆は日付を合わせて、無理やり7月に行うことを主張したためです。そんなことで古くからの伝統が破られるはずはありません。日本のほとんどの地域では、そういった政府の意向を拒絶し、今日まで、お盆を8月（つまり旧暦でいう7月）に行っているのです。

lunisolar calendar：太陰太陽暦 scrap：〜を廃止する	die hard：なかなか消えない

　子どもに関する興味深い年中行事として、節分と七五三があります。節分では、子どもたちが煎った豆を家の内と外にまき、邪気や災厄を追い払います。鬼の面を着けた大人が子どもたちに近寄っていき、子どもたちはこの鬼に豆を投げつけ、ついには家から追い出す、といったことをする家もあります。
　七五三は、3歳と7歳の女の子と3歳と5歳の男の子が、着物などで正装し、健康を祈って親と一緒に神社へお参りする儀式です。この行事は幼児死亡率がとても高かったときに生まれました。

roasted beans：煎り豆 ward off 〜：〜を寄せ付けない evil spirit：邪気	misfortune：災厄 pelt with 〜：〜を投げつける mortality rate：死亡率

クリスチャンでもない日本人が、クリスマスやバレンタインデーに大騒ぎするのはなぜでしょう。中元や歳暮と同様、人間関係の潤滑油として贈り物をし合う日本人の習慣にピッタリはまったから、と考えるとわかりやすいでしょう。

The Japanese also celebrate annual events like Christmas and Saint Valentine's Day. Although it may seem strange that a country with few Christians would adopt Christian customs, these two dates fit well with Japanese culture. Christmas and St. Valentine's Day are similar to some traditional Japanese events such as *chugen* and *seibo* in that gifts are exchanged. The exchange of gifts has been an important way for the Japanese to show gratitude to others and to foster human relations. These imported events allow Japanese people to exchange gifts among family members and close friends.

 *chugen* → p.116   *seibo* → p.116

日本人は、クリスマスやバレンタインデーのような日も祝います。キリスト教信者が少ない国でキリスト教の習慣が行われているのは不思議に思われるかもしれませんが、実は日本の文化によくなじむものなのです。クリスマスやバレンタインデーは贈答習慣として、中元や歳暮などに相通ずる側面があります。日本では、日ごろの感謝の気持ちを表したり、より良い人間関係を築くために、贈答品をやり取りするのが昔からの習慣です。これらの海外から入ってきた行事が、家族や親しい友達の間で贈答品を交わす良い機会となっているのです。

fit well with ～：～によく合う
gratitude：感謝の意

foster：～を育む

祭り　*matsuri* | festivals

Matsuri refers to festivals. There are numerous *matsuri* in Japan throughout the year. Although there are differences according to the region, most are held in order to show thanks for the harvest and to pray for prosperity. The typical *matsuri* is characterized by participants parading through town while carrying portable shrines called *mikoshi* or hauling festival floats called *dashi*.

お盆　*obon*

Obon is a Buddhist annual event observed from August 13 to 15, or in some areas from July 13 to 15. Many families hold reunions at this time. The purpose is to welcome their ancestors' spirits that are believed to return to visit their families.

節分　*setsubun*

Setsubun is a traditional ceremony to ward off evil and is held in early February. People throw beans to drive away demons while chanting "Oni-wa-soto, fuku-wa-uchi," meaning "Out with demons! In with good luck!" It is customary for family members to eat the same number of beans as their age.

七五三　*shichigosan*

Shichigosan, translated as 7-5-3, is held on November 15. Parents take their three-year-old boys and girls, five-year-old boys, and seven-year-old girls to the local tutelary shrines to pray for their safe and healthy future. After the visit, long candy sticks called *chitoseame* are purchased at the shrine and then distributed to relatives and neighbors.

日本では1年中、数え切れないほどの祭りが行われており、その内容も地域によってさまざまですが、ほとんどの祭りは収穫に感謝し、繁栄を祈るために行われます。典型的な祭りでは、参加者が、神輿（みこし）と呼ばれる持ち運び式の神社を担いだり、山車（だし）と呼ばれる祭り用の台車をひいたりしながら、町中を練り歩きます。

お盆は、8月13日から15日、地域によっては、7月13日から15日にかけて行われる仏教の年中行事の一つです。多くの家族がこの時期に集まります。祖先の霊が家族のもとに戻ってくると信じられており、その霊を迎えるのがこの行事の目的です。

節分は、邪気を追い払うための伝統的儀式で、2月初旬に行われます。鬼を追い払うために「鬼は外！　福は内！」（鬼は出て行け！　福は家の中へ）と唱えながら、豆をまきます。家族は、それぞれ自分の年齢と同じ数の豆を食べるのが習慣となっています。

七五三は、11月15日に行われる行事です。親は、3歳の男児と女児、5歳の男児、7歳の女児を地元の神社へ連れていき、子どもたちの安全と健康を願います。お参りが終わった後、「千歳飴」と呼ばれる長い棒状の飴を神社で買って、親戚や近所の人に配ります。

中元と歳暮　*chugen* and *seibo*

Chugen is a summer gift, and *seibo* is a winter gift. They are given to superiors, customers, and other people who have provided favors. Some typical *chugen* and *seibo* items are food, beverages, daily necessities such as soap and towels, and gift coupons.

 **Related Key Words**｜関連キーワード

MP3 32

年賀状　*nengajo*｜New Year's greeting cards

Nengajo are New Year's greeting postcards. People usually prepare the cards at the end of the year so that they can be delivered on New Year's Day. In addition to a New Year's message, the card usually has a photograph or graphic image. Postcards designed exclusively for this purpose have a lottery number, which adds to the enjoyment of exchanging these cards.

年始参り　*nenshimairi*｜New Year's visit

Nenshimairi is a New Year's courtesy visit to relatives, friends, superiors, and customers. People exchange these visits in order to wish for continued favor for the new year. Children typically receive money gifts called *otoshidama* from the adults during these visits.

初詣　*hatsumode*

Hatsumode is one's first visit of the year to a shrine or temple. A large shrine like Meiji Jingu in Tokyo will have over 3 million visitors in the first few days of the year.

中元は夏季の贈答品で、歳暮は冬季の贈答品です。中元と歳暮は、上司や顧客、お世話になった人たちに贈ります。中元と歳暮の品としては、食品、飲料、石鹸やタオルなどの日常生活品、商品券などが一般的です。

年賀状は、新年の挨拶をするためのハガキです。年賀状を送る人たちは年賀状が元日に配達されるように、通常、年末に準備をします。年賀状には、新年の挨拶に加えて、写真や絵などを添えるのが普通です。年賀状専用のハガキには抽選のくじ番号がついていて、年賀状をやり取りする楽しみを増してくれます。

年始参りは、親戚、友人、上司、顧客などに対して行う新年の儀礼訪問です。訪問し合うことによって、新しい年にも変わらず引き立ててもらうことを願います。年始参りでは、「お年玉」と呼ばれるお金の贈り物が大人から子どもたちへ贈られることが一般的です。

初詣は、神社やお寺に新年最初のお参りをすることです。東京の明治神宮のような大規模な神社には、三が日の間に300万人以上の人が参詣します。

新年会　*shinnenkai* | new year party

Shinnenkai is a new year party held among company colleagues and friends. The aim of the party is to celebrate the new year. A typical party involves eating and drinking at an *izakaya*.

花見　*hanami* | cherry blossom viewing

Hanami is cherry blossom viewing, which is done in spring when the cherry blossoms (*sakura*) are in full bloom. News organizations regularly report on the *sakura* front, which is the line showing where the trees most recently bloomed. Since the blossoms last only about a week, areas known for cherry trees can become very crowded. Often there are parties under the trees where people eat, drink, and socialize.

七夕　*tanabata*

Tanabata is a festival held on July 7, or in some areas August 7. The festival is based on a Chinese folk legend in which two stars—the Weaver Star (Vega) and the Cowherd Star (Altair)—love each other but can meet only once a year on this day. People decorate and display bamboo branches with long, narrow strips of colored paper upon which they inscribe their wishes and romantic aspirations.

紅葉狩り　*momijigari*

Momijigari is a traditional pastime of viewing the changing colors of autumn leaves. Visiting local parks, hiking, and driving in the mountains are popular ways of viewing the beautifully colored leaves.

忘年会　*bonenkai* | year-end party

Bonenkai is a year-end party, or more literally, a "forget-the-year party." Most companies will organize such parties, but there are many parties among colleagues and friends, as well. The aim of the party is to forget the unfortunate incidents and hardships of the past year.

新年会は、会社の同僚や友人の間で開かれる宴会で、新年の訪れを祝うために行われます。新年会は、居酒屋を利用し、飲食を楽しむ形式が典型的です。

花見は、桜が満開になる春に行われる、花を見る行事です。この時期、報道機関は、桜が開花し始める地点をたどる桜前線をニュースにのせます。桜の花の見頃は、ほんの1週間足らずなので、桜で有名な場所は、大勢の人で混み合います。桜の木の下で飲食をしながら、皆で楽しむ宴会を開くこともよくあります。

七夕は7月7日、地域によっては、8月7日に行われる祭り。中国の故事に由来し、それによると、織女星（ヴェガ）と牽牛星（アルタイル）の2つの星は互いに思い合いながら、1年に1度だけ、七夕の日にしか逢うことができません。人々は細長い色紙に願い事や夢を書きつけ、長い竹の枝に結んで飾り付けます。

紅葉狩りは、秋の紅葉を眺める昔ながらの行楽の一つ。人々は近くの公園を散策したり、ハイキングしたり、また山にドライブに出かけたりして、美しい紅葉を鑑賞します。

忘年会は、年末に開かれる宴会のことですが、文字どおりには「旧年を忘れる宴会」ということになります。ほとんどの会社で忘年会を催しますが、同僚や友人たちともよく開きます。忘年会は、1年の間に起きた不幸な出来事や災難を忘れるためのものなのです。

除夜の鐘　*joya-no-kane*

Joya-no-kane is the new year ceremony held at Buddhist temples. Beginning just before midnight on New Year's Eve, the temple bell is rung 108 times. Symbolically, each peal of the bell dispels one of the 108 earthly desires.

年越しそば　*toshikoshi-soba*

Toshikoshi-soba is the year-end dish of buckwheat noodles customarily eaten on New Year's Eve. People eat these long noodles in the hope that they will lead a long and fortunate life.

神輿　*mikoshi* | a portable shrine

Mikoshi are portable shrines used at festivals. The deity resting at the local tutelary shrine temporarily reposes in the *mikoshi* during the festival. Festival participants parade through the town carrying *mikoshi* on their shoulders, shouting "*Wasshoi, wasshoi*" to animate their procession.

山車　*dashi* | a festival float

Dashi are festival floats. These tall, elaborately decorated floats are hauled by festival participants. Some *dashi* are designed for people in festival costumes to dance and play instruments on them.

お宮参り　*omiyamairi*

Omiyamairi is the custom of taking a baby to the local tutelary shrine on the 20th, 30th, 50th, or 100th day after birth, depending on the area. The baby is usually carried by the paternal grandmother and accompanied by both parents to be recognized as a member of the local *Shinto* community. The baby is often made to cry in the ceremony in order to be heard by the tutelary deity.

除夜の鐘は、仏教寺院で行われる新年の行事。大みそかの深夜直前あたりから、寺の鐘を108回つきます。その一つきごとに1つ、合わせて108の煩悩を追い払うという意味があります。

年越しそばは、慣習として大みそかに食べるそばを指します。この長い麺のそばを食べることで、長寿と幸福を願うという意味合いがあります。

神輿は祭りで用いられる持ち運び式の神社。祭りの期間中、土地の神社の氏神が一時的に宿るとされます。祭りの参加者は、神輿を肩に担いで、「ワッショイ、ワッショイ」と声を上げて祭りを盛り上げ、町中を練り歩きます。

山車は祭りで使われる台車です。祭りの参加者が、細部まで飾り立てられた背の高い山車をひいて回ります。山車には、上に祭りの衣装を着た人が乗って、踊ったり楽器を奏でたりできるように作られているものもあります。

お宮参りは、地域によって、子どもの誕生から20日目、30日目、50日目、100日目に子どもを地元の神社に連れていってお参りをする習慣のことです。赤ん坊は、たいてい父方の祖母に抱きかかえられ、両親に伴われて参拝し、土地の神社の氏子として認めてもらうのです。この儀式では、しばしば氏神様に聞こえるようにと、赤ん坊に泣き声を上げさせます。

ひな祭り　*Hina Matsuri* | Doll Festival

Hina Matsuri is the Doll Festival held on March 3. Families display special *hina* dolls, which wear Heian Period clothing. This day is a chance to celebrate the growth of girls and wish for their health and happiness. At the festival, girls treat their guests with special sweet *sake* called *amazake* and some special food, including rice cakes called *hishimochi* and snacks called *hina-arare*.

彼岸　*higan*

Higan is a Buddhist memorial service for the deceased. It is held twice a year—during the weeks of the Vernal and Autumnal Equinoxes.

 **Related Vocabulary** | 関連語彙

■ 初日の出：the new year's first sunrise
■ たこ揚げ：kite flying
■ こま回し：top spinning

■ 帰省ラッシュ：the homecoming rush during holiday seasons
■ 出初式（でぞめしき）：the New Year's fire brigade display

3月3日に行われる女の子の祭り。平安時代の衣装をまとった独特のひな人形が家に飾られ、女子の成長を祝い、健康と幸せを祈ります。ひな祭りでは、女の子たちは、甘酒と、ひし餅やひなあられで客をもてなします。

彼岸は、故人の供養のために行われる法事で、年2回、それぞれ春分の日と秋分の日を中心とする週に行われます。

■海開き：the opening of a beach to swimmers
■花火大会：a fireworks display
■運動会：an athletic meet

■文化勲章：Order of Culture
■月見：moon viewing
■里帰り：returning to *one's* hometown
■大みそか：New Year's Eve

 # Dialogue | 対話

MP3
33

I thought we were just going to look at flowers!

J : What's wrong with you? You don't look well at all.

F : I've got a hangover—too much *sake* last night.

J : Ah, you went to a *hanami* party, didn't you?

F : I was told it was a flower viewing party. I thought we were going to look at flowers. Why didn't anyone tell me that it's also a drinking party?

J : Oh, stop complaining. No one forced you to drink.

F : Yes, they did! Some complete strangers asked us to join them. They gave us food, and they kept pouring *sake* for us. As soon as we left the first group, another group of people invited us over.

J : So, did you have a good time?

F : Are you kidding? I had a great time. And the flowers were so beautiful. I've never seen anything like it. I want to go again.

J : You better be quick. The blossoms don't last long. When you're feeling better, I'll tell you a little bit about *mujo*. It has to do with impermanence.

F : I hope this headache isn't permanent.

J＝日本人女性、F＝外国人男性を表します。

花を見に行くだけ、と思ってたんだ！

J： どうしたの？　気分が良くないみたいね。

F： 二日酔いなんだ。きのうの晩、飲みすぎちゃって。

J： あら、お花見に行ったのね。

F： 花を見る会だと言われたから、ただ花を見に行くだけ、と思っていたのに。飲み会だって、なんで誰も言わなかったのかなあ。

J： ぐちらないでよ。誰もお酒を無理強いしたわけじゃないでしょ。

F： いいや、無理強いされたよ。ぜんぜん知らない人から、仲間に入れようって誘われて、そしたら食べ物をくれるわ、お酒を注ぎ続けられるわ、という調子。そこを退散したと思ったら、すぐにまた別のグループから誘われたりして。

J： それで、楽しかったんでしょ？

F： もちろん！　最高だったよ。桜の花もとてもきれいだったし。あういうのは見たことなかったなあ。もう一度行きたいよ。

J： それなら、急いだほうがいいわよ。桜の花はすぐに散ってしまうから。今度、あなたの気分が良いときに、「無常感」について話してあげるわ。物事にはすべて終わりがあるってよ。

F： たしかに。この頭痛には終わりがあってほしいね。

---

hangover：二日酔い
Are you kidding?：まさか。
⇒「からかってるの？そんなこと聞くまでもな
いでしょ？」といった意味。

have to do with～：～と関係がある
impermanence：永続しないこと

Introduction | 概説

MP3
34

日本人の宗教観は、「寛容」なことで知られていますが、人生の二大イベントである結婚式と葬式にそれが表れているようです。

In Japan, many weddings are conducted according to *Shinto* tradition, while most **funerals** follow Buddhist tradition. This mix of religions poses no dilemma for the Japanese, who tend to be open-minded regarding religious practices and customs.

🔍 *Shinto* → p.144   funeral → p.130

神前結婚式は現在でもよく行われていますが、その発端は、大正天皇の皇太子時代の結婚式にあるようです。そのほか、キリスト教式、海外挙式など、最近の日本の結婚式には、実にさまざまな形式があります。

The *Shinto*-style wedding is patterned after the 1900 wedding of the Crown Prince, who was later known as the Emperor Taisho. A highlight of the *Shinto* ceremony is *san-san-ku-do*, where the bride and groom drink *sake* together. Wedding ceremonies are sometimes held at **shrines**, but more often they are held at hotels which provide both a room for the religious ceremony and a hall for the reception. Although many Japanese weddings are performed according to *Shinto* customs, Western elements, such as exchanging rings and cutting a cake, may be included. These days more Japanese couples choose to have the entire wedding in the Christian style, even though they aren't Christian. Another trend is for couples to get married overseas. With fewer guests invited and the honeymoon combined with the wedding ceremony, they save money.

🔍 *san-san-ku-do* → p.130   *sake* → p.82   shrines → p.144

　日本では、多くの結婚式が神式で行われていますし、葬式のほとんどが仏式で行われています。このように2つの宗教が混在していても、宗教儀式や慣習に関して寛容な日本人は矛盾を感じたりしません。

pose a dilemma for 〜：〜を板ばさみ状態にする

　神式の結婚式は、1900年の当時の皇太子（後の大正天皇）の結婚式に倣（なら）ったものです。神前結婚式のハイライトは三三九度で、新郎新婦がともに酒を飲む場面です。結婚式は神社で行われることもありますが、宗教的儀式場と宴会場の両方を提供できるホテルで行われるのが一般的です。多くの日本人が結婚式を神式で行いますが、西洋の風習である結婚指輪の交換やケーキのカットなどが取り入れられています。また、キリスト教徒でないのに、結婚式の全過程をキリスト教式で行う日本人も増えています。別の流行としては、海外で結婚式を挙げるカップルも増えています。招待客の数を少なくし、ハネムーンを兼ねることで、経費を削減できるのです。

be patterned after 〜：
　〜に倣う、〜を手本にする
highlight：山場

bride：新婦
groom：新郎

結婚は2つの家の結合と考えられ、本人の意思と関係なく決められた時代がありました。ただし、現在の「見合い」には、結婚する可能性のある相手を紹介する、という以上の意味合いはありません。

A Japanese wedding was originally considered a union of two families. For this reason, arranged marriages, called *miai kekkon*, were the norm until the end of World War II. Although the term *miai* still exists, it is more of an introduction service today—people freely choose their marriage partners.

🔍 *miai* → p.130

葬式は、仏教の儀式にのっとって行われるのが一般的です。

Japanese **funerals** are performed according to Buddhist customs. After a death, a **funeral** wake, called a *tsuya*, is held. Incense and candles are lit and other customs follow. The family and friends eat and drink as they reminisce about the deceased. On the **funeral** day, the body is cremated. The actual Buddhist ceremony involves a Buddhist monk reciting sutras. The deceased is given a posthumous Buddhist name.

結婚式と葬式、この人生の一大事を神道と仏教という二刀流で受け入れている国民性を、宗教という視点から考えようとすると無理があるかもしれません。生活になじんだ文化だとする考え方もあることに触れましょう。

Although weddings and **funerals** are basically religious ceremonies, the Japanese tend not to perform these rituals with any deep religious feeling. Rather, the ceremonies are part of the customs and culture that have been handed down through many generations.

日本人の結婚式は、かつては2つの家族の結合と考えられていました。そのため、見合い結婚は第二次世界大戦が終わるまで、ごく当たり前のことだったのです。見合いという言葉は現在でも使われていますが、現代の見合いは、結婚相手の紹介サービスのようなものです。見合いをした人は、自分の意思で結婚相手を選びます。

the norm：当たり前のこと

　日本の葬式は、仏教の儀式に基づいて行われます。人が亡くなると、通夜と呼ばれる儀式が行われます。線香やろうそくが灯され、その他の儀式が続きます。遺族や友人は、故人をしのんで食事をし、酒を酌み交わします。葬式の当日には、遺体は火葬されます。仏葬では、僧侶が読経をし、故人に死後の名前である戒名を与えます。

incense：お香、線香
the deceased：故人
cremate：〜を火葬にする
recite：〜を唱える

sutra：お経
posthumous name：
　戒名（宗派によっては、法名、法号とも）

　結婚式も葬式も、基本的に宗教的儀式なのですが、日本人はこれらの儀式を、深い信仰心から行っているわけではありません。むしろ、これらの儀式は、幾多の世代にもわたって引き継がれてきた習慣や文化の一部だと考えることができます。

hand down 〜：〜を（後世に）伝える

葬式 *soshiki* | funeral

Soshiki is a funeral. Most Japanese funerals are based on Buddhist rites, and are conducted at either a temple or a funeral hall. In recent years, people often rely on companies that specialize in handling funeral preparations.

三三九度 *san-san-ku-do*

San-san-ku-do is the nuptial exchange of *sake* and literally means "three-three-nine times." Using three cups of increasing size, the bride and groom take turns sipping *sake* three times from the three different cups, making nine sips for each of them in total.

見合い *miai*

Miai, or *omiai*, is an arranged meeting of a man and woman interested in marriage. The meeting is usually arranged by a go-between called a *nakodo*. Although the first meeting is arranged, the pair decide themselves whether to have subsequent dates.

Related Key Words | 関連キーワード

MP3
36

香典 *koden*

Koden is the money gift given to the bereaved family by those attending a funeral. The money is usually used to help cover funeral expenses.

ほとんどの日本人の葬式は、お寺や斎場において、仏式で行われます。近年では、葬式の準備を専門とする業者を利用する人が多くなってきています。

三三九度は、酒を飲み交わす結婚の儀式で、文字どおりには「三度・三度・九度」ということです。小、中、大の3つの盃を使い、新郎と新婦が交互にそれぞれの大きさの盃から3度ずつ、合計9度、酒を飲みます。

見合い、もしくはお見合いは、結婚を希望する男女が出会う機会を取り持つことです。見合いは、たいてい「仲人」と呼ばれる人物によってお膳立てされます。最初の出会いこそ、このようにお膳立てされますが、その後デートをするかどうかを決めるのは、見合いをした男女自身です。

香典は、葬式に参列した人たちから遺族に贈られるお金です。この香典は、たいてい葬式の諸費用を賄うのに使われます。

角隠し *tsunokakushi*

Tsunokakushi is a hood or white silk cloth that fits on the wig of a bride wearing traditional Japanese wedding attire. The hood is said to hide her "horns of jealousy."

結納 *yuino*

Yuino is the betrothal money given by the male to his fiancé. In some areas, it is customary that half of this gift is then returned. However, more recent *yuino* ceremonies involve only the formal presentation of the engagement ring and the exchange of an engagement oath in the presence of the go-between and the couple's parents.

Related Vocabulary | 関連語彙

- 国際結婚：international marriage
- 披露宴：a wedding reception
- 引出物：a gift given to those who attend a wedding reception
- ご祝儀：a congratulatory money gift
- せんべつ：a farewell money gift
- 四十九日：the 49-day mourning period
- 初七日：a Buddhist memorial service held on the 7th day following a person's death
- 焼香：offering incense
- 霊柩車：a Japanese hearse
- 喪中：in mourning
- 厄年：years of calamity

角隠しは、日本伝統の結婚式の衣装をまとう新婦の結髪（けっぱつ）に付ける頭巾または白絹の布のことです。角隠しは、「嫉妬の角」を隠すためのものといわれています。

結納は、婚約を交わした際に、夫となる男性から妻となる女性へと贈られるお金です。一部の地域では、結納の半額を返却するのがしきたりになっています。しかし、最近の結納の儀式では、仲人と双方の親が同席して、婚約指輪を贈り、婚約の誓いを交わすだけの場合が多くなっています。

■還暦：celebration of *one's* 60th birthday
■お辞儀：bow
■正座：sitting down with the buttocks resting on top of the ankles
■敬語：an honorific / an honorific expression

■棟上げ式（むねあげしき）：a framework-raising ceremony
■名刺：a business card
■印鑑、はんこ：a personal seal
■実印：a registered personal seal
■しきたり：a ritual / a tradition / a convention

Dialogue | 対話

MP3 37

You don't really think I was forced to get married, do you?

F : Your wedding pictures are so beautiful.

J : Thank you. It doesn't even look like me, does it? I was so uncomfortable. Besides the *kimono*, I was wearing a rather heavy wig.

F : Tell me about the wedding. What was it like?

J : Well, it's becoming less common these days, but my husband and I did *miai* kekkon—that's an arranged marriage.

F : Is that legal?

J : Oh, you don't understand. It isn't a forced marriage. It's more like an introduction service. I dumped the first two guys I met through *miai*. Anyway, we were married in a small **shrine** in a hotel. Drinking *sake* is part of the marriage rite—it's called *san-san-ku-do*, which means 3-3-9 times.

F : What do you mean by 3-3-9?

J : There are three different sized *sake* cups. First the groom takes three sips and then the cup is passed to the bride who also takes three sips. Next, a larger cup is used and the bride goes first. And finally the largest cup is used, so three sips times three cups comes to nine. Oh, and I should mention that odd numbers are considered auspicious at weddings. Even the money gift should be an odd number of bills.

F : Why?

J : Even numbers can be split in half, so that's considered bad luck for the future of the marriage.

F : Okay, that makes sense.

無理やり結婚させられたわけじゃないわよ

F： 結婚式の写真、とてもきれいだね。

J： ありがとう。とても私には見えないでしょう。本当に大変だったのよ。着物だけじゃなくて、かつらも重くって。

F： 結婚式について教えてよ。どんな感じだったの？

J： 実はね、このごろはだんだん少なくなってきてるんだけど、私と夫は見合い結婚、つまり仲を取り持ってもらったのよ。

F： それは法的に許されることなのかい？

J： ああ、勘違いしないで。結婚を強要されたわけではないの。見合いは、相手を紹介してくれるだけなの。お見合いをした最初の２人の男性は蹴ったわ。それはそれとして、結婚式はホテルにある小さな神社で挙げたのよ。結婚の儀式の一つとしてお酒を飲むの。それを三三九度というのよ。

F： 三三九って何を意味するの？

J： 大きさが違う３種類の盃があって、最初に新郎が３口飲むの。その盃を新婦に渡して新婦が３口飲むの。次に、もう少し大きな盃を使って今度は新婦から。最後に一番大きな盃で飲むってわけ。３口ずつ３つの盃から飲むから９回飲むことになるわ。そうそう、結婚式で奇数は縁起が良いって思われていることを言い忘れていたわ。結婚式で贈るご祝儀も、奇数枚のお札を入れるのよ。

F： どうしてだい？

J： 偶数は半分に割ることができるでしょ。だから今後の結婚生活には縁起が悪いとされているわけ。

F： ああ、それは納得。

J : After the ceremony, there is a formal reception. I switched into a Western wedding gown. And, believe it or not, there was a second reception—we call it *nijikai*. The second one was more casual and we could invite more of our friends.

F : Are Japanese weddings expensive?

J : Terribly expensive. Some young couples save money by having a small ceremony overseas—Hawaii is a popular destination.

F : Ah, a combination wedding / honeymoon. Now that's killing two birds with one stone.

J : Killing birds? What do you mean?

J：結婚式の後に正式な宴会があるのよ。私はドレスに着替えたわ。信じられないでしょうけど、2度目の宴会も開いたの。二次会って呼ぶけど。二次会ではもうちょっとくだけた格好をして、友人をたくさん招待したわ。

F：日本の結婚式ってお金がかかるの？

J：恐ろしく高いわ。若いカップルの中には、予算を抑えるために海外でささやかな結婚式を開く人たちもいるの。ハワイが人気ね。

F：なるほど。結婚式とハネムーンを一度にやろうということか。まさに一石二鳥というわけだね。

J：鳥を殺すの？　どういう意味？

---

wig：かつら
legal：合法な
dump：〜を捨てる、蹴る
rite：儀式
odd numbers：奇数
auspicious：縁起の良い

even numbers：偶数
that makes sense：納得だ、なるほど
believe it or not：信じようと信じまいと
reception：披露宴
killing two birds with one stone：
　一石二鳥 [ことわざ]

 **Introduction** | 概説

日本人にとっての宗教は、たとえば欧米人とキリスト教との関係とは違って、独特の距離感、受け入れ方があります。日本人の精神世界には、神道と仏教の２つが大きくかかわってきました。

Shinto and **Buddhism** are the two major religions in Japan. *Shinto* is indigenous to Japan, while **Buddhism** was imported from China through Korea in the 6th century. Although the two religions are different, most Japanese people accept both and will alternate between the religions depending on the situation. For example, weddings are often performed by a *Shinto* priest, while **funerals** are handled by a Buddhist monk.

Q *Shinto* → p.144   Buddhism → p.144   funeral → p.130

かつて神道と仏教は、神仏習合といってお互いに融合していました。両者は明治初期の神仏分離令で明確に分離されますが、今でも、神仏習合の名残が見られます。

When **Buddhism** came to Japan, people started to see that Buddhist and *Shinto* deities often had complementary roles. Later, there was an interpretation that *Shinto* deities were the manifestations of Buddhist deities, which allowed for a peaceful merging of the two religions. At some **temples** *Shinto* deities were enshrined, and some *Shinto* **shrines** added **temples** to their grounds. In the 19th century, however, the new Meiji government ordered that *Shinto* be separated from **Buddhism**. The two religions have been officially separated since then, but the mixed nature remains. For example, *torii* gateways found on the

　神道と仏教は日本の二大宗教です。神道は日本固有の宗教ですが、仏教は6世紀に中国から朝鮮を経て日本へ伝えられました。この2つは異なる宗教ですが、ほとんどの日本人が両者を受け入れ、状況によって使い分けます。たとえば、結婚式はたいてい神道の神主が執り行うのに対し、葬式は仏教の僧が執り行う、といった具合です。

| indigenous：その土地に固有の | *Shinto* priest：神主、神官 |
| alternate between 〜：〜を使い分ける | Buddhist monk：僧侶 |

　仏教が日本に伝来したとき、日本人は仏教と神道の神々が相互補完的な役割を持つと見なすようになりました。のちに、神道の神々は仏教の神々が仮の姿となって現れたものであるという解釈が生まれ、神道と仏教は軋轢を起こさずに融合することが可能となりました。お寺に神道の神々が祀られることもありましたし、神社の境内に寺が建てられることもありました。しかし19世紀、新たに誕生した明治政府は、神道を仏教から分離することを命じたのです。それ以来、神道と仏教は公的には分離されてきましたが、神仏習合の性質が残っています。たとえば、お寺の境内に鳥居が見られることがありますが、これは神仏習合の時代の名残なのです。

grounds of **temples** are a remnant of the time when the two religions mixed.

🔍 temples → p.144   shrines → p.144   *torii* → p.146

日本人にとっての神の概念を説明しておいたほうがよいでしょう。神道の神は、キリスト教などの一神教の神と違って超越した存在ではなく、自然や祖先が神格化されたものといえます。

For the Japanese, the gods, or *kami*, are much closer to man and nature than in most other religions. The *kami* can be represented in nature and in one's ancestors. Japanese are just as likely to practice religion in their own home as they are to go to ***Shinto* shrines**, called ***jinja***, or Buddhist **temples**, called *tera*. Traditional homes often have ***Shinto*** family altars, called *kamidana*, and Buddhist altars, called *butsudan*. These altars are for worshiping deities and family ancestors.

🔍 *jinja* → p.144   *tera* → p.144

この日本人と宗教とのかかわりは、生活に根付いた社会習慣ともいうべきものであり、観念的な宗教心とは別物と考えたほうがよいでしょう。

In Japanese culture there are many rituals and ceremonies associated with religion. Besides weddings and **funerals**, most Japanese people will visit a **temple** or **shrine** on **New Year's Day** or soon after. In the summer, many people participate in the ***matsuri*** and ***bon*** festivals. Nevertheless, these events are held more out of tradition than from any deep religious feeling.

🔍 New Year's Day → p.98   *matsuri* → p.114   *bon* → p.114

deity：神
complementary：補完的な
allow for 〜：〜を可能にする

be enshrined：祀られる
remnant：名残

　日本人にとって、神は、ほかの多くの宗教に比べると、人間や自然に極めて近い存在です。自然の中や先祖の霊に神を見いだすこともあるのです。日本人は神社やお寺にお参りに行くのと同じくらい、家でも宗教儀式を行います。昔ながらの家には、神棚と呼ばれる家庭用の神殿や、仏壇と呼ばれる仏式の祭壇があります。神棚や仏壇は神や先祖を敬うためのものです。

be represented in 〜：〜に現れる

altar：祭壇

　日本文化には、宗教に関連して数多くの儀式や祭儀があります。結婚式や葬式のときだけでなく、ほとんどの日本人は、元日または三が日のうちにお寺や神社に参詣します。夏には、祭りやお盆にも参加します。とはいっても、それらの行事は、あつい信仰心からというより、むしろ伝統行事という側面から行われています。

associated with 〜：〜と関連のある
participate in 〜：〜に参加する

religious feeling：信仰心

神道の儀式は日本の文化とも深く結び付いています。その例の一つとして、地鎮祭が挙げられるでしょう。

Shinto is closely tied to Japanese culture, and there are many instances where *Shinto* rites or rituals might appear. For example, most construction work begins with a *Shinto* purification of the site called *jichinsai*. This ritual is meant to ensure the safety of the construction workers as well as the happiness of the future occupants. But it is also a ritual to ask the gods of the land for permission to use the land.

 *jichinsai* → p.146

神道は日本文化と深く結び付いており、神道の祭礼や儀式が伴われる事例が多々あります。たとえば、ほとんどの建設作業は、地鎮祭といって、建設現場を清める神道の儀式から始まります。この儀式は、建設作業員の安全を願い、完成後の居住者の幸せを祈るためのものですが、同時に、その土地を使用することに対して、許しを請うための儀式でもあるのです。

be meant to *do*：～するためのものである

神道　*Shinto* | Shintoism

Shinto is the indigenous religion of Japan. *Shinto* is a polytheistic religion and has neither a founder nor firm religious principles. Along with Buddhism, *Shinto* has exerted a strong influence on Japanese politics, society, culture, and art. Today, celebrations for births, marriages, and other occasions are conducted at *Shinto* shrines by *Shinto* priests called *kan-nushi*.

仏教　*Bukkyo* | Buddhism

Bukkyo is the Japanese term for Buddhism. Buddhism was introduced to Japan through China and Korea in the 6th century. It has exerted a strong influence on Japanese politics, society, culture, and art. Across the country, various kinds of Buddhist deities are worshiped at temples, which are called *tera*. Many *tera* also have graveyards, and Buddhist monks conduct funerals and other services for the deceased.

寺　*tera* | Buddhist temples

Tera are temples where Buddhist deities are enshrined. Buddhist monks at the temples offer various religious services to followers. The layout, structure, and deities enshrined are different according to the Buddhist sect or school, but a typical large *tera* has a graveyard, a pagoda, a statue hall, a lecture hall, and several gates.

神社　*jinja* | *Shinto* shrines

Jinja are *Shinto* shrines. *Shinto* deities are enshrined in *jinja*. *Shinto* priests at *jinja* offer various religious services to their followers. Many *jinja* offer various religious goods such as *omamori*, or good luck talismans, and *omikuji*, which is a strip of paper telling a fortune. People visit *jinja* to celebrate births and marriages, or more casually, to pray for good health, good luck, happiness, and protection from misfortune.

144

神道は日本固有の宗教です。神道は多神教で、開祖もいませんし、確固とした教義があるわけでもありません。仏教とともに、神道は、日本の政治、社会、文化、芸術に大きな影響を与えてきました。今日では、出産、結婚、その他の祝い事は神社で神主によって神式で行われます。

仏教は、6世紀に中国と朝鮮を経て日本へ伝わりました。仏教は、日本の政治、社会、文化、芸術に大きな影響を与えてきました。日本中の寺でさまざまな種類の仏が信仰の対象になっています。多くの寺には墓があり、寺の僧が葬式やその他の法事を行います。

寺は、仏が祀（まつ）られていて、僧侶が信者に対してさまざまな法事を行ってくれるところです。寺の伽藍（が　らん）配置や建築構造、祀られている仏は宗派によって異なりますが、典型的な寺には、墓地、塔、金堂、講堂、複数の門などがあります。

神社は神道の神が祀られていて、信者のために神主がさまざまな宗教的儀式を執り行うところです。多くの神社では、お守りや、運勢が書かれたおみくじなど、いろいろなものを授けています。信者たちは、出産や結婚、あるいはもっと気軽に、健康、開運、幸福、災厄除けなどを祈願しに、神社に参詣します。

鳥居　*torii* | *Shinto* shrine gate

Torii are gates to *Shinto* shrines. These gates consist of two upright posts connected at the top by two crosspieces. They are believed to keep evil spirits out of the shrine precincts and to purify those passing through the gate.

地鎮祭　*jichinsai*

Jichinsai is the *Shinto* ceremony of land purification. This ceremony precedes construction projects in order to appease the deities that may reside at the site. The purification helps to ensure that the construction will be safe and successful.

 **Related Key Words** | 関連キーワード　

新興宗教　*shinko shukyo* | new religious groups

Although *shinko shukyo* can be defined in different ways, it basically refers to new religious groups that have formed in Japan since the 19th century. Although these religions have been influenced by *Shinto* and Buddhism, they have independent religious principles and practices.

紙垂　*shide*

Shide is a strip of white paper cut roughly into the shape of a lightning bolt. It is used in *Shinto* rituals. The *shide* is often attached to a *shimenawa*, a sacred rice straw rope, which is found at the border of a sacred area. One type of *shide* is also attached to the *tamagushi*, which is a sacred branch used by priests to remove impurities.

鳥居は神社の門です。鳥居は、上部に2本の梁を通した2本の柱から成っています。鳥居は、境内に邪気を寄せ付けず、鳥居を通過する人たちを清めると信じられています。

地鎮祭は、土地を清めるための神道の儀式です。建設工事に先立ち、建設予定地に座しているとされる神を鎮めるために行われます。この清めの儀式によって、工事が安全でつつがなく進められることを祈願するのです。

新興宗教の定義にはいろいろありますが、基本的には19世紀以降に日本で生まれた、新しい宗教団体を意味します。新興宗教には神道や仏教の影響が見られますが、個別の教義や宗教的儀式があります。

紙垂は、切り込みを入れて雷のような形にした白い紙で、神道の儀式で用いられます。紙垂は一般に、聖域との境界を示すしめ縄に付けられます。また、お祓いに用いられる玉串と呼ばれる神聖な枝にも、紙垂の一種が付けられています。

仏像　*butsuzo* | Buddhist statues

Buddhist statues represent various sacred deities in Buddhism, including Buddhas, bodhisattvas, and guardian gods called *Myo-o* and *Tembu*. The name Buddha refers to those who have attained the state of enlightenment. They include *Shaka*, the founder of Buddhism, and many others described in Buddhist scriptures. Two of the most famous Buddha statues are the great statues of Buddha at Todaiji Temple in the city of Nara and Kotokuin Temple in the city of Kamakura. Bodhisattvas (Buddhas-to-be) refer to sacred ascetic monks appearing in Buddhist scriptures. One of the most popular bodhisattvas is *Kannon*, a deity of mercy. There are various *Kannon* statues, some of which have numerous faces and more than two arms.

地蔵　*jizo*

Jizo is one of the bodhisattvas. There are various types of *jizo* statues, but they are usually small with no hair. Some hold a priest's staff in the right hand and a precious orb in the left hand. *Jizo* is a deity of salvation. In Japan the *jizo* is regarded as a guardian of deceased children, including unborn babies.

お守り　*omamori* | a good luck talisman

Omamori is a good luck talisman which is available at shrines and temples. A typical *omamori* is a small tablet covered with cloth, on which wishes are written.

おみくじ　*omikuji* | fortune paper

Omikuji is a strip of paper with a fortune printed on it. It is available at shrines and temples. On the *omikuji*, good luck is indicated by the *kanji* character *kichi*. Bad luck is represented by the *kanji* character *kyo*. If the fortune is unfavorable, the strip of paper is often tied to a nearby tree to leave the bad luck behind.

仏像はさまざまな仏の彫像で、如来や菩薩のほか、明王・天部と呼ばれる守護神などがあります。如来は悟りの境地に到達した仏で、仏教の開祖である釈迦のほか、経典に出てくる数多くの如来があります。最もよく知られているものに奈良の東大寺の大仏と、鎌倉の高徳院の大仏があります。菩薩は経典に出てくる苦行僧のことで、将来的に如来になる仏という意味があります。最も人気があるのは、慈悲の仏とされる観音菩薩です。観音菩薩像にはいろいろな種類があり、なかには多くの顔と3本以上の手を持つものがあります。

地蔵は菩薩の一人です。地蔵の像は多様ですが、よく見かけるのは小さな像で剃髪しているものです。右手に錫杖、左手に宝珠を持っている地蔵もいます。地蔵は救済の菩薩で、日本では特に、水子を含めて、親より早世した子どもの守護神とされています。

お守りは、神社やお寺で受けられます。典型的なお守りは、祈願が書かれた小さな銘板を布で覆ったものです。

おみくじは、運勢が書かれている紙切れです。おみくじは、神社やお寺で受けられます。おみくじでは、幸運は漢字の「吉」で表され、不幸は漢字の「凶」で表されます。もし運勢があまり良くなければ、不運を置き去りにするということで、おみくじを近くの木に結び付けます。

法事　*hoji*

Hoji is a Buddhist memorial service. In Buddhism, there are periodic memorial services for the deceased and the service is conducted by the temple they belong to. These memorial services also function as a family reunion. *Obon* in August and *higan*, in both spring and autumn, are some of those occasions.

注連縄　*shimenawa* | a sacred *Shinto* rope

Shimenawa is a sacred rope used in the *Shinto* religion. It is often found in front of shrines or other sacred locations. The *shimenawa* at Izumo Shrine in Shimane Prefecture weighs several tons and is one of the largest in Japan.

線香　*senko* | incense

Senko, also known as *ko*, is incense. *Senko* is burned at Buddhist temples, funerals, and home altars. Recently, a wide variety of incense is also available for aromatic and therapeutic purposes.

Related Vocabulary | 関連語彙

- 七福神 : the seven deities bringing wealth and long life
- 菩薩 : a Bodhisattva
- 大仏 : a great statue of Buddha
- 五重塔 : a five-story pagoda
- お神酒 (おみき): rice wine offering for *Shinto* rites
- 儒教 : Confucianism
- 道教 : Taoism
- 破魔矢 (はまや): sacred arrow bringing good luck
- 境内 : precinct / grounds
- 密教 : esoteric Buddhism
- 玉串料 : offering for *Shinto* rites
- お布施 : offering for Buddhist monks / Buddhist idea of giving offerings to others

法事は、故人を供養する儀式のことです。仏教では、故人に対して定期的な法事が行われ、その儀式は信徒が属するお寺によって執り行われます。これらの法事は、また、親族の懇親のための役割も果たしています。8月の盂蘭盆会（うらぼんえ）や、春と秋の彼岸会（ひがんえ）も法事の一部です。

注連縄（しめなわ）は、神道で用いられる神聖な綱で、神社の前や神聖な場所の前によく配置してあります。島根県の出雲大社の注連縄は、日本最大級で、重さが数トンあります。

線香は「香（こう）」ともいわれます。線香は、お寺、葬儀、家庭の仏壇などでたかれます。最近では、芳香剤やアロマテラピー用に、さまざまな種類の香も市販されるようになっています。

- ■舎利 (しゃり): remains / remains of Buddha
- ■拍手 (かしわで): hand-clapping performed to worship in *Shinto*
- ■さい銭：monetary offering for Buddhist and *Shinto* deities
- ■一神教：monotheism
- ■多神教：polytheism
- ■神学：theology
- ■無神論者：an atheist
- ■教義：dogma / religious principles
- ■お経：sutra / Buddhist scripture
- ■誓詞：swear (before a *Shinto* deity) / pledge (before a *Shinto* deity)
- ■数珠 (じゅず): a Buddhist rosary

 **Dialogue 1**｜対話

Is that a temple or a shrine?

F : What's the difference between a **temple** and a **shrine**?

J : Oh, that's easy. A temple is for Buddhism and a shrine is for Shintoism.

F : No, that's not what I mean. How do you tell one from the other?

J : I should've known better. Your questions are never so easy. Let's see, a **shrine** has a *torii*, which is a tall, open gate with two pillars and a pair of cross-beams connecting them at the top. You might have seen pictures of the beautiful red *torii* at Miyajima.

F : Yes, I have. The one on the water?

J : Right. A **temple** is more likely to have a gate with doors and it might have a cemetery on the grounds. **Funerals** and memorial services are usually held at **temples**. Of course, **temples** will often have statues of Buddha or *jizo*. A **shrine** would more likely have statues of foxes or *komainu*, which is a cross between a lion and a dog.

F : Okay. I think I got it. Oh, there's another thing I wanted to ask you about. I was looking at a map the other day and I noticed that the symbol for Buddhist **temples** is the Nazi swastika. Why is that?

J : In Japanese that is called *manji*, and it's been a Buddhist symbol for hundreds of years. It has been used in other cultures as well. If you look closely, you'll see that the Nazi symbol is the reverse of the *manji*.

F : I wonder if the Nazis copied it?

J : Hmm, good question, but I can't help you with that one.

あれはお寺なの？　神社なの？

F：お寺と神社はどこが違うの？

J：あら、それは簡単よ。お寺は仏教の施設で、神社は神道の施設なの。

F：いや、そういうことではなくて、どうやって見分けるの？

J：そうよね。あなたの質問がそんなに簡単なはずがないわね。そうね、神社には鳥居があるわ。鳥居は高い、扉の付いてない門で、てっぺんが２本の梁_{はり}でつないである２本の柱でできているの。宮島のきれいな赤い鳥居を見たことがあるでしょう。

F：うん、あるよ。水に浮かんでいるやつだろう？

J：そうよ。お寺には扉付きの門があることが多く、境内には墓地があったりもするわ。お葬式や法事はたいていお寺で行われるのよ。それに、お寺には如来さまやお地蔵さまの仏像があることが多いわ。神社にはキツネの像や、獅子と犬が混じったみたいな狛犬と呼ばれる像があることが多いわね。

F：うん、わかったよ。そうそう、もう一つ聞きたかったことがあるんだ。この前、地図を見ていたら、お寺の記号がナチスドイツの国章のかぎ十字だってことに気がついたんだ。どうしてかぎ十字なの？

J：日本では「まんじ」と呼ばれていて、何百年も前からお寺の象徴として使われてきたの。ほかの文化圏でも同じよ。よく見るとわかるけど、ナチスドイツの国章はまんじのかぎが逆向きになってるわ。

F：ナチスドイツがまねしたのかな。

J：うーん、難しい質問ね。それはさすがにわからないわ。

---

tell one from the other：両者を区別する
should have known better：愚かだった
⇒know betterで「分別をわきまえている」。
pillar：柱
cross-beam：梁
Miyajima：宮島
⇒広島県にある小島で厳島（いつくしま）とも。
水上の大鳥居は島内の厳島神社のもの。

cross between *A* and *B*：
　AとBを融合したもの
swastika：かぎ十字、まんじ、卍
⇒ナチスドイツの国章は逆卍で卐の形となる。卍は吉祥を表すものとされ、仏像の胸に描かれる。卍と逆卍のいずれもあるが、日本では主に卍として、寺の記号などに用いられる。

 **Dialogue 2** | 対話

How do I pray at a shrine?

F : I went to a **shrine** the other day, but I wasn't sure what the procedures are. Can you tell me what to do?

J : Sure. After you pass under the *torii* gate, you'll come across a water basin. It's often adorned with a dragon. Don't worry, they usually don't bite.

F : Very funny.

J : Use the water to rinse your hands and mouth. This is a purification ritual. You will see something similar at the beginning of a *sumo* match.

F : Oh, yes. I remember seeing that on TV.

J : When you approach the **shrine**, you'll see an offertory box. The Japanese consider the five yen coin lucky, but I'm not sure if the gods will answer your prayers for such a small amount.

F : Why is five yen lucky?

J : Five yen is pronounced "go en." This sounds like a Japanese word for good luck.

F : Alright. And then do I ring the bell?

J : Yes, ring the bell, then bow twice, then clap twice. This is to get the attention of the gods. Then you offer your prayer. Finally bow once more before you leave.

F : I don't think I'll be able to remember all that.

J : I think you can just watch other people and follow their lead. And anyway, no one is going to get upset if you do things in the wrong order.

F : Okay, thanks for explaining.

神社ではどうやってお参りするの？

F：先日、神社に行ったんだけど、お参りの仕方がよくわからないの。どうするか教えてちょうだい。

J：いいとも。まず鳥居をくぐると、手水鉢があるはずだよ。龍の図柄で飾られていることが多いけど、普通は噛みつかないから心配しないで。

F：あら、おかしい。

J：鉢の水を使って手と口を軽く洗うんだ。これは清めの儀式。相撲の取り組みが始まるときにも似たような仕草を見るはずだよ。

F：ええ。見たことあるわ。

J：神殿の前に行くと、さい銭箱がある。日本人は5円玉が幸運の硬貨だと思っているけど、あまりに小額なんで、神さまが願いを聞いてくれるかどうかは微妙だね。

F：どうして5円が幸運なの。

J：5円玉は「御縁」と発音が同じだからね。日本人にとっては幸運という響きがあるんだ。

F：わかったわ。そこで鈴を鳴らすわけ？

J：そう、鈴を鳴らして、それから二礼二拍。これは神さまに気づいてもらうため。その後お祈りをして、最後に一礼して終わり。

F：全部は覚えきれないみたい。

J：ほかの人がどうやっているかを見て、まねをするといいよ。いずれにせよ、順番を間違えたところで誰も怒ったりしないから。

F：よくわかったわ。ありがとう。

10
Religion 対話

---

water basin：水鉢	bow：礼をする、お辞儀をする
be adorned with ～：～で飾られている	clap：手を打つ
rinse：～を軽く洗う、～をゆすぐ	

Sports and Leisure
スポーツ・余暇

 **Introduction** | 概説

見るスポーツも自分でやるスポーツも大人気。また、カラオケ、パチンコ、居酒屋で一杯といったアフターファイブの娯楽もよりどりみどり。「働き者」といわれる日本人庶民の豊かな余暇について説明します。

Despite all the workaholic stereotypes, the Japanese take their leisure activities seriously. Traditional sports like *sumo* and martial arts like *judo*, *kendo*, *karate*, and *aikido* share popularity with baseball, soccer, volleyball, skiing, tennis, and golf. An evening out might include singing Japanese songs at *karaoke* or watching the latest flick. If one gets tired of gambling at a Japanese *pachinko* parlor, Western-style horse racing is available. The local *izakaya* may be crowded with after-work revelers, but so is the Italian restaurant next door. Anyone who says that the Japanese don't know how to enjoy themselves has obviously never been to Japan.

🔍 *sumo* → p.160　　　　*judo* → p.160　　　　*kendo* → p.160
　　karate → p.160　　　*aikido* → p.160　　　*karaoke* → p.162
　　pachinko → p.162　　*izakaya* → p.82

なかでも野球は日本人の好むスポーツです。日本選手の大リーグでの活躍にファンは大喜びです。サッカーも、4年毎のワールドカップに向け、Jリーグが盛り上がりを見せています。

Baseball is Japan's most popular sport, so much so that even the high school tournaments are televised. In recent years, many talented Japanese players have left Japan to play in Major League Baseball, demonstrating the high skill levels of Japanese baseball players.

　働きすぎだという日本人に対する固定観念とは裏腹に、日本人は余暇活動には余念がありません。伝統的なスポーツである相撲や、伝統武道である柔道、剣道、空手、合気道などと並んで、野球、サッカー、バレーボール、スキー、テニス、ゴルフなども人気があります。カラオケで日本の曲を歌ったり、最新の映画を見に行ったり、と夜の街の娯楽もさまざまです。日本のオリジナルであるパチンコ店での賭け事に飽きたら、西洋式の競馬があります。近くの居酒屋は仕事帰りに酒盛りをする人で混み合っていますが、その隣にあるイタリアンレストランも大変な人気です。日本人は余暇の過ごし方を知らないなどと言う人がいたら、きっとその人は、日本に来たことがないに違いありません。

stereotype：固定観念	flick：映画
martial art：武道	reveler：酒盛りをする人

　野球は日本で最も人気のあるスポーツです。その人気の高さゆえ、高校野球さえテレビ放送されるほどです。近年では、日本を離れ、メジャーリーグでプレーする野球選手も多くなり、日本人野球選手のレベルの高さを証明しています。

Soccer is also a hot sport in Japan. In 1993, J. League, or the Japan Professional Football League, officially kicked off, which has inspired a lot of children to join youth teams. Also, Japanese soccer fans have come to enjoy the World Cup Soccer Tournament held every four years.

ここで、国技としての相撲について、少し触れておきましょう。古代から占いの手段として行われてきた相撲は、江戸時代になると寺社の寄付集めを目的とした観戦スポーツとして発展していきました。最近では外国人力士の活躍も目立ち、新たな歴史を刻みつつあります。

The traditional sport of *sumo* has a long history, first being mentioned in an ancient 8th century mythology text. Originally a means of religious fortune telling, *sumo* developed into a professional spectator sport in the early **Edo Period**. The first professional tournament was held to raise funds for restoring **shrines** and **temples**. Even today *sumo* features many ancient ceremonies and rites of purification. Despite its ancient beginnings, the success of foreign wrestlers has increased the popularity of *sumo* overseas.

🔍 Edo Period → p.26　　　shrines → p.144　　　temples → p.144

日本の国技には柔道もあります。近年ではより国際的なスポーツへと変化しつつありますが、日本の武道に欠かせない「礼」は今でもしっかり守られています。

The sport of *judo*, now popular worldwide, originated in Japan and was once dominated by Japanese competitors. However, as foreign *judo* enthusiasts have increased in number, their presence and success has become larger in the Olympic Games and other international competitions. The rules have also been revised over the years, which some say has changed the nature of *judo*. Nevertheless, courtesy, or *rei*, a key element of Japanese martial arts, is still well-observed even in the international arena.

サッカー熱も日本では高まっています。1993年には日本のプロサッカーリーグであるJリーグが正式に開幕し、多くの子どもたちがユースチームに参加するようになりました。また、日本のサッカーファンは、4年毎に開催されるワールドカップを心待ちにしています。

so much so that 〜：あまりにそうなので〜

日本の伝統スポーツである相撲には長い歴史があり、8世紀に編纂された記紀神話には相撲に関する最初の記載があります。相撲は、もともと吉凶を占う手段であったものが、江戸初期にプロの観戦スポーツへと発展したものです。最初のプロ相撲大会は、寺社の復興資金を集める目的で開かれました。そのため、相撲には、今でも儀礼や清めの儀式が数多く見られます。このように、相撲の起源は古代にさかのぼるものの、外国人力士が角界で名を上げるようになったため、人気は海外でも高まっています。

mythology：神話
a means of 〜：〜の手段
fortune telling：吉凶の占い

spectator sport：観戦スポーツ
raise funds：資金を集める
purification：清め

今では世界中で人気がある柔道は、日本で創始されたスポーツで、かつては日本人の柔道選手による独壇場でした。しかし外国人の熱心な柔道家も増え、オリンピック競技大会や他の国際大会では外国人柔道家が活躍し、その存在も大きくなってきました。その間、規則も変更され、柔道の本質自体が変化したと言う人もいます。それでも、日本の武道に欠かせない要素である「礼」は、国際舞台においてもしっかり守られています。

the nature of 〜：〜の性質、本質

courtesy：礼、礼儀

相撲　*sumo*

Sumo is traditional Japanese wrestling. The match is decided when one wrestler forces the other out of the circle of a clay ring, called a *dohyo*, or causes him to touch the surface of the *dohyo* with any part of his body other than the soles of his feet.

柔道　*judo*

Judo is a Japanese martial art. It takes the form of unarmed combat between two contestants. Techniques include throwing and grappling in a way that uses the opponent's weight and power against him or her. Since its invention in the late 19th century, *judo* has been valued as a method of exercise, moral training, and self-defense. It is now an Olympic sport.

剣道　*kendo*

Kendo is the Japanese martial art of fencing. It was originally practiced by *samurai* warriors to improve their swordsmanship. The contestants use a bamboo sword called a *shinai*, a protective mask called a *men*, gloves called *kote*, body armor called *do*, and a waist protector called a *tare*. Points are scored by hitting the opponent's head, wrist, or body.

空手　*karate*

Karate is a martial art which developed in the Ryukyu Kingdom, which is now known as Okinawa Prefecture in the southwest part of Japan. It is a form of unarmed self-defense whose techniques include arm strikes called *uchi*, thrusts called *tsuki*, and kicks called *keri*. In the Tokyo Olympic Games in 2020, *karate* will be an Olympic sport for the first time.

合気道　*aikido*

Aikido is a Japanese martial art. It is an unarmed self-defense whose techniques include immobilizing holds and throws that take advantage of the opponent's momentum and strength.

相撲は、レスリングに似た日本の伝統的な競技です。勝敗は、相手の力士を土俵と呼ばれるリングの外へと追い出すか、足の裏を除く相手の体の部分を地に着かせたときに決まります。

柔道は日本の武道の一つです。柔道では2人の競技者が武器を持たずに闘います。柔道には、相手の体重や力を利用する投げ技と寝技があります。19世紀後半に創始されて以来、柔道は、身体の鍛錬、精神の修養、護身術として価値を認められてきました。今ではオリンピック種目に加えられています。

剣道はフェンシングに似た日本の武道です。剣道はもともと侍が剣術を磨くために練習したものです。競技者は、竹刀と呼ばれる竹製の剣、面と呼ばれる防御マスク、小手と呼ばれるグローブ、胴と呼ばれる腹部のよろい、垂と呼ばれる下腹部のプロテクターを用います。得点は、相手の頭部（面）、手首（小手）、あるいは腹部（胴）を打つことで与えられます。

空手は、今では日本南西部の沖縄県として知られる琉球王国で発達した武道の一つです。空手はウチと呼ばれる腕による打撃や、ツキと呼ばれる相手を一突きする攻撃、そしてケリと呼ばれる足蹴りによる技などを使う、武器を使用しない護身術の一つです。東京2020オリンピックでは、空手が初めてオリンピック競技になります。

合気道は日本の武道の一つです。相手の勢いや力を利用して相手の動きを封じ、相手を投げる技を使う、武器を使用しない護身術の一つです。

カラオケ　*karaoke*

Karaoke, or karaoke, is a form of entertainment where people sing to the accompaniment provided by a *karaoke* machine. Some establishments rent out small soundproof rooms, called *karaoke-boxes*, that have *karaoke* machines. They cater to small groups and also serve food and drinks.

パチンコ　*pachinko*

Pachinko is a type of gambling using a pinball machine. It is played in a *pachinko* parlor, where players can win various prizes. Players manipulate a handle and try to steer small steel balls into a winning hole to get more balls. The balls won can be exchanged for various prizes, including food and drinks, electrical appliances, and cigarettes. Only those over seventeen can enter a *pachinko* parlor.

 **Related Key Words｜関連キーワード**

道場　*dojo*

Dojo is a hall for practicing Japanese martial arts. The floor of a *dojo* is different according to the type of sport practiced. *Judo*, *aikido*, and *karate dojo* have *tatami*-matted floors, and *kendo dojo* have wooden floors.

マージャン　*majan*｜mahjong

Mahjong is a table game introduced from China. The game is played by four players who draw and discard the mahjong tiles until they can complete a winning hand. Sometimes mahjong is played for money, but this is technically illegal in Japan.

将棋　*shogi*

Shogi is a board game introduced from China. It is quite similar to Western chess, but *shogi* is unique in that the players can use the pieces they captured from the opponent. Like chess, the game ends with the checkmate of the king.

カラオケは、機械の伴奏に合わせて歌を唄う娯楽です。カラオケ機器を置いた小型の防音室を有料で貸す、カラオケボックスと呼ばれる店もあります。カラオケボックスの客は少人数のグループで、食べ物や飲み物も出されます。

パチンコは、パチンコ専門店で遊ぶピンボールゲームの一種で、勝てばさまざまな景品を獲得できます。プレーヤーは、ハンドルを操作しながら小さな鉄球を入賞口に入れ、鉄球の数を増やすようにします。出玉は、飲食物、電気製品、タバコなどのいろいろな景品と交換することができます。18歳未満はパチンコ店に入場できません。

道場は、日本の武道を行うホールのことです。道場の床は、行われるスポーツの種類によって異なります。柔道、合気道、空手の道場には畳敷きの床が、剣道の道場では板張りの床が用いられます。

マージャンは、中国から伝来した卓上ゲームの一つです。マージャンは4人で行われ、役が揃うまでマージャン牌を取ったり捨てたりするゲームです。マージャンは時に賭け事として行われますが、日本では本来、賭けマージャンは違法行為です。

将棋は、中国から伝わった盤上ゲームの一つです。将棋は、西洋のチェスによく似ていますが、相手から取った駒を使うことができるという点で独特です。チェスと同様に、王の駒を詰めたときにゲームは終わります。

Dialogue | 対話

MP3 46

Are those fat guys really athletes?

F : I was surprised to learn that baseball is so popular in Japan. I always thought *sumo* was the biggest sport.

J : Both soccer and baseball are popular in Japan. But *sumo* is still very popular—especially as a spectator sport. *Sumo* was originally a religious event used to foretell the future. Look at that. Do you see how they throw salt into the ring? That's a purification ritual.

F : I really get a kick out of the outfits—not just the wrestlers but the referee as well.

J : The referee is called the *gyoji*, and his attire is from ancient times. The wrestlers are wearing what's called a *mawashi*.

F : It doesn't seem fair that the small guys have to wrestle the big, fat ones.

J : There are numerous techniques to throw and thrust opponents. So, even though there are no weight divisions in *sumo*, the smaller wrestlers can beat the bigger ones.

F : What are the rules?

J : There are few rules. A wrestler cannot punch, but they do slap each other. Also, they can't pull the opponents' hair or choke them. And to win, a wrestler has to push the opponent out of the ring or knock him down.

F : It seems like the matches are on television every day. How does one become champion?

J : The grand tournaments, or *basho*, last 15 days and are held six times annually. The wrestlers have one match per day, and the one who wins the most matches becomes the winner of the tournament. The wrestlers are promoted or demoted according to the results. The highest rank is called *yokozuna*, or grand champion.

あの太った人たちは本当にスポーツ選手なの？

F：日本で野球が大人気なことを知って驚いたのよ。日本では相撲が一番の人気スポーツだといつも思ってたから。

J：日本では、サッカーも野球も人気があるよ。でも、相撲も、特に観戦スポーツとしてまだまだ根強い人気を保ってるんだ。相撲は元来、吉凶を占う宗教的な行事だったのさ。ほら、見て。力士が塩をまいているのが見えるかい？　あれは清めの儀式なんだ。

F：私はあの衣装が面白いと思ってたの。力士だけでなく、レフェリーのもね。

J：相撲のレフェリーは「行司」と呼ばれていて、あの衣装は古代から受け継がれてきたものなんだ。力士がつけているのは「まわし」と呼ばれるものだよ。

F：小さい力士が、大きくて太った力士と格闘しなくてはならないのは、不公平だと思うんだけど。

J：相手を投げたり、突いたりする技が数え切れないほどあるんだ。だから、たとえ相撲が体重別の対戦でなくても、小さい力士は自分より大きい力士に勝つこともできるんだよ。

F：ルールはどうなっているの？

J：ほとんどないね。パンチは禁止されているけど平手打ちはいいんだ。それに相手の髪を引っ張ったり、首を絞めるのも禁じ手だね。勝つには相手を土俵の外へ押し出すか、倒さないとだめなんだ。

F：試合は連日テレビ放映されているようね。優勝者はどうやって決まるの？

J：「場所」と呼ばれる大相撲大会は15日間続き、それが1年に6回行われるのさ。各力士は、毎日1試合闘って、勝ち星を最も多く上げた力士が、その場所の優勝者になるんだよ。力士は自分の取り組みの結果で昇進したり、降格したりする。最高位が「横綱」と呼ばれているんだ。

foretell：〜を予言する	weight divisions：重量別の区分
purification ritual：清めの儀式	knock down：〜を倒す
get a kick out of 〜：〜を面白いと思う	promote：昇格する
outfit, attire：衣装	demote：降格する

Arts and Crafts
美術・工芸

 ## Introduction | 概説

MP3 47

日本の美術史を振り返ると、そこに、海外の影響を取り入れながらも、独自のものとして発展させるという、日本人の稀有な能力が見えてきます。

Japan is like most other countries in that artistic expression has been affected by many different factors. Certainly Chinese culture and **Buddhism** influenced early Japanese art. Nevertheless, Japan absorbed and incorporated the ideas that came from overseas and created its own unique style. This can be seen in many of Japan's artistic techniques including *chanoyu*, *ikebana*, and *ukiyo-e*.

🔍 Buddhism → p.144   *chanoyu* → p.172   *ikebana* → p.172
ukiyo-e → p.172

特徴的なのは、自然が作品に巧みに生かされていることでしょう。盆栽や日本庭園などは、世界に例を見ない日本独自の世界です。

Images of the seasons and nature appear over and over again in Japanese art—the cherry blossoms, the colorful fall foliage, Mt. Fuji blanketed with snow. Some common art materials come directly from nature—bamboo and lacquer, to name just a few. The art of *bonsai* and the **Japanese garden**—both of which require meticulous care over a period of years—are also examples of the Japanese appreciation of nature's beauty.

🔍 *bonsai* → p.172   Japanese garden → p.174

　日本もほかの国々同様、その芸術表現はさまざまな要因の影響を受けてきました。たしかに、中国文化や仏教は初期の日本の芸術に影響を与えました。しかし、日本人の場合は、外国からもたらされた発想を吸収・統合し、日本独自の様式を創造したのです。このことは、茶の湯や生け花、浮世絵など、日本の芸術手法の多くに見ることができます。

absorb：〜を吸収する	incorporate：〜を取り入れる、〜を統合する

　季節と自然の描写が、日本の芸術作品には繰り返し登場します。たとえば、桜の花、色とりどりの紅葉、雪を山頂に戴いた富士山などです。よく用いられる素材には、竹や漆など、自然の素材をそのまま利用した例も数多くあります。長年にわたる入念な手入れが必要な盆栽や日本庭園もまた、日本人の自然を愛でる傾向を示す良い例です。

foliage：（集合的に）葉 blanketed with 〜：〜で覆われた bamboo：竹 lacquer：漆	to name just a few： 　少数の例を挙げただけでも meticulous：入念な

日本の美術工芸の粋は、なんといっても江戸時代の文化にあります。そこには、藩の貴重な収入源として、各地の特産物生産を奨励した台所事情がかかわっていたことは見逃せません。

Japanese crafts and craftsmanship attained extraordinary levels of quality in the **Edo Period**. Many feudal lords encouraged craft making in their region as a way to create revenue. Items such as **ceramics**, **lacquerware**, **woven fabrics**, and dolls were made and in some cases mass-produced. Even today, local regions have their own uniquely designed crafts. At present, more than 200 items are designated as Traditional Craft Products by the Minister of Economy, Trade and Industry under the Act on the Promotion of Traditional Craft Industries.

🔍 Edo Period → p.26   ceramics → p.174
  lacquerware → p.174   woven fabrics → p.174

江戸時代、庶民の間で人気を博した浮世絵が、印象派の画家たちを中心に西洋美術に影響を与えたことを紹介しましょう。

A genre of art called *ukiyo-e* was especially influential during the **Edo Period**. Translated as "pictures of the floating world," these woodblock prints featured beautiful women, *kabuki* actors, *sumo* wrestlers, and landscapes. Some prints could be called the prototypes of today's *manga*. It is also well-known that *ukiyo-e* techniques influenced Western impressionist artists. Because *ukiyo-e* allowed mass production, the prints were available to ordinary people. When Japan began its rapid modernization at the end of the 19th century, the art of *ukiyo-e* rapidly declined.

🔍 *kabuki* → p.186   *sumo* → p.160   *manga* → p.210

　日本の工芸品は、江戸時代に驚異的なレベルへと到達しました。当時、多くの大名は、藩の財源として、領土内で工芸品生産を奨励するようになりました。陶磁器、漆器、織物、人形などの工芸品が生産され、地域によっては、大量生産も手がけられました。今日でも、各地に地域独特の意匠を凝らした工芸品があります。現在、伝統的工芸品産業の振興に関する法律のもとで、200種類以上が経済産業大臣から伝統的工芸品に指定されています。

revenue：歳入　　　　　be designated as 〜：〜に指定される

　浮世絵と呼ばれる様式は、特に江戸時代に大きな影響力を持っていました。「浮世を描いた絵」という意味の浮世絵は木版画で、主に、美女、歌舞伎役者、力士、風景などが好んで描かれました。なかには、現代のマンガの原型といえるものもあります。また、浮世絵の技法は、西洋の印象派の画家たちに影響を与えたこともよく知られています。浮世絵は大量生産が可能であったため、一般大衆でも手が届きました。19世紀末に日本が急速な近代化を迎える中で、浮世絵芸術は急速に衰えていきました。

genre：様式、ジャンル　　　　prototype：原型
woodblock print：木版画

近年、日本の美術工芸が国内外で人気です。なかには日本の伝統工芸に従事するために、日本に定住する外国人もいます。

Recently, there has been an increased interest in Japanese arts and crafts at home and abroad. Domestic art exhibitions are drawing ever more visitors, and there are an increased number of younger crafts-people. The Japanese **tea ceremony**, or *chanoyu*, has become increasingly popular outside of Japan, and some foreign craftspeople have settled in Japan to engage in traditional Japanese craft making.

 tea ceremony → p.172

　最近は、日本の美術工芸への関心が国内外で高まっています。国内の展示会は過去最大の動員数を記録していますし、若い工芸士も多くなってきています。茶の湯は海外でもますます人気になってきていますし、日本に定住して日本の伝統的な工芸に従事する外国人工芸士もいます。

at home and abroad：国内外で	engage in 〜：〜に従事する
craftsperson：工芸士（複数形は craftspeople）	

茶の湯　*chanoyu* | tea ceremony

Chanoyu is the Japanese tea ceremony. The tea is made by adding hot water to powdered green tea, called *matcha*, and whisking it into the water. The ceremony emphasizes the host's hospitality towards the guests and the guests' appreciation to the host. Influenced by *Zen* Buddhism, *chanoyu* creates a feeling of serenity and discipline.

生け花　*ikebana* | flower arrangement

Ikebana is Japanese flower arrangement. Although there have been many different ways of arranging flowers in its long development, the basic idea is to create a form symbolic of the harmony between man and nature. Japanese flower arrangement is unique in that the practice itself is regarded as a way to discipline oneself and acquire good manners.

盆栽　*bonsai*

Bonsai is the Japanese art form of growing miniature potted trees. Dwarfing a tree requires pruning, repotting, pinching off new growth, and the wiring of the branches and trunk. Some *bonsai* have been tended for hundreds of years and are very valuable. They are usually kept outdoors in a garden or displayed in a *tokonoma*—the alcove in a traditional Japanese room.

浮世絵　*ukiyo-e*

Ukiyo-e is a type of art which predominantly uses woodblock printing. Developed during the Edo Period, the prints depicted beautiful women, *sumo* wrestlers, *kabuki* actors, landscapes, and so on.

茶の湯は、お茶を出したりいただいたりする日本式の作法です。茶の湯のお茶は、抹茶と呼ばれる粉末の緑茶にお湯を加え、かき混ぜてお湯に溶きます。茶の湯では、客人に対する主人のもてなしの心と、客人の主人に対する感謝の心が大切にされます。茶の湯は禅の影響を受けており、平常心と自己を鍛錬する気持ちを育みます。

生け花は、花を飾る日本式の手法です。生け花の長い歴史の中で、数多くの異なる手法が生まれましたが、その基本理念は、人と自然の調和を象徴的に表す形を作りだすことにあります。日本の生け花は、花を生けるという行為そのものが、自己鍛錬や行儀作法の修得の方法であると考えられている点で独特です。

盆栽は、小型の鉢植えの樹木を育てる芸術形式です。樹木の発育を抑えるには、剪定、別の鉢への植え替え、新芽の摘み取り、針金で枝や幹を縛ることなどが必要です。盆栽には、何百年も手入れされてきた、とても貴重なものもあります。盆栽は通常、屋外の庭に置いたり、和室の床の間に飾ったりします。

浮世絵は主に木版で描かれる絵です。浮世絵は江戸時代に発達しました。それらには美女、力士、歌舞伎役者、風景などが描かれています。

日本庭園　*nihon teien* | Japanese gardens

Teien refers to gardens. Japanese-style gardens are basically landscape gardens characterized by a layout which seeks to duplicate natural scenes. Such gardens typically have abundant greenery, hills, streams and ponds, stone lanterns, and tea houses.

陶磁器　*tojiki* | ceramics

Tojiki is a general term for ceramics referring to both *toki*, which is pottery, and *jiki*, which is porcelain. Japan has a long history of producing ceramics, and each district has its own special *tojiki*.

漆器　*shikki* | lacquerware

Shikki is lacquerware. Japan was once one of the biggest producers of lacquer in the world, and this naturally contributed to the development of Japan's lacquerware production. Although today Japan relies mostly on imported lacquer, lacquerware production remains popular. Lacquerware includes bowls, trays, layered boxes, chopsticks, and accessories such as broaches and combs.

織物　*orimono* | woven fabrics

Orimono is a general term for woven fabrics. Japan has long been famous for producing silk fabrics. One of the most famous types is *Nishijin-ori*, produced in the Nishijin district of Kyoto. Nishijin products are very popular as the material for *kimono*, *obi* sashes, purses, and many other items.

日本式の庭園は、基本的に風景式庭園で、自然風景の再現に主眼を置いた作庭方式が特徴です。このような庭園は緑に覆われており、築山、遣り水、池、石灯籠、茶室などが配置してあるのが一般的です。

陶磁器は、陶器と磁器の両方の焼き物を意味する一般用語です。日本の陶磁器製造の歴史は古く、各地でそれぞれ独自の陶磁器が作られています。

日本はかつて世界有数の漆の産地であったため、漆器製造が発達したのは自然の成り行きでした。今日、日本は、漆のほとんどを輸入に頼っているものの、漆器製造は依然として盛んです。漆器には、椀、盆、重箱、箸、ブローチや櫛といった装飾品などがあります。

織物は、糸を織り上げて作った製品を指す一般用語です。日本は、昔から絹織物の生産でよく知られていました。最もよく知られた銘柄に、京都の西陣で作られる西陣織があります。西陣で製造される着物、帯、財布、その他多くの製品は、とても人気があります。

枯山水　*karesansui*

Karesansui is a dry-style garden consisting mainly of rocks and sand. The rocks represent mountains, and the sand represents water. These gardens are often found at *Zen* Buddhist temples, and their symbolic elements are based on *Zen* Buddhist philosophy.

借景　*shakkei*

Shakkei is a Japanese garden construction technique aimed at integrating the background scenery of the garden into its layout. Representative samples can be observed at Shugakuin Rikyu, or Shugakuin Imperial Villa, and at the garden attached to Rokuonji, also known as Kinkakuji, or the temple of the Golden Pavilion, both in Kyoto.

染物　*somemono* | dyed textiles

Somemono is a general term for dyed textiles. Although there are a number of dyeing techniques, one of the most famous methods is *Yuzen-zome*, which originated in Kyoto. In *Yuzen*, textiles are dyed in elaborate patterns. *Yuzen* textiles are quite popular as the material for *kimono*.

大和絵　*Yamato-e*

Yamato-e is a term referring to a traditional Japanese painting style which dates back to the 9th century. *Yamato-e* paintings not only have Japanese themes but also are distinctively Japanese in style. The paintings appear on narrative handscrolls, *fusuma* sliding doors, and *byobu* folding screens.

枯山水は、岩と砂を主体に用いて、水を使わない様式の庭園です。岩は山を表し、砂は水を表します。枯山水式の庭園は、禅宗の寺によく見られ、その象徴的な要素は禅の哲学に基づいています。

借景は、庭園の背景を庭の設計に取り込むことをねらった日本の作庭技術の一つです。代表的な借景式庭園は、京都にある修学院離宮や、金閣寺とも呼ばれる鹿苑寺庭園などに見られます。

染物は、織物を染めた製品を指す一般名称です。染色技術にはさまざまなものがありますが、最も有名な手法に、京都で創始された友禅染があります。友禅は、織物を精巧な模様に染めたもので、着物の素材として、とても人気があります。

大和絵は伝統的な日本様式の絵画で、その起源は9世紀にさかのぼります。大和絵は日本的な題材を取り上げているだけでなく、日本独特の様式を持っています。大和絵は、絵巻物、襖、屏風などに描かれています。

水墨画（墨絵）　*suiboku-ga (sumi-e)*

Suiboku-ga, or *sumi-e*, is a term referring to Chinese-style india ink painting, which was introduced to Japan in the 14th century and became popular among *Zen* Buddhist monks. The style is characterized by the use of contrast made by shades of ink and brush strokes.

書道　*shodo* | calligraphy

Shodo is Japanese calligraphy. In *shodo*, shades of ink and brush strokes are important to write artistic characters. People practice it not only to improve their writing skills, but also to discipline themselves.

日本刀　*nihon-to*

Nihon-to, or Japanese swords, were the traditional weapons of the *samurai* class. There are several types of sword, but the most common is the *katana*, which has a single edge and a curved blade. In modern Japan, high-quality swords made by a well-known craftsman can easily cost several thousands of dollars.

水墨画（墨絵）は中国様式の墨絵を意味する用語で、こうした絵は14世紀に日本にもたらされ、禅僧の間で広まりました。水墨画の様式は、墨汁の明暗と筆遣いが生むコントラストを利用するのが特徴です。

書道では、墨の明暗と筆遣いが、美しい文字を書くために重要です。書道は、単に書の技術を磨くだけでなく、自己鍛錬としても学ばれています。

日本刀は武士が使用した日本の伝統的な武器でした。日本刀にはいくつかの種類がありますが、典型的なものは片刃で刀身が反っている刀です。現在、著名な刀鍛冶が作る高級な刀は安くても数十万円します。

Ukiyo-e influenced van Gogh!

F : Guess what? This weekend, I'm going to a **tea ceremony**.

J : That's great. You might wonder why we make such a fuss over a cup of green tea, but you have to remember, the ceremony has a religious origin. That goes for *ikebana* too. Are there any other Japanese arts or crafts that you're interested in?

F : Oh, yes. I've always loved the famous image of Mt. Fuji being dwarfed by an ocean wave.

J : That would be an *ukiyo-e* by Hokusai. That image is from his *36 Views of Mt. Fuji*, which he did in the early 1800s. Did you know that Japanese *ukiyo-e* influenced several great Western impressionist artists such as Vincent van Gogh and Claude Monet?

F : No, I didn't know that.

J : You see, toward the end of the 19th century, old *ukiyo-e* prints were used as wrapping paper for items that were being exported to Europe. The unique designs attracted the attention of artists.

F : That's amazing. But why were *ukiyo-e* prints being used as wrapping paper?

J : A painter like Hiroshige or Hokusai would create a painting. Then a craftsman would make woodblocks so that the work could be duplicated. The prints were mass-produced for ordinary people. I guess it wasn't much different than wrapping something in old newspaper.

F : Did the prints include text?

J : Oh, yes. In fact, Japan had a very high literacy rate compared to the rest of the world back then.

浮世絵から影響を受けたヴァン・ゴッホ！

F：ねえ、聞いてよ。今週末、お茶会に行くんだよ。

J：すてきね。たかが1杯の緑茶に何を大げさな、と思われるかもしれないけど、茶の湯は宗教から生まれてきたということを覚えておく必要があるわ。生け花も同様。ほかに興味のある日本の美術や工芸はある？

F：ああ、もちろん。ぼくは以前から、富士山が大波で小さく見える構図の有名な絵が気に入っていたんだ。

J：それは北斎の浮世絵ね。その絵は1800年代初期に北斎が描いた『富嶽三十六景』の一つ。浮世絵が有名な印象派の画家たちに影響を与えたって知ってる？　ゴッホやモネなんかよ。

F：へえ、それは知らなかったな。

J：19世紀の終わり近くには、ヨーロッパへの輸出品の包装紙に古い浮世絵が使われていたの。その独特のデザインが画家たちに注目されたのよ。

F：すごいね。でもなぜ浮世絵を包装紙に使っていたの？

J：広重や北斎などの浮世絵師が原図を描いて、職人が木版を作る仕組みだから、複製品が作れたわけ。そうやってできた木版画が庶民向けに大量生産されていたのよ。読み終わった新聞に何かを包むのとあまり変わらなかったんだと思うわ。

F：文章も印刷されていたの？

J：もちろん。事実、当時の日本は、世界のほかの国々と比べて識字率がかなり高かったんだから。

---

might wonder why 〜：
　なぜ〜だろうと思うかもしれない
make a fuss over 〜：〜で大騒ぎする
dwarf：〜を縮小する
The 36 Views of Mt. Fuji：富嶽三十六景
⇒江戸後期の浮世絵師、葛飾北斎の代表作。
Vincent van Gogh：
　ヴィンセント・ヴァン・ゴッホ（1853 〜 90）

⇒浮世絵に影響を受けたオランダ印象派の画家。
Claude Monet：クロード・モネ（1840〜1926）
⇒フランス印象派の画家で、浮世絵のコレクターとしても知られる。
woodblocks：木版
duplicate：〜を複製する
literacy rate：識字率

 **Introduction | 概説**

日本が世界に誇る伝統的な舞台芸術として、能と歌舞伎、そして狂言や文楽があります。それぞれ家柄と厳しい修業に支えられ、継承されてきた伝統芸として、今日も生き続けています。

The classical Japanese dramatic arts include *kabuki*, *noh*, *kyogen*, and *bunraku*. The most popular today is *kabuki*, which developed during the **Edo Period**. The actors belong to acting families which pass on the tradition from father to son—there are no female performers.

🔍 *kabuki* → p.186　　*noh* → p.186　　　　　　*kyogen* → p.186
　bunraku → p.186　　Edo Period → p.26

能では、面を着けた役者の表情は見る者にはわかりませんが、その所作に集中することで、いっそう劇的緊張感が高められます。滑稽かつ洗練された所作が特徴の狂言は、能の幕間などに演じられます。文楽は人形劇で、高度な技術で人形に人の情感を見事に表現させます。

Noh is performed with actors wearing masks and includes song and dance. *Kyogen* is a comic performance that is often performed between *noh* plays. *Bunraku* is a form of puppet theater. The main puppets are manipulated from behind by three puppeteers. One of the most famous Japanese playwrights, Chikamatsu Monzaemon, wrote many of his plays for *bunraku*. One popular theme involves lovers who cannot marry because of social pressures. Unable to live apart, they commit suicide.

日本の古典的な演劇芸術には、歌舞伎、能、狂言、文楽などがあります。今日、最も人気があるのは歌舞伎で、江戸時代に発達しました。歌舞伎俳優は特定の家系に属し、伝統の芸は父から子へと伝承されます。女性の演技者はいません。

pass on *A* from *B* to *C*：ＡをＢからＣへ伝承する

能は能面を着用した演者が謡や舞踊とともに演じます。狂言は滑稽さを含んだ演劇で、しばしば能の幕間に演じられます。文楽は人形劇の一種です。文楽の主要な人形は背後から3人で操ります。日本における最も有名な劇作家の一人である近松門左衛門は、文楽の台本を数多く書きました。人気のある題材に、社会的重圧のために一緒になれない恋人同士を語ったものがあります。2人は別れて生きるしかないならと、心中してしまいます。

comic：滑稽な
puppet theater：人形劇
manipulate：〜を操る

puppeteer：人形遣い
playwright：劇作家
commit suicide：自殺する

音楽については、和楽器をいくつかを紹介しましょう。音楽は世界の共通言語といいますが、似たような楽器を外国の楽器の中から探すのはそれほど難しくありません。

Traditional music ranges from the festive *bon'odori* dance music that can be heard throughout Japan in the summer to the very formal *gagaku*, which was originally performed for the Imperial Court. Some of the common traditional musical instruments are the *biwa* and the *shamisen*, which are guitar-like instruments, the *koto*, which is a 13-string zither, the *shakuhachi*, which is a bamboo flute, and a variety of *taiko*, or Japanese drums.

🔍 *bon* → p.114　　　　*shamisen* → p.188　　　　*koto* → p.188
shakuhachi → p.188

日本の伝統芸能の継承者として、芸者の存在は重要です。その他、伝統芸能以外にも、さまざまな芸能ジャンルが日本で盛んであることを指摘しておきましょう。

Traditional Japanese music and dance have also been handed down by *geisha*, professional female entertainers. Although the number of *geisha* has declined over the years, *geisha* culture is now drawing renewed attention as a popular tourist attraction.

In addition to the traditional Japanese arts, there are many other types of performance available—especially in the large cities. Opera, Broadway shows, classical music, jazz and rock concerts—it's difficult to find a performance genre that Japan has ignored.

🔍 *geisha* → p.188

　伝統音楽には、毎年夏に各地で行われる盆踊りの音楽から、もともとは宮廷音楽であった格式ある雅楽まで、さまざまな種類があります。最もよく見かける伝統的な楽器としては、ギターに似た琵琶や三味線、チターに似た13弦の琴、フルートに似た竹製の尺八、それに、さまざまな種類の太鼓などがあります。

range from A to B：AからBにわたる　　　　zither：チター
the Imperial Court：宮廷

　日本の伝統的な音楽や舞踊は、女性の職業芸能人である芸者によっても継承されてきました。芸者の数は年々減ってきましたが、ここにきて観光の目玉として新たな注目を浴びるようになっています。

　伝統芸術に加え、特に大都市では、オペラ、ブロードウエーのショー、クラシック音楽、ジャズ、ロックコンサートなど多くの舞台や音楽を楽しむことができます。日本にない舞台芸術の分野は、ほとんど見当たらないといっていいでしょう。

hand down 〜：〜を継承する

歌舞伎 *kabuki*

Kabuki is a traditional dramatic art which developed in the 17th century. In *kabuki*, all the roles are played by male actors. Other features of *kabuki* include exaggerated makeup, elaborate costumes, sophisticated stage sets, and the *hanamichi*, which is a runway that extends into the audience. Themes of *kabuki* are mainly based on historical events and the traditional lives of commoners.

能 *noh*

Noh is a traditional dramatic art which developed in the 14th century. It is characterized by the masks that the actors wear, elaborate costumes, simple stage sets, and distinctive narrative chants. Many themes of *noh* are related to encounters with supernatural beings, which deliver the symbolic messages to the audience.

狂言 *kyogen*

Kyogen is a traditional Japanese stage art. It developed along with *noh* around the 14th century. *Kyogen* features comical and satirical stories written from the commoners' viewpoint and is in sharp contrast to *noh*, which features serious stories.

文楽 *bunraku*

Bunraku is a type of traditional puppet theater which developed in the 18th century and was quite popular among the commoners of the time. *Bunraku* is characterized by skillful manipulation of puppets and distinctive narrative ballads. The themes of *bunraku* deal with warriors, nobility, and the lives of commoners. Some of the most famous *bunraku* plays are based on true stories involving double suicides. Even today these stories are regarded as some of the greatest Japanese literary achievements.

歌舞伎は17世紀に発達した伝統演劇です。歌舞伎では、すべての配役が男優によって演じられます。歌舞伎の特徴は、派手な隈取、凝った衣装、精巧な舞台装置、観客席へと延びた花道などにあります。歌舞伎の題材は、歴史上の出来事や当時の庶民の生活に基づくものが中心です。

能は14世紀に発達した伝統演劇です。能の特徴は、演者が着用する面、凝った衣装、簡素な舞台装置、独特の詠唱歌にあります。能の題材は、超自然的な存在との遭遇を扱ったものが多く、その遭遇を通じて観客に象徴的なメッセージを伝えます。

狂言は、日本の伝統的な舞台芸術です。狂言は能とともに14世紀ごろに発達しました。狂言は、庶民の視点から描かれた滑稽で風刺的な物語を扱い、能が扱う深刻な題材と好対照を成しています。

文楽は18世紀に発達した伝統的な人形劇の一種で、当時の庶民にとても人気がありました。文楽の特徴は、巧みな人形操作と独特の語り唄にあります。文楽は題材として、武士、公家、庶民生活などを取り上げています。心中事件など実際の恋物語に基づいた作品が最もよく知られています。これらの物語は、今日でも日本文学の傑作とされています。

三味線　*shamisen*

Shamisen is a 3-string instrument similar to a guitar. The instrument is mainly played to accompany traditional songs or narrative ballads. There are several different playing styles for *shamisen*, one of which is *Tsugaru Jamisen*, a style characterized by its strong beat and sound.

琴　*koto*

Koto is a 13-string musical instrument used for playing traditional music. It is laid on the floor and plucked with finger- and thumb-picks. Each string is supported by an independent bridge, which can be moved to change the pitch.

尺八　*shakuhachi*

Shakuhachi is a traditional Japanese wind instrument made of bamboo. The name *shakuhachi* is derived from the standard length of the instrument. Although sizes do vary, the standard length is about 55 centimeters, or 1.8 feet. It has five holes and is played vertically. The *shakuhachi* is used for accompanying traditional music and folksongs, and is characterized by its hoarse, melancholy sound.

芸者　*geisha* and *geiko*

Geisha or *geiko* are traditional, female Japanese entertainers, whose skills include traditional Japanese music and dance. *Geiko* is the term used in the western part of Japan including Kyoto. They are dispatched to exclusive Japanese restaurants to entertain guests. *Maiko* is a term used in Kyoto to refer to an apprentice *geisha*, who is usually called a *hangyoku* in other areas. It takes a *hangyoku* or *maiko* several years of training in performance skills and manners to become a full-fledged *geisha* or *geiko*.

三味線は、3弦の楽器でギターに似ています。三味線は、また、伝統的な唄や語り唄の伴奏として用いられます。三味線にはさまざまな演奏スタイルがあり、その一つに、強烈なビートと音を特徴とする津軽三味線があります。

琴は13弦の楽器で、伝統的な音楽の演奏に用いられます。琴は床に置いて、指につけた爪で弾きます。各弦は、それぞれ別個の柱（駒）で支えられており、その柱を移動することで弦の音程を変えることができます。

尺八は、日本の伝統的な竹製の管楽器です。尺八の名称は、標準的な尺八の長さに由来します。実際、長さはまちまちですが、一般的なものは1.8フィート（＝一尺八寸）で、約55センチメートルあります。尺八には5つの穴があり、縦に持って演奏されます。尺八は、伝統的な音楽や民謡の伴奏に用いられ、その枯れた、悲しげな音色が特徴です。

芸者・芸妓は伝統的な女性の職業芸能人で、日本の伝統音楽や伝統舞踊などに長けています。芸妓は京都を含む西日本で用いられる名称です。芸者は客をもてなす高級料亭に派遣されます。舞妓は見習いの芸者を指す京都で使われる名称で、ほかの地域では半玉と呼ばれます。半玉や舞妓が一人前の芸者や芸妓になるには、数年にわたる芸や作法の稽古が必要です。

※芸妓は、芸者と芸妓を合わせて意味する場合、「げいぎ」と読みます。

演歌　*enka*

Enka is a genre of Japanese music that is most popular among the older generations. Many of the songs have sad themes, such as lost love or death. *Enka* is characterized by distinctive five-scale tunes, a unique singing style, and the use of traditional Japanese instruments.

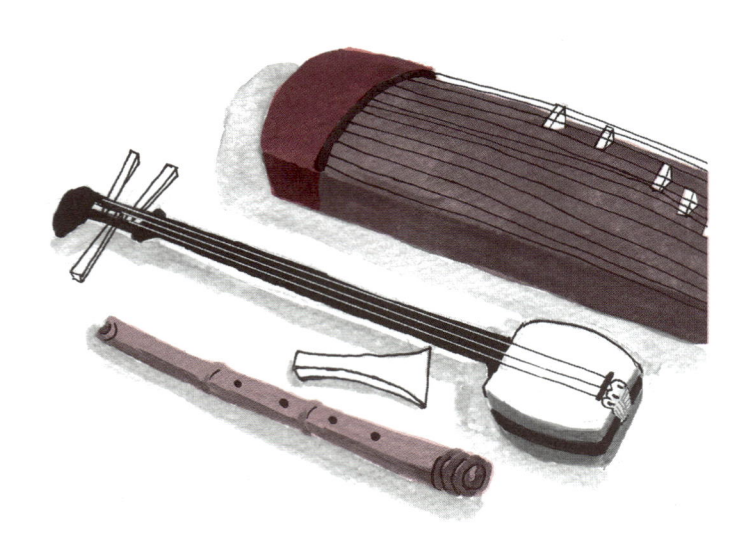

演歌は日本の音楽ジャンルで、中年以上の層に非常に人気があります。多くは失恋や人の死といった悲しい話を題材としています。演歌は、独特の５音階旋律、特有な歌い回し、さらに日本の伝統的な楽器を使うことが特徴です。

Dialogue | 対話

Bunraku is not for kids.

F : I'd really like to see a *kabuki* performance, but I'm afraid I won't be able to understand anything.

J : You don't have to worry about that. You can borrow an earphone which provides an English explanation of the story. You'll really enjoy *kabuki*. The elaborate *kimono* and makeup are visually stunning, and the music is played using traditional Japanese instruments. Did you know that all the roles, including female roles, are played by men?

F : Why is that?

J : When *kabuki* began in the early 1600s, women were featured. I believe some scandal caused them to be banned.

F : That's too bad. Is it expensive to see *kabuki*?

J : It depends on the program and casting, but in some programs you can get seats for less than 3,000 yen. Also, it's rather casual. At some theaters, you can buy a *bento* at food stands in the lobby, and have it at your seat during the intervals.

F : Okay, I'll do that. Also, on TV I saw a play where the actors were wearing masks. What was that?

J : That's *noh*. It's even older than *kabuki*. Another classical Japanese dramatic art is *bunraku*, which is a puppet performance. But it's not for kids—the themes are adult-oriented.

F : Would you like to go see *kabuki* with me?

J : Sure. It's been years since I've seen *kabuki*.

文楽は子ども向けじゃないのよ

F : ぜひ歌舞伎を見てみたいんだけど、何一つわからないんじゃないかと思って心配なんだ。

J : それは心配ないわ。英語で筋書き解説を聞けるイヤフォンを借りることができるの。きっと楽しめるはずよ。凝った着物の衣装や隈取なんかは見ていて圧倒されるし、伝統的な和楽器を使って音楽が奏でられるの。ねえ、すべての役を男優が演じることは知っている？

F : どうしてそうなの？

J : 歌舞伎が始まった17世紀の初めは、女優が中心だったの。それが、なんらかのスキャンダルがあって禁止されたんじゃなかったかな。

F : それは残念。歌舞伎の入場料は高いの？

J : 出し物や出演者によるけど、3,000円以下の席がある出し物もあるわ。それに、それほど堅苦しいものでもないの。劇場によってはロビーの販売コーナーでお弁当を買って、観客席で幕間に食べることもできるわ。

F : わかった。そうしてみるよ。そういえば、テレビで、俳優が面を着けている演劇を見たことがあるけど、あれは何？

J : それは能。能は歌舞伎よりもさらに古いものよ。古典的な日本の演劇がもう一つあって、文楽という人形劇よ。といっても子ども向けのものではなく、内容は大人向け。

F : 歌舞伎に一緒に出かけないかい？

J : いいわよ。歌舞伎なんて、私、何年ぶりかしら。

---

feature：〜を主演させる
ban：〜を禁止する

puppet performance：人形による演技
adult-oriented：大人向きの

Literature
文学

 **Introduction** | 概説

日本人の活字好きは、識字率の高さにも現れています。日本人の活字文化の歴史をざっと振り返ってみましょう。

The Japanese are some of the most prolific readers in the world. Books, magazines, newspapers, and of course *manga* comics are widely read. Many foreign books and publications are translated and available in Japanese bookstores. Although the writing system of Japan uses three different character sets, Japan boasts a literacy rate above 99%.

🔍 *manga* → p.210

中国から「漢字」がもたらされたのは4世紀とされます。その後、日本独自の詩「和歌」を集めた『万葉集』が編纂されました。

The Chinese writing system was imported to Japan in the 4th century. The first known Japanese literary works emerged in the 8th century. Two early works of note are the anthology of *waka* poems called *Man-yoshu*, and the earliest written history of Japan, the *Kojiki*. Both were compiled in the 8th century.

🔍 *waka* → p.198

世界初の小説として『源氏物語』が日本で生まれたことは、その作者、紫式部の名とともに、日本の文学を語るときに欠かせない出来事です。

The Chinese writing system that Japan adopted consists of complex ideograms called *kanji*. Since the Japanese and Chinese languages are completely different, the Japanese first used the Chinese characters as phonetic symbols to write Japanese text. Around the 10th century,

　日本人は、実によく活字を読む国民です。本や雑誌、新聞、そしてもちろんマンガも幅広く読まれています。多くの外国の本や出版物が翻訳されており、国内の本屋で入手できます。日本語の表記法では、3種類の異なる文字を使いますが、識字率は99パーセント以上という高さを誇っています。

prolific reader：多読する人　　　　　literacy rate：識字率

　中国の表記体系が日本に伝わったのは4世紀です。日本最初の文学作品は8世紀に登場します。特筆すべき初期の作品は、和歌を集めた『万葉集』、ならびに日本最初の史書である『古事記』で、いずれも8世紀に成立しました。

anthology：歌集

　日本が取り入れた中国語の表記法は、複雑な表意文字の「漢字」でした。日本語と中国語は全く異なるため、日本人は最初のころ、中国の文字を表音記号として用いて日本文を書いていました。10世紀ごろには、日本独自の表音記号である「かな」が使われていました。11世紀の平安時代の貴族女性は、こ

original Japanese phonetic characters called *kana* were being used. The Heian Period court ladies of the 11th century used *kana* when they wrote *kyutei bungaku*, or court literature. Some of the most notable writers were Murasaki Shikibu, who wrote the novel *Genji Monogatari*, or *The Tale of Genji*, and Sei Shonagon, the writer of the essay *Makura-no-Soshi*, *The Pillow Book*. These works provide deep insight into the Imperial Court during that period.

🔍 *kanji* → p.198   *kana* → p.198   *kyutei bungaku* → p.198
  Genji Monogatari → p.200   *Makura-no-Soshi* → p.200

さまざまな文化が花開いた江戸時代。文学も例外ではありませんでした。

In the **Edo Period**, many of Japan's traditional arts matured, and literature was no different. This was the time that *haiku* poetry developed into its present form.

🔍 Edo Period → p.26   *haiku* → p.200

時代が明治に至り、ようやく書き言葉に口語体が用いられるようになりました。現代では、海外の作品が数多く翻訳されると同時に、日本人作家の作品も欧米を中心に数多く紹介されていることも忘れてはなりません。

Well into the Meiji Period, most Japanese literature was written in a classical style which partially used the Chinese language. As the country modernized, the written language was changed to more closely reflect the spoken language. Nevertheless, Japan still uses three types of characters—*kanji*, *hiragana*, and *katakana*. *Katakana* are mostly used to write non-Chinese loan words.

In modern times, numerous Japanese writers have received international recognition. Mishima Yukio, Abe Kobo, Murakami Haruki, and others have had their works translated into foreign languages. Two Japanese authors have won the Nobel Prize in Literature —Kawabata Yasunari (1968) and Oe Kenzaburo (1994).

のかな文字を使って宮廷文学を生み出したのです。最も有名な作家は、小説『源氏物語』を著した紫式部と、随筆『枕草子』を著した清少納言です。これらの作品は、当時の宮廷世界について深い洞察を行っています。

ideogram：表意文字　　　　　　　　　phonetic character：表音文字
phonetic symbol：表音記号　　　　　　insight into ～：～への洞察

　江戸時代には数々の伝統的な芸術が大成していきますが、文学も例外ではありませんでした。俳句が現在の形へと発展したのはこの時代でした。

　明治時代に入っても、文学作品は中国語を取り入れた古典的な漢文調で書かれているものがほとんどでした。近代化が進むにつれ、書き言葉は話し言葉に近い形に変化していきます。それでも、日本ではいまだに、漢字、ひらがな、カタカナという3種類の文字を用いています。カタカナは特に、中国語以外の外来語を表記するときに用いられています。

　現代では、数多くの日本人作家が国際的な評価を得るようになってきました。三島由紀夫、安部公房、村上春樹などの作品は数か国語に翻訳されています。また、川端康成（1968）と大江健三郎（1994）の2人の日本人作家がノーベル文学賞を受賞しています。

loan word：外来語　　　　　　　　　the Nobel Prize：ノーベル賞

和歌 *waka*

Waka is a Japanese poetic style that has a 5-7-5-7-7 syllable pattern. *Waka* has become synonymous with the term *tanka* which literally means "short poem." The style was developed between the 6th and 8th centuries. The most notable *waka* collection is *Kokin-wakashu*, which was compiled in the 10th century.

漢字 *kanji*

Kanji are Chinese characters used in Japanese writing. They are most often used for nouns, verb stems, and adjective stems in the Japanese writing system. The characters are ideograms and often have several readings.

かな *kana*

Kana are simplified *kanji* that are used as phonetic characters in the Japanese writing system. *Hiragana* and *katakana* are the two types of *kana* characters. *Hiragana* are used to supplement *kanji* or to provide the readings of *kanji*. *Katakana* are used mainly for foreign words.

宮廷文学 *kyutei bungaku*

Kyutei bungaku is a form of literature developed around the Imperial Court in the 11th century. Some of the famous pieces include the novel *Genji Monogatari*, written by Murasaki Shikibu, and the essay *Makura-no-Soshi*, written by Sei Shonagon. Both works significantly influenced Japanese literature and are highly praised even to this day.

和歌は、五・七・五・七・七の音節パターンを持つ日本の詩形態です。和歌は、文字どおり「短い歌」という意味の短歌と同義です。和歌は、6世紀から8世紀にかけて発達しました。最も有名な和歌集は『古今和歌集』で、10世紀に編集されました。

漢字は、日本語の表記で使われる中国の文字です。漢字は、日本の表記法では名詞や動詞・形容詞の語幹を表記するときに多く用いられます。漢字は表意文字で、多くの場合、複数の読み方があります。

かなは漢字を簡略化したもので、日本語の表記法において表音文字として用いられます。かなには、ひらがなとカタカナの2種類があります。ひらがなは、漢字を補足するため、あるいは漢字の読みを記すために用いられます。カタカナは主に、外国語を表記するときに用いられます。

宮廷文学は、11世紀に宮廷を中心に発達した文学の形式です。著名な作品には紫式部の小説『源氏物語』、清少納言の随筆『枕草子』などがあります。この2作品は、日本の文学に多大な影響を与え、今日に至るまで高い評価を得ています。

源氏物語　*Genji Monogatari* | The Tale of Genji

The Tale of Genji is the world's oldest full-length novel, composed of 54 chapters. Written by a court lady named Murasaki Shikibu around the 11th century, the novel, which centers around the hero Hikaru Genji's romance with court ladies, describes the refined lifestyles of court nobility. With strong emphasis on the transience of life, *The Tale of Genji* is regarded as a timeless masterpiece.

枕草子　*Makura-no-Soshi* | The Pillow Book

The Pillow Book is an essay written around the 11th century by a court lady named Sei Shonagon. It describes her deep insights into what she saw, experienced, and felt in her court life with vividness and sharp wit. Along with *The Tale of Genji*, it is regarded as one of the greatest court literature works.

俳句　*haiku*

Haiku is a Japanese poetic style that has a 5-7-5 syllable pattern. Each *haiku* must include a seasonal term called *kigo*. Matsuo Basho, of the 17th century, is one of the most notable *haiku* poets.

 Related Vocabulary | 関連語彙

- ■詩：poetry / a poem
- ■随筆：an essay
- ■日記文学：literature based on a diary
- ■私小説：a novel that is based on the author's experiences
- ■推理小説：a mystery novel / a detective story
- ■暴露本：an exposé
- ■実話本：a non-fiction novel

『源氏物語』は世界最古の長編小説で、54帖から成っています。11世紀ごろに宮廷に仕える女性の紫式部が著した小説で、主人公の光源氏と宮廷女性との恋を中心に、洗練された宮廷貴族の生活を描き出しています。『源氏物語』は、もののあわれを強調しており、不朽の名作とされています。

『枕草子』は、11世紀に宮廷に仕えた女性の清少納言が著した随筆です。『枕草子』は、彼女が見たり経験したり感じたりしたことに対する彼女の深い洞察を、優れた写実性と鋭い機知で描いており、『源氏物語』とならんで、宮廷文学の最高傑作とされています。

俳句は日本の詩形態の一つで、五・七・五の音節パターンを持っています。俳句には、季語と呼ばれる季節を表す語が必ず含まれています。17世紀の松尾芭蕉は、最も有名な俳人の一人です。

■連載小説：a running story
■日本語教育：Japanese-language teaching
■貸し本屋：a book rental shop

■古本屋：a second hand bookstore / a used bookstore

Dialogue | 対話

MP3 57

We composed *haiku* in literature class.

F : When I was a student, I had a literature class where the teacher made us compose *haiku* poems.

J : Is that right? In the United States?

F : Yes. I hated poetry, but for some reason I enjoyed doing the *haiku*—maybe because they're so short.

J : Did you know that every *haiku* has a symbolic reference to a season called *kigo*?

F : No. What do you mean?

J : The cherry blossom represents spring, for example. And the summer could be represented by *furin*, or a wind chime. Using a *kigo* is one of the ways such a short, simple poem can hold so much meaning.

F : That's interesting. Isn't there some limit on the number of lines or syllables?

J : Yes, a *haiku* has three lines in a five, seven, five syllable pattern. If you make *haiku* in English, though, you don't need to be strict about the syllable count. But you should stick to three lines.

F : What about the … the … umm …

J : *Kigo*?

F : Yes. Do I need to use *kigo*?

J : Some people say it's not necessary because non-Japanese might come from a place where the climate is very different. But I still think it's a nice touch to have a *kigo* term.

F : I agree. Say, what Japanese authors do you like?

J : I like Natsume Soseki and Kawabata Yasunari. Many of their novels and stories have been translated into English. I recommend that you pick up *I Am a Cat* by Soseki. You'll enjoy it.

F : Thanks, I'll do that.

文学の授業で俳句を作ったよ

F：学生のとき、文学の授業を取ってたんだけど、そこで先生が俳句を作る課題を出したことがあるよ。

J：ほんと？　アメリカで？

F：うん。詩を作るのは嫌いだったんだけど、なぜか俳句を作るのは好きだったな。たぶん俳句は短かったからだと思うけど。

J：すべての俳句には、必ず季節を象徴する季語が入っているのは知ってる？

F：いや。どういうこと？

J：たとえば、桜の花は春の意味なの。夏を意味するには風鈴などが使われるわ。季語は、短くて簡潔な詩に、とても深い意味を持たせるための手法の一つよ。

F：面白いね。行数や音節数に制限はあるの？

J：ええ。俳句は、3行で五・七・五の音節で作られるの。でも英語で俳句を作る場合、音節の数は気にしなくていいわ。その代わり、3行詩の形は取ったほうがいいいわね。

F：それじゃ、あの、えーっと、何だっけ？

J：季語？

F：そう、そう。季語は使わないといけないの？

J：季語は必要ないと言う人もいるわ。だって、外国人なら日本と全く気候が違うところの出身かもしれないし。でも、個人的には季語があったほうが、雰囲気が出ると思うわ。

F：僕もそう思う。ところで、日本人作家では誰が好き？

J：夏目漱石や川端康成が好き。彼らの作品の多くが英語に翻訳されているわね。漱石の『吾輩は猫である』はお勧めよ。きっと面白いから。

F：ありがとう。読んでみるよ。

compose：（詩など）を書く
for some reason：なぜか
symbolic：象徴的な
syllable：音節

be strict about ～：～に厳密に従う
stick to ～：～を保つ
nice touch：良い感じ
pick up ～：～を手に取る

Introduction | 概説

MP3 58

日本文化というと伝統的なイメージが強いですが、最先端を行くポップカルチャーも また日本文化の重要な一面です。

Japanese culture is steeped in history, but that hasn't slowed the rapid changes in fashion, trends, and other popular culture. Some of these trends have become popular overseas.

マンガやアニメといったポップカルチャーには、日本の社会が反映されているだけで なく、日本の伝統文化の影響が強く見られます。また、携帯、スマートフォンなどの 先端技術がポップカルチャーの普及を後押ししています。

There is a tendency to associate pop culture, which is an abbreviation of popular culture, with the activities and interests of younger generations. Nevertheless, it reflects the society as a whole and also has a connection with traditional culture. If we look at the romantic tales of early Japanese literature such as *The Tale of Genji*, and the exaggerated depictions in **Edo Period** *ukiyo-e*, it's easy to see how earlier forms of culture have influenced the *manga* and *anime* of today.

We can also see that Japanese society today invokes a strong work ethic, which likely contributes to the escapist plots common in *manga* and *anime*. Furthermore, many people have long train commutes in Japanese urban areas. Besides reading, you will see numerous people on trains killing time on their cell phones, or *keitai*. Smartphones are increasingly being used to download content, including pop music, games, and *manga*.

The Tale of Genji → p.200   Edo Period → p.26   *ukiyo-e* → p.172

manga → p.210   *anime* → p.210

日本文化には長い歴史が染み込んでいますが、それがファッションや流行などのポップカルチャーの目まぐるしい変化にブレーキを掛けるものではありません。日本のポップカルチャーには海外で人気になってきたものもあります。

be steeped in 〜：〜が染み込んでいる

ポップカルチャーは、英語のpopular cultureの略で、若い世代の活動や興味が連想される傾向があります。それでも、ポップカルチャーは日本の社会全体を映し出しており、伝統文化とも結び付いています。『源氏物語』といった日本文学黎明期の恋愛小説や、江戸時代の浮世絵の誇張的な描写手法を見ると、昔の文化が現代のマンガやアニメに与えてきた影響を容易に感じ取れます。

また、現代の日本社会が求める労働倫理観が強いために、マンガやアニメではどうしても、現実逃避的な筋書きになる傾向があるとも思えます。さらに、日本の都市部では通勤時間が長い人が多く、電車の中では、読書に加え、携帯電話で時間をつぶす人が大勢います。ポップミュージック、ゲーム、マンガなどのコンテンツをダウンロードする目的で、スマートフォンが使われることがますます多くなっています。

abbreviation：省略、略語
work ethic：労働倫理観
escapist：現実逃避的な

plot：（映画などの）筋
kill time：時間をつぶす

日本のポップカルチャーは海外でも注目されるようになりました。特に、マンガやアニメは年齢層を超えて、世界的に高く評価されています。

It is important to note that aspects of Japanese pop culture have been embraced overseas. Some Japanese *manga* comic books have been translated and published abroad. Interestingly, the books read from right to left just as they do in Japan.

Japanese *anime* has certainly become well-known overseas. Many middle-aged Americans watched *Astro Boy* and *Kimba the White Lion* as children, both created by famed Japanese artist Tezuka Osamu. In modern times, the *anime Pokémon*, or *Pocket Monsters*, has been exported to over 50 countries. In 2002, Miyazaki Hayao won the Academy Award for Best Animated Feature with a film titled *Spirited Away* in English. In trademark Miyazaki fashion, the movie combined stunningly beautiful graphics with a social message, and did so with a plot that can be enjoyed by both children and adults alike.

コスプレやキャラクターグッズも日本独特のポップカルチャーの一部です。ポップカルチャーに没頭する人は「オタク」と呼ばれることもあります。

Cosplay, or *kosupure*, which is a contraction of the words "costume play," and collecting character goods are two genres of popular culture that grew from *manga* and *anime*, and both are now widely practiced overseas. The people who most embrace the various aspects of popular culture are sometimes referred to as *otaku*, or geeks. The word *otaku* started out as an insult, but increasingly is used to refer to someone who has a passion about something—especially something related to pop culture.

🔍 *kosupure* → p.210   *otaku* → p.210

重要なのは、日本のポップカルチャーには、海外で人気を博すようになった
ものもあることです。外国語に翻訳され、海外で出版されている日本発のマ
ンガ本もあります。面白いことに、これらのマンガ本は日本流に右から左へと
読まれています。

　日本製のアニメは間違いなく海外でも有名です。現在の米国人中年層の多
くが、日本の有名なマンガ家、手塚治虫が作った『鉄腕アトム』(*Astro Boy*)
や『ジャングル大帝』(*Kimba the White Lion*) を子どものころに見ていま
す。現代では、ポケモンこと『ポケットモンスター』というアニメが50以上の
国へ輸出されていますし、2002年には宮崎駿が『千と千尋の神隠し』(*Spirited Away*) でアカデミー長編アニメ賞を受賞しました。宮崎駿のアニメは独
特のスタイルを持っており、驚異的に美しい画像と社会性のあるメッセージが
一つになり、しかも、それらが子どもも大人も楽しめるようなストーリーで展
開します。

15

Popular Culture and Mass Media

概説

embrace：〜を支持する

　costume playを略したコスプレとキャラクターグッズの収集は、マンガや
アニメから派生したポップカルチャーで、いずれも海外で広く受け入れられて
います。さまざまな分野のポップカルチャーに熱中する人たちは、時にオタク
と呼ばれます。オタクという語はもともと軽蔑的な表現でしたが、特にポップ
カルチャーなどの特定の分野に没頭する人たちを意味して用いられることが多
くなっています。

contraction：短縮形　　　　　　　geek：変人
genre：様式　　　　　　　　　　　insult：侮辱（の言葉）

日本にはあらゆるメディアがあふれ、インターネットの利用も拡大しています。

As for mass communication, the Japanese have ample access to radio, television, film, newspapers, magazines, and of course the Internet. The news media is occasionally criticized for sensationalizing the news and invading the privacy of those involved in newsworthy events. As for the Internet, many Japanese people have access to high speed Internet connections, and most teenagers are just a few clicks away from the Internet via their smartphones.

マスコミについて言えば、ラジオ、テレビ、映画、新聞、雑誌、そしてもちろんインターネットなど、日本ではありとあらゆるメディアが利用できます。ニュースメディアは、センセーショナルな報道や、関係者のプライバシー侵害が非難の的にされることもあります。インターネットの世界では、高速接続回線を利用する人が多くなり、ほとんどのティーンエージャーが、スマートフォンのボタンを押すだけでインターネットにアクセスしています。

a few clicks away from 〜：数回クリックするだけで〜が利用できる

マンガ   *manga*

Manga are comics. Although there were various comics before the war, it was in the postwar era that *manga* gained enormous popularity. There are a wide variety of *manga* themes, and they appeal to all age groups.

アニメ   *anime*

Anime is Japanese hand-drawn or computer animation. The term is now part of the English lexicon. Various Japanese animated films have become internationally known, some winning international film contests.

コスプレ   *kosupure* | cosplay

Kosupure, or cosplay, is the practice of dressing up as a character from *manga*, *anime*, or some other source. The word derives from "costume play." Originating in Japan, the practice of *kosupure* has spread to many other countries.

オタク   *otaku*

Otaku literally means "your home" or "you" and has a negative connotation similar to the English terms "geek" or "nerd." The term refers to those devoted to certain aspects of subculture, including such things as *manga*, *anime*, video games, or *aidoru*. Outside of subculture topics, those that immerse themselves in some particular field are also sometimes referred to as *otaku*.

Related Key Words | 関連キーワード

MP3
60

ヴィジュアル系   *Visual-kei*

Visual-kei, or visual style, is a trend among Japanese musicians to add a powerful

マンガとはコミックのこと。戦前にもいろいろなマンガがありましたが、大人気を博すようになったのは戦後のことです。マンガではさまざまな題材が取り上げられ、すべての年齢層に受けています。

アニメは、手描きやコンピューターで作成した日本流のアニメーションを意味します。今ではanimeとして英語にもなっています。日本発のさまざまなアニメ映画が、国際映画コンテストで賞を獲得し、世界的に知られるようになっています。

コスプレ (cosplay) は、マンガやアニメなどに出てくるキャラクターに扮することで、英語のcostume playからきています。コスプレは日本が発祥ですが、今では多くの国々にも広まっています。

オタクの原義は「お宅 (家)」や「あなた」で、英語で言うgeek (変人) やnerd (ダサい奴) に似た否定的な意味合いで用いられていました。オタクは、マンガやアニメ、テレビゲームやアイドルなどの特定のサブカルチャーに没頭する人たちを指します。また、サブカルチャー以外の分野でも、特定の分野に熱中する人たちをオタクと呼ぶことがあります。

ヴィジュアル系とは、日本のミュージシャンが強烈な視覚的要素を取り入れた格好

visual element to their image. Typically, the musicians or the group wear heavy makeup and unusual costumes.

ケータイ小説　*keitai shosetsu*

Keitai shosetsu are novels written by mobile phone users sending text messages through their phones. The style originated in Japan and is now popular in other countries as well. Some *keitai shosetsu* have become so popular that they have been published as hard copy books.

メイドカフェ　maid cafe

A maid cafe is a type of cosplay cafe where the waitresses wear maid outfits similar to those of classic English or French maids. They play the role of a house servant to give customers the illusion of being a real master, using overly polite words and behavior while pampering the customers.

アキバ系　*akiba-kei*

Akiba-kei, or Akihabara style, is a term that describes men who spend most of their free time in the Akihabara district. Akihabara is known for having shops that sell electronics, video games, *anime*, and other *otaku* goods.

マンガ喫茶　*manga kissa* | *manga* cafe

Manga kissa, or *manga* cafes, began as 24-hour coffee shops which had *manga* comics for customers to read at the cafe. The modern *manga* cafes today have Internet access, movies, and video games, and private booths.

アイドル　*aidoru* | idol

In Japanese, *aidoru*, derived from the English word idol, usually refers to a young and attractive media personality who has become extremely popular. Those that reach idol status include pop musicians, actors, and models.

をする傾向を指します。わかりやすい例で言えば、ミュージシャンやバンドが派手な化粧をして異様な格好をするものです。

ケータイ小説は、携帯電話の利用者が携帯電話から文書を送る形で書かれる小説です。ケータイ小説の様式は日本で生まれ、今ではほかの国でも人気になっています。なかには人気が出て、書籍として出版されたケータイ小説もあります。

メイドカフェは、ウエートレスが昔の英国やフランス風のメイドの格好をしている一種のコスプレ喫茶です。メイドは、使用人の役割を演じ、極端に丁寧な言葉や振る舞いで客を手厚くもてなすことで、客に本当に主人になったかのように感じさせます。

アキバ系は、東京の秋葉原駅周辺で自由時間のほとんどを過ごしている男性を指す言葉です。秋葉原は、家電製品、テレビゲームのソフト、アニメなどを含むオタク関連グッズを販売している店が集まっていることで知られます。

マンガ喫茶は、お客が読むためのマンガを備えた24時間営業のカフェから始まりました。最近のマンガ喫茶はインターネットアクセス、映画、テレビゲームなどのほか、個室などのサービスも備えています。

日本語のアイドルは英語のidolからきており、大人気になった若くて魅力的なマスコミの芸能人を指します。アイドルの地位を獲得する人たちには、ポップミュージシャン、俳優、モデルなどがいます。

癒し系　*iyashi-kei*

Iyashi-kei, or healing style, is a term referring to a form of media entertainment having the effect of making the audience feel relaxed. *Iyashi-kei* can be expressed through *manga*, *anime*, music, or even the personality of an idol. For example, *iyashi-kei anime* depicts people's lives in a relaxing way, without any conflict or drama.

カワイイ　*kawaii*

The word *kawaii* means cute or adorable, and can be used to describe a wide variety of things like comic characters, clothing styles, or behavior. The idea of *kawaii* has become such an important part of Japanese culture that it is now referred to as *kawaii* culture. Increasingly, certain aspects of *kawaii* are being found overseas. Japanese pop culture and cosplay events have been held in many foreign cities.

ゆるキャラ　*yuru kyara*

Yuru kyara is the Japanese expression to describe mascot characters. The mascots are created to represent a place, event, or organization. They are designed to be *kawaii*. The mascots typically use designs that represent local culture, history, or produce. For example, Hikonyan is a mascot representing the castle town of Hikone. The character is a white cat wearing a *samurai* helmet. After the character was created, tourism to Hikone increased.

ABCD Related Vocabulary | 関連語彙

- ■インディーズブランド：independent brand
- ■ゲームセンター：game arcade / video arcade
- ■興行収入：box-office profits
- ■ワイドショー：a gossip show
- ■折り込み広告：inserts / circulars inserted in newspapers
- ■全国紙：a national newspaper
- ■地方紙：a local newspaper

癒し系は、観客や視聴者をリラックスさせる効果を持つマスコミ上の娯楽を意味します。癒し系には、マンガ、アニメ、音楽、さらにはアイドルの性格などによる表現手法があります。たとえば、癒し系アニメの場合、葛藤や事件などは扱わず、人々の生活をゆったりと描くような作品を意味します。

「カワイイ」という言葉は、マンガのキャラクターやファッションや振る舞いなど、幅広い事柄を意味するときに使われます。カワイイの概念は日本文化の重要な部分になってきており、今では、カワイイ文化と呼ばれたりします。カワイイ文化の一部は、海外でますます評価されてきています。日本のポップカルチャーやコスプレに関するイベントが、外国の多くの都市で開催されるようになりました。

ゆるキャラは、マスコットキャラクターを意味する日本語です。ゆるキャラは、地域や行事や組織などを象徴するもので、カワイイ風に作られています。ゆるキャラは、普通、地域の文化や歴史や産物などを意味するデザインがなされています。たとえば、城下町の彦根を象徴するゆるキャラはひこにゃんです。ひこにゃんは兜をかぶった白い猫です。ひこにゃんが生まれてから、彦根の観光収入は増加しました。

■新聞の見出し：a news headline
■風刺漫画：a caricature
■映画監督：a film director
■（映画の）封切り：a first run of a film /
a release of a new movie

■衛星放送：satellite broadcasting

Cool Japan

F : I was reading a magazine I received at the tourist office, and it kept referring to "Cool Japan." What exactly does that mean?

J : Many years ago there was a magazine article about Japan's "gross national cool." It was about how Japanese culture was influencing people outside of Japan. Since then the government of Japan has picked up on this as a way to promote interesting and modern aspects of Japanese culture.

F : I see. One of the articles in the magazine was about a place called Akihabara. Is that the center of cool Japan?

J : Not really. I think you can find interesting and unusual things all over Japan—especially in big cities like **Tokyo** or Osaka. Akihabara used to be a great place to buy electronics, and it still is. These days it is also known to be a place where *otaku* go for character goods or video games. There are even **maid cafes** there.

F : What do you mean by *otaku*?

J : It is translated as nerd or geek. Basically, *otaku* are people who are somewhat obsessed with something like *anime* or computer games.

F : Well, what do you think is cool about Japan?

J : Well, I'm the wrong person to ask about that. But if you are interested in seeing the modern side of Japan, I can suggest a few places.

F : Yes, please.

クールジャパン

F : 観光案内所でもらった雑誌を読んでいたんだけど、「クールジャパン」って繰り返し書いてあるんだ。正確にはどういう意味?

J : もう何年も前だけど、日本の「国民総かっこよさ」に関する雑誌記事があったわ。日本文化が外国の人たちにどれほど影響を与えているかってことだったわね。それ以来、日本の政府が日本文化の面白くて新しい側面を売り込む方法として使ってきたの。

F : なるほど。その雑誌の記事の一つが秋葉原って地域のことだったな。そこってクールジャパンの中心地かい?

J : そうでもないわ。今では一風変わった興味深いものは日本全国にあるの。特に、東京とか大阪などの大都市にね。秋葉原はかつて家電製品が人気の場所だったのよ。今でもそれは変わらないけど、このごろはオタクがキャラクターグッズやゲームソフトを買いに行く場所として有名ね。メイドカフェだってあるわよ。

F : オタクって何だい?

J : 英語だと、nerd や geek ってところね。オタクは基本的に、アニメやテレビゲームみたいなものに夢中になっている人のこと。

F : それで、君は日本の何がクールだと思っているの?

J : そうね、私に聞いてもわからないわ。でも、新しい側面の日本に興味があるならいくつかお勧めの場所があるわよ。

F : 教えて。

J : I recommend you go to a place called Odaiba. It's a popular place with young people, but people of any age can enjoy it. You can see a robot exhibition, you can ride a very large Ferris wheel, and there is even a historic fort that is now a park. And the night views are fantastic!

F : That sounds interesting. How do I get there?

J : You can take a train, but I'm going to recommend the water bus. There are several boats, but two were designed by a famous Japanese animator. They have very futuristic designs—I guess you could say that they are … well, they're cool!

J : お台場というところに行くのがいいわね。若い人に人気がある場所だけど、年齢に関係なく楽しめるわ。ロボットの展示があったり、巨大な観覧車があったり、今は公園になっている要塞の史跡があったり。夜景は特に美しいわね!

F : 面白そうだね。どうやって行くの?

J : 電車で行けるけど、水上バスがお勧めね。いくつかボートがあるけど、そのうち2つは、有名な日本のアニメーターがデザインしたのよ。すごく未来的なデザインで、そうね、言い表すなら……そう、クールだわ!

gross : 総〜	be obsessed with 〜 : 〜に夢中である
pick up on 〜 : 〜を継続する	Ferris wheel : 観覧車
nerd : 専門ばか (geekとともに、コンピューターオタクなどを意味する)	fort : 要塞
	futuristic : 未来的な

 **Introduction** | 概説

MP3
62

日本人をひとからげにして、その性格をこうだと断じるのに抵抗を感じる人は多いでしょう。しかし、諸外国との比較において、顕著な特徴の一つに、日本人の「群れる」傾向を指摘することができるでしょう。

Japan contains a wide variety of people with different personalities. Nevertheless, it is possible to generalize about some common attributes of the Japanese character.

An important characteristic of the Japanese is group solidarity. There are many groups that one might belong to—one's family, a group of classmates, one's company, and of course the country itself. Japanese people put much importance on their involvement in these various groups, and exclusion from a group is a serious problem for some Japanese people.

この集団志向の傾向は、「本音」と「建前」という二本立ての行動原理をつくり出しました。これが、外国人の目から見ると、不可解な日本人的あいまいさ、という特質としてとらえられているようです。

The importance of the group has a powerful effect on Japanese behavior. The strong work ethic and the tendency to conform are both explained by the Japanese desire to have good relations within their groups. Because of the importance of maintaining group harmony, the Japanese often speak in ambiguous ways. They might employ *tatemae*, which is the polite behavior that is expected in public. Their true feelings, or *honne*, are kept hidden. All cultures do this, of course, but non-Japanese find it especially difficult to interpret Japanese *tatemae*.

🔍 *tatemae* → p.224　　　*honne* → p.224

　日本には、性格の異なるさまざまな人がいます。ですが、日本人の性格を、ある共通した特質という枠で一般化することはできます。

　特筆すべき日本人の性質として、集団志向が挙げられます。人はそれぞれ多くの集団に、家族、クラス、会社、そして当然、日本という国の一員として属しています。日本人はこれらのさまざまな集団にかかわることをとても重視します。ですから、ある集団から排除されるのは、人によって深刻な問題となります。

generalize about 〜：〜について一般化する	solidarity：団結
attributes：特質	exclusion from 〜：〜からの排除

　この集団を重視する傾向は、日本人の行動様式に強い影響を与えています。強い労働倫理観や、他人と合わせようとする傾向は、どちらも、日本人に集団内で円満な人間関係を保ちたいという願望があるからだと説明できます。集団内での和を保つことを重んじるばかりに、日本人はあいまいな返答をしがちです。一般に求められる儀礼的な振る舞いとして、「建前」を通すこともあり、その実、自分の気持ち、つまり「本音」は表に出さないようにするのです。もちろん、これは、あらゆる国の文化においても見られることですが、外国人にとって、日本人の「建前」を見抜くことは、ことさら難しいようです。

work ethic：労働倫理観	employ：〜を使う
conform：他人に合わせる	kept hidden：表に出されないで
ambiguous：あいまいな	interpret：〜を解釈する

ここでもう一つ、世界に名高い、日本人の「義理と人情」の世界も紹介しなければならないでしょう。

One interesting aspect of Japanese group dynamics is *giri*. *Giri* is one's obligations to society or to an individual—especially with regard to returning favors. On some occasions, *giri* comes into conflict with *ninjo*, which is one's true and natural feelings.

🔍 *giri* → p.224　　　　　*ninjo* → p.224

さらに、このような日本人の文化背景に大きな影響が認められる儒教の教えについて、言及しておきましょう。端的にいえば、階級意識です。家族や社会構造での厳密な上下関係が、連綿として受け継がれてきたのです。

Confucianism had an influence on the development of Japanese culture, and therefore the Japanese are very aware of hierarchical structures. This extends to all levels of society. It is uncommon for a Japanese person to directly disagree with a doctor, a professor, or an employer. Even the language is affected by one's place in the social order. For example, younger employees must speak respectfully to older employees, and shopkeepers use very polite language when speaking to customers.

最後に、「甘えの構造」について。日本が、世界に通用する自立した個人が育つ社会へと発展していくことは可能でしょうか。

Another interesting aspect of Japanese behavior is *amae*, which roughly translates as a desire to depend upon others. In the social hierarchy, it is expected that seniors look out for their juniors. This interdependence is more pronounced in Japanese society than in the West because the Japanese place less emphasis on individual independence.

🔍 *amae* → p.224

日本人の集団心理の原動力となっているもののうち、興味深い側面は、「義理」の概念です。義理とは、社会や個人に対する義務、特に、恩恵を受けた相手に報いを果たすというものです。時に、この義理は、個人の素直な心情に従った気持ちである「人情」と矛盾する場合があります。

　儒教の教えは日本文化の発展に強い影響を与え、そのため日本人は、階級意識が極めて強い面があります。この意識は社会のあらゆる階層に見られます。多くの日本人にとって、たとえば、医者や教授や経営者に直接異議を唱えることはあまりありません。言葉遣いも、社会階層における個人の立場によって規定されます。たとえば、若い従業員は、年配の従業員に対して丁寧な言葉遣いをしなければなりませんし、店の店員は客に対し、非常に丁寧な言葉を使います。

　日本人のもう一つの興味深い行動様式は、「甘え」の概念ですが、これはおおまかにいえば、他人に頼ろうとする願望です。日本の社会階層では、年長の者が年下の者の面倒を見ることが求められます。日本社会におけるこのような相互依存は、欧米社会よりも顕著であり、このことは、日本人が、個人の自立をあまり重視しないという傾向にあることで説明がつきます。

本音と建前   *honne* and *tatemae*

Honne is one's true feelings, and *tatemae* is the polite behavior that one presents in public. Japan is a group-oriented society in which *tatemae* is used to maintain harmonious relations within one's various groups.

義理と人情   *giri* and *ninjo*

Giri is social obligations that should be observed to maintain good interpersonal and social relations, and *ninjo* is human feelings including sympathy and affection that human beings naturally possess. A common theme in Japanese literature involves the dilemma people face when *giri* and *ninjo* conflict with each other.

甘え   *amae*

Amae is the desire to depend upon others. Although a child depending on his or her mother is the most obvious example of *amae*, this relationship is reflected in Japanese society in many adult relationships. *Amae* is more common in Japanese society because the culture places less emphasis on independence and self-reliance.

Related Key Words | 関連キーワード

MP3
64

粋   *iki* | a sophisticated lifestyle / chic

Iki, a sophisticated lifestyle, is a Japanese aesthetic ideal which avoids extremes. This concept developed among commoners during Japan's feudal ages, and it presents a stark contrast to conservative, stern, and often inhumane *samurai* values.

「本音」は自分の本当の気持ちで、「建前」は人前で振る舞うべき儀礼的な態度のことです。日本は集団志向的な社会であり、「建前」は、社会において、自分が関与するさまざまな集団と良好な関係を保つのに利用されています。

「義理」は、円滑な人間関係や社会との関係を保つために果たさねばならない社会的義務のことで、「人情」は、人間が本来備えている同情心や慈愛などの人間的な感情のことです。人が相反する「義理」と「人情」の板ばさみに直面する姿は、日本の文学作品においてよく取り上げられるテーマです。

「甘え」は、他者への依存心のことです。子どもの母親への依存は、「甘え」の最もわかりやすい例ですが、これが日本の社会においては、多くの大人同士の関係にも見られるのです。「甘え」が日本の社会で顕著なのは、独立心や自尊心をあまり重視しない文化構造によります。

あかぬけた生活様式を意味する「粋」は、極端に走らないという日本人の美的観念です。「粋」の概念は日本の封建時代に、保守的で厳格、時に非人間的な武士の価値観とは対照的なものとして、一般庶民の間で発達しました。

ガラパゴス症候群　*Garapagosu shokogun* | Galapagos syndrome

Galapagos syndrome is used by the Japanese to refer to a product that has been designed for the Japanese market and differs from similar products made outside Japan. The term is increasingly used to refer to younger generations of Japanese who are inward looking. One example of this is that many younger workers say they do not want to be posted overseas. Another example is a tendency for some people to avoid social contact.

草食系男子と肉食系女子
soshoku-kei danshi and *nikushoku-kei joshi* |
herbivorous men and carnivorous women

Soshoku-kei danshi is a term used to describe young Japanese men who are feminine in the sense that they are gentle, like shopping, wear cosmetics, and aren't aggressive toward the opposite sex. On the other hand, *nikushoku-kei joshi* are women who are active, have careers, and are more outspoken than earlier generations of Japanese women.

ゆとり世代　*Yutori sedai* | Yutori generation

Yutori sedai refers to the generation of the Japanese who were educated in a way that was less demanding than previous generations. It covers people born between the late 1980s and the early years of the 21st century. They are sometimes criticized for their less aggressive nature, but are also said to have high abilities in some areas, such as IT literacy.

ABCD Related Vocabulary | 関連語彙

- ■村八分：ostracism
- ■人の和：harmony among people
- ■人間関係：interpersonal relationships
- ■暗黙の了解：tacit approval
- ■目配せ：a conspiratorial wink
- ■照れ隠し：to conceal *one's* embarrassment
- ■指切り：making a pledge by hooking each other's little finger
- ■お世辞：compliment / flattery

ガラパゴス症候群は日本人が使う言葉であり、日本市場向けに作られた製品で、海外の類似製品と互換性がないものを指します。さらには、この言葉は内向的な日本の若い世代を意味する場合にも用いられています。一例として、多くの若い労働者が海外赴任を望んでないことを指します。また、社会との接触を避ける傾向のある人も指します。

草食系男子は、温厚で買い物好き、化粧をして異性に対して消極的など、女性っぽい若い日本人男性を表すときに用いられる言葉です。一方、肉食系女子とは、活動的でキャリアがあり、上の世代の女性よりも率直に物を言うような女性を意味します。

ゆとり世代は、以前に比べ、ゆとりのある教育を受けた日本人の世代を意味します。世代の範囲は、1980年代末から2000年代初期にかけて生まれた人たちに相当します。あまり積極的でないなど、時折批判の対象にもなりますが、たとえばITリテラシーが高いなど、優れた能力を持っているとも評価されます。

■不幸中の幸いでした。：It could have been worse.
■身内：family circle
■仲間はずれにされる：be left out in the cold

■武士道：the way of *samurai* warriors
■無常：transience / impermanence
■恩義：debt of gratitude
■恥：dishonor
■以心伝心：unspoken understanding

Dialogue | 対話

MP3 65

Please speak your mind!

F : No offense, but sometimes I just don't understand Japanese people.

J : Don't worry. Things will be better after you learn Japanese.

F : That's not what I mean. I even have trouble with Japanese people who speak English well. I wish they would just speak their minds.

J : Well, the Japanese don't express their opinions as strongly as most other cultures do. We tend to speak in ambiguous ways in order to avoid any conflict with others. It's a way for us to maintain harmony in our various groups. You've heard of the group mentality of the Japanese, haven't you?

F : Yes. But, sometimes it takes a long time just to decide a simple thing. Last night it took five minutes of discussion just to decide what kind of restaurant we would go to.

J : I think you're exaggerating just a bit.

F : Well, it seemed like five minutes.

J : Japanese people like to reach a consensus on things. Once there is agreement, everyone's reading from the same page. I think you can see how such a thing might be useful in some situations—business for example.

F : I suppose.

J : Some people say the emphasis on group harmony among the Japanese is one reason why crime rates are so low in Japan. People generally follow the rules and try not to cause trouble with others.

言いたいことは、はっきり言いましょう！

F : 悪気があって言うわけじゃないけど、ときどき、日本人のことがわからなくなるんだよ。

J : 心配しないで。日本語を覚えれば、うまくやっていけるわ。

F : そういうことじゃないんだよ。英語がうまい人と話していてもわからなくなるんだよ。みんなが、言いたいことをもっとはっきり言ってくれればなあと思うんだ。

J : 日本人は、相手とのいざこざを避けるために、自分の意見を言うとき、あまりほかの国の人たちのような強い言い方をしないのよ。日本人にとっては、いろいろな集団の中で和を保つ方法なの。日本人の集団志向について聞いたことがあると思うけど。

F : うん。でも、簡単なことを1つ決めるのにも、長い時間がかかるときがあるよね。昨夜も、どのレストランにするか決めるのに、5分も話し合ったんだよ。

J : それは少し大げさじゃないかしら。

F : う～ん。5分ぐらいに思えたんだよ。

J : 日本人は何事においても、全員の意見が一致するのが好きなのよ。一度同意すれば、みんなが物事について同じ解釈をすることができるし。状況によっては、たとえばビジネスでは、そういうやり方が有効だということがわかると思うけど。

F : そうかもしれないね。

J : 日本の犯罪率がとても低いのは、集団の調和を大切にすることが理由の一つと言う人もいるわ。みんな概して規則を守るし、他人に迷惑をかけないように気を付けるしね。

F : That's a good point. I have to admit, I've always felt safe in Japan.

J : I'm glad you feel that way. Now stop your whining.

F : Huh? Hey!

J : Didn't you just tell me you wished the Japanese would speak their minds? You got your wish.

F : Very funny.

F： それは一理あるね。日本にいると、安全だっていつも感じていることは認めるよ。

J： そう感じてもらえてるとうれしいわ。じゃ、ぐちを言うのはこれでやめなさい。

F： ええ？　待ってよ!

J： 日本人が言いたいことをはっきり言ってくれればなあって言ったばかりじゃない？　願いはかなったはずよ。

F： 面白いことを言うじゃないか。

---

speak *one's* mind：自分の考えを述べる
No offense.：悪気はありません。
conflict：いざこざ
group mentality：集団志向

exaggerate：〜を誇張する
read from the same page：
　何かについて同じ解釈をする
whine：不平をたらたらと言う

MP3
66

📖 Introduction｜概説

日本の政治機構の説明では、立憲君主国、三権分立制、二院制などがキーワードになります。

Japan is a constitutional monarchy with a parliamentary system. There are three independent branches of government—the legislative, the judiciary, and the administrative. The legislative branch is the Diet, which consists of the House of Representatives and the House of Councilors. The members are elected by the Japanese people.

As for the judiciary branch, the highest court is the Supreme Court. Other courts are high courts, district courts, family courts, and summary courts. The Chief Judge of the Supreme Court is designated by the Cabinet and then appointed to office by the **emperor**. This, however, leads to one of the biggest criticisms of the judiciary branch. Since those judges are somewhat like employees of the government, they have an incentive to not rule against the government in administrative lawsuits that involve the government.

🔍 emperor → p.26

首相は国会によって指名されますが、日本では、女性が首相になった例はまだありません。

The prime minister is designated by the Diet and then appointed to office by the **emperor**. He is typically the leader of the majority party. So far, Japan has never had a female prime minister. The prime minister appoints the Cabinet. The majority of the Cabinet must be Diet members, and all of them must be civilians.

　日本は、議会制度を持つ立憲君主国です。政府は三権分立制をとっており、それぞれ、立法府、司法府、行政府となります。立法府は国会で、衆議院と参議院の二院制をとっており、国会議員は国民によって選ばれます。

　司法制度の最上位にある裁判所は最高裁判所です。下級裁判所には、高等裁判所、地方裁判所、家庭裁判所、簡易裁判所があります。最高裁判所長官は、内閣が指名し、天皇が任命します。しかし、このことが、日本の司法制度に対する強い批判の原因ともなっています。最高裁の裁判官は政府から雇われているような立場に近いので、政府に関わる行政訴訟において政府に不利になるような判決を出したがらないのです。

constitutional monarchy：立憲君主国	the Diet：（日本の）国会
parliamentary：議会の	the House of Representatives：衆議院
branch：部門	the House of Councilors：参議院
legislative：立法府の	the Cabinet：内閣
judiciary：司法府の	have an incentive to 〜：〜する気になる
administrative：行政府の	administrative lawsuits：行政訴訟

　日本の首相は国会によって指名され、天皇によって任命されます。通常は、多数党の党首が首相の指名を受けます。これまでのところ、女性の首相はまだ登場していません。首相は閣僚を任命します。閣僚（国務大臣）は、その過半数が国会議員であり、全員が文民でなければなりません。

the majority party：多数党	civilian：文民

第二次世界大戦後に制定された新憲法、および、中央政府・地方政府の力関係も特徴的です。

The current **Japanese Constitution** came into effect in 1947. It contains three principles: sovereignty of the people, respect for human rights, and renunciation of war. Furthermore, the **Emperor of Japan** is described as "the symbol of the State and of the unity of the people."

The government is centralized, with most local governments dependent on the state for financial subsidies. There are 47 prefectures in the country. The government is also characterized by a strong bureaucracy, which has powerful regulatory functions.

 Japanese Constitution → p.236

国防に関しては、自衛隊と米国軍が連携して任務にあたっていますが、自衛隊の規模は実は世界有数です。

Because of constitutional constraints, Japan's security forces are called the **Self-Defense Forces** (SDF). They often operate in tandem with United States military forces. The cooperation between the two security forces is outlined by the **Japan-U.S. Security Treaty**. Japan spends approximately 1% of GDP on the SDF, which is recognized by experts as being one of the top ten strongest military forces in the world.

 Self-Defense Forces → p.236   Japan-U.S. Security Treaty → p.236

日本の現行憲法は1947年に発効しました。日本国憲法の3原則は、国民主権、基本的人権の尊重、戦争放棄です。さらに、日本の天皇は、「日本国の象徴であり日本国民統合の象徴」と表現されています。

　日本政府は中央集権的で、ほとんどの地方政府は政府の助成金に頼っています。日本には47の都道府県があります。政府はまた、官僚の権力が強いことも特徴で、官僚は強力な規制機能を有しています。

constitution：憲法	dependent on 〜：〜に依存している
come into effect：発効する	subsidy：助成金
sovereignty：主権	bureaucracy：官僚
renunciation：放棄	regulatory：統制の

　憲法上の制約があるため、日本の安全保障を守る軍隊は自衛隊と呼ばれています。自衛隊は、米国軍と行動を共にすることが多く、両者の協力関係は、日米安全保障条約に定められています。日本は国内総生産のおよそ1パーセントを防衛費につぎ込んでおり、軍備において自衛隊は世界の軍隊の上位10位以内に入ると専門家は認識しています。

constraint：制限	GDP (gross domestic product)：
in tandem with 〜：〜と連携して	国内総生産

日本国憲法　*Nihon-koku kenpo* ｜ Japanese Constitution

Nihon-koku kenpo refers to the Japanese Constitution, which took effect in 1947. Some of the characteristics of the Japanese Constitution are that it defines the emperor as a symbol of the nation, affirms the sovereignty of the people, renounces war as a means of settling international disputes, forbids military forces, and guarantees human rights.

自衛隊　*Jieitai* ｜ Self-Defense Forces

Jieitai refers to Japan's Self-Defense Forces (SDF). There are three branches: the Ground Self-Defense Force (GSDF), the Maritime Self-Defense Force (MSDF), and the Air Self-Defense Force (ASDF). As the name implies, the role of the SDF is to defend Japan from threats and to ensure the nation's peace and independence.

日米安全保障条約
Nichibei-anzen-hosho-joyaku ｜ Japan-U.S. Security Treaty

Nichibei-anzen-hosho-joyaku is the Japan-U.S. Security Treaty, which was first signed in 1951 and then updated in 1960. The agreement ensures the security of Japan and allows U.S. military forces to maintain a presence in Japan.

平和維持活動　*heiwa iji katsudo* ｜ peacekeeping operations

Heiwa iji katsudo refers to peacekeeping operations (PKO). In 1992, the Diet passed the PKO Cooperation Bill, which allows the Self-Defense Forces to participate, with some limitations, in peacekeeping operations.

日本国憲法は1947年に施行されました。日本国憲法の特徴としては、まず、天皇を日本国の象徴と規定していること、主権在民を保障していること、国際紛争解決の手段として交戦権を放棄すること、軍隊の保有を認めていないこと、人権を保障していることなどが挙げられます。

自衛隊には、陸上自衛隊、海上自衛隊、航空自衛隊の3つがあります。自衛隊の役割は、その名が示すとおり、日本への脅威に対して日本を防衛すること、ならびに、日本の平和と独立を護ることです。

日米安全保障条約は1951年に最初に調印され、1960年に改定されました。同条約は、日本の安全保障を約定し、米軍の日本駐留を認めています。

1992年に、国会は「国際連合平和維持活動等に対する協力に関する法律」を通過させた結果、自衛隊は、制限枠内での平和維持活動参加が認められるようになりました。

非核三原則

Hikaku sangensoku | Japan's three anti-nuclear principles

Hikaku sangensoku are Japan's three anti-nuclear principles. Japan will not possess, develop, or permit into the country any nuclear weapons. The principles were proposed in 1968 by then Prime Minister Sato Eisaku and were adopted in 1971. As the only nation to have suffered from a nuclear attack, these principles are an important way for the country to express its abhorrence of nuclear weapons.

Related Vocabulary | 関連語彙

- 三権分立：division of powers
- 国会：the Diet
- 予算案：a budget bill
- 内閣：Cabinet
- 内閣府：Cabinet Office
- 国家公安委員会：National Public Safety Commission
- 警察庁：National Police Agency
- 総務省：Ministry of Internal Affairs and Communications
- 法務省：Ministry of Justice
- 外務省：Ministry of Foreign Affairs of Japan
- 文部科学省：Ministry of Education, Culture, Sports, Science and Technology
- 財務省：Ministry of Finance
- 厚生労働省：Ministry of Health, Labour and Welfare
- 環境省：Ministry of the Environment

非核三原則は、核兵器に対する日本の3つの原則を示したものです。原則では、日本はいかなる核兵器も、保有せず、開発せず、日本に持ち込ませないとしています。非核三原則は1968年に時の首相・佐藤栄作が提案し、1971年に採択されました。核攻撃を世界で唯一経験した国として、これらの原則は、核兵器に対する日本人の嫌悪感を表す重要な手段となっています。

- ■農林水産省：Ministry of Agriculture, Forestry and Fisheries
- ■経済産業省：Ministry of Economy, Trade and Industry
- ■国土交通省：Ministry of Land, Infrastructure, Transport and Tourism
- ■防衛省：Ministry of Defense
- ■観光庁：Japan Tourism Agency
- ■復興庁：Reconstruction Agency
- ■消費者庁：Consumer Affairs Agency
- ■公正取引委員会：Japan Fair Trade Commission
- ■宮内庁：Imperial Household Agency
- ■首脳会談：a summit meeting
- ■国交回復：a rapprochement

I'm curious about the Self-Defense Forces.

F : Did you vote for the current prime minister?

J : In Japan, we don't vote directly for the prime minister. He's designated by the Diet. I wish we did vote for the prime minister. It might make things a little more interesting.

F : What is the voting age?

J : The voting age is eighteen. Unfortunately, voter turnout is rather low for the younger generations. This worries me a lot.

F : Why?

J : Japan is aging. If the older generations dominate politics, then nothing will change. We need younger people to bring fresh ideas into government.

F : I agree with you on that. In your opinion, what is the biggest problem facing the Japanese government these days?

J : The government needs to get the economy back on track, and it also needs to consider the problems of the aging society.

F : What about local governments? Do they have a big impact on communities?

J : Not really. There is a lot of talk about decentralization, but change seems to come slowly in Japan.

F : I'm curious about the military. Why is it that you have to say **Self-Defense Forces**? Why don't you just say "military"?

J : That's a difficult question. According to the **Japanese Constitution**, Japan cannot have military forces. So instead we have the **Self-Defense Forces**.

自衛隊に興味があるんだ

F：君は今の首相に投票したのかい？

J：日本では、首相を直接投票で選ぶことはできないの。首相は国会によって指名されるのよ。首相に対する投票権があればと思うけど。そうすると、少しは面白い結果になると思うわ。

F：選挙権は何歳で与えられるんだい？

J：今は18歳。残念ながら、若い人たちの投票率が低いのよ。とっても心配だわ。

F：どうして？

J：日本は高齢社会でしょ。年配の人たちが政治を独占すると何も変わらないわ。若い人たちが政府に新しい考えを吹き込む必要があると思うの。

F：それはたしかだね。日本政府が、最近直面している最大の問題は何だと思う？

J：景気を立て直す必要があるわね。それに、高齢化社会の問題を考えていく必要もあるわ。

F：地方自治体はどうなんだい？　地域社会に対して大きな影響力を持っているのかな。

J：それほどでもないわ。地方分権化の議論は盛んだけど、日本では物事はゆっくりにしか進展しないから。

F：軍隊に興味があるんだけど。なぜ、わざわざ自衛隊と呼ぶ必要があるんだい？　わかりやすく「軍隊」と呼べばいいのに。

J：それは難しい問題だわ。日本国憲法では、日本は軍隊の保有が許されていないの。だから、軍と呼ぶ代わりに自衛隊と呼んでいるのよ。

17

Government 対話

F : Yeah, right. If it looks like a duck, walks like a duck, and sounds like a duck, then it must be a duck.

J : Actually, you have a point. Japan only spends about 1% of GDP on defense, but that's still a lot of money. Most experts say that the Japanese **Self-Defense Forces** are in the top ten worldwide. But remember, our neighbors are Russia and China—both have large militaries and both have nuclear weapons.

F : Yeah, and I think North Korea has nukes now too?

J : They do. Japan was the first country to have nuclear weapons used against it in warfare. I'm hoping that no other country ever has to endure such horrible weapons.

F : なるほど。だけど、アヒルに見えて、アヒルのように歩いて、アヒルの鳴き声で鳴くのなら、それは間違いなくアヒルだよ。

J : そうね、そのとおりだわ。日本の防衛費はGDP比率でたったの1パーセントだけど、それでも巨額ね。ほとんどの専門家が、日本の自衛隊は世界のトップ10以内だと言ってるわ。でも、隣国がロシアや中国ってことも忘れちゃいけないのよ。軍も強大だし、核兵器も持っているからね。

F : そうだね、それに、北朝鮮も今は核保有国だろう？

J : そう。日本は戦争で核兵器が使用された最初の国だもの。ほかの国には決してそんな恐ろしい目にあってほしくないわ。

vote for 〜 : 〜に投票する
voting age : 投票年齢
voter turnout : 投票率
get 〜 back on track :
　〜を元の軌道に戻す
aging society : 高齢化社会
impact on 〜 : 〜への影響
decentralization : 地方分権化

If it looks like a duck, ... it must be a duck.
⇒比喩表現。軍隊のように見えて、軍隊のような活動をしているのであれば、それは軍隊に違いない、という意味。
have a point : 一理ある
nuke : 核兵器 (a nuclear weapon の略語。動詞としても使われる)

 ## Introduction | 概説

MP3
70

戦争で工業生産力の大半を失った日本。戦後の日本は、経済の復興にすべての力を注ぎ、ついには米国に次ぐ経済大国へと上り詰めたのです。

After World War II, a devastated Japan focused on its economic development policy of "catch up and overtake." With few natural resources, the country focused on manufacturing products for export. By the time of the 1964 Tokyo Olympic Games, Japan had recovered and was experiencing rapid economic growth. By 1968, Japan had become the world's second largest economy. Japan is well known for producing high-quality products such as electronics and automobiles.

1980年代のバブル経済の崩壊によって、日本にはさまざまな問題が残ってしまいました。社会の高齢化も問題を深刻化させています。

Despite having many strengths, the Japanese economy has been sluggish for many years. In the late 1980s, an asset price bubble developed, mostly because of sky-rocketing real estate and stock prices. When the **bubble economy** burst, banks were left holding billions in bad loans. Since then, the government has tried to stimulate the economy by increasing public works spending, reducing interest rates, and initiating deregulation.

Unfortunately, those policies weren't completely effective. Currently, Japan has a large public debt, low consumer confidence, and faces increasing global competition. In addition, an aging society is causing various problems for both government and industry.

　第二次世界大戦後、荒廃した日本は「米国に追いつき、追い越せ」というスローガンのもとで、経済発展に専念することになりました。日本は天然資源が少ないために、輸出向け製品の製造に注力しました。1964年、東京オリンピックが開催されるころには、日本は復興を成し遂げ、高度経済成長期を迎えました。1968年には日本は世界第2位の経済大国となりました。日本は、電子製品や自動車などの高品質製品を作ることでよく知られています。

devastated：荒廃した	overtake：追い越す
catch up：追いつく	

　日本には数多くの強みがあるにもかかわらず、日本経済は何年も停滞が続いています。1980年代末に、地価や株価が暴騰したことが主な原因で、資産のバブルが膨れ上がりました。バブルが崩壊したときに、銀行は多額の不良債権を抱え込むこととなったのです。それ以来、政府は、公共投資を増加し、金利を引き下げ、規制緩和を主導しながら、景気を刺激する努力を重ねてきました。

　残念ながら、これらの政策に完璧な効果があったとはいえませんでした。現在、日本は巨額の負債を抱え、消費意欲も低く、ますます激化する国際競争に直面しています。加えて、社会の高齢化によって、政府にも産業にもさまざまな問題が生じてきています。

🔍 bubble economy → p.250

企業では、雇用制度が大きく変化し、各方面でリストラが断行されました。一方、政府は、予算の無駄遣いが指摘され、天下りの問題も頻繁に取り上げられています。

Many Japanese corporations, once the engines of Japan's rapid growth, have struggled to stay competitive. One result is that Japanese employers are reevaluating the **lifetime employment system** and the **seniority ranking system**. Global competition and technological advances are forcing companies to focus more on performance and skills, rather than age, when considering employee promotions. As companies **restructure**, many older workers are finding themselves unemployed. At the same time, new graduates are finding that there are fewer full-time job opportunities available.

The government's handling of the economy has been criticized for wasteful spending. A large amount of money has been doled out to government-related entities and has been used on unnecessary projects and facilities. One of the causes of this problem is the practice of *amakudari*, which encourages the trading of favors between government and industry. Reform of the civil-service system to stop *amakudari* has been a challenge for the government.

🔍 lifetime employment system → p.250   seniority ranking system → p.250
   restructure → p.250   *amakudari* → p.252

sluggish：不景気な	stimulate：〜を刺激する
sky-rocket：急上昇する	interest rate：利率
real estate：不動産	deregulation：規制緩和
bad loan：不良債権	consumer confidence：消費意欲

　かつて日本の高度成長の原動力であった多くの日本企業は、競争力を維持するのに懸命になっています。その結果として、日本の企業は、終身雇用や年功序列などの制度を見直し始めています。激化する国際競争とテクノロジーの進歩で、従業員の昇進を考える際に、年齢よりも業績や技能を重視せざるを得なくなってきているのです。リストラが進行するにつれ、年配の労働者はますます失業の危険にさらされるようになってきています。一方で新卒者は、正社員としての雇用機会をますます得にくくなってきています。

　政府の経済対策は無駄遣いが多いと批判されてきました。政府関連の団体に莫大な資金が流れ、不必要な建築物や事業に費やされてきました。その一因は、政府と企業の間でお互いに都合の良い取引を助長する、天下りという慣行にあります。公務員制度の改革による天下りの根絶が、政府の重大な課題となっています。

engine：中心的原動力	be doled out to 〜：〜に分配される
reevaluate：〜を見直す	entity：団体、組織

しかし、客観的に見れば、日本経済はまだまだ強力です。現在の苦境は、次なる飛躍への萌芽ともなり得るのです。

Despite the negative business and economic news, Japan is still a powerful economic force in the world. The challenges the country faces now may result in changes that will benefit both Japan and her workers. A future worker shortage may result in more equal opportunities for women. The pressures of globalization may force the government and companies to become more streamlined and more efficient. Also, a promotion system based on merit will inspire workers to increase their knowledge and skills. Even job instability may have long term benefits, as more Japanese strike out on their own to start new businesses.

ビジネスや経済に関する暗いニュースがある一方で、日本はまだまだ強力な経済大国として世界に君臨しています。現在の日本に立ちはだかる難題が、いずれ、日本と日本の労働者を救う変革をもたらすかもしれません。今後の労働力不足は、女性により均等な雇用機会を提供するでしょうし、国際化への重圧のもとで、政府や企業はより効率化を目指して、合理化を進めざるを得なくなるでしょう。さらに、実力主義に基づく昇進制度は、雇用者が自主的に知識と技能を磨くきっかけとなると思われます。雇用不安の問題も、長期的には恩恵とさえなる可能性もあります。事実、自立して新しいビジネスを始めようとしている日本人もますます多くなってきています。

streamline：合理化する
merit：功績、手柄

strike out on *one's* own：自立する

バブル経済 *baburu keizai*｜bubble economy

A bubble economy occurs when certain asset values rise to unusual levels. In the late 1980s, real estate and stock prices rose dramatically in Japan. To say that the "bubble burst" is to say that the values declined.

終身雇用 *shushin-koyo*｜lifetime employment system

Shushin-koyo is the lifetime employment system. Employees are guaranteed employment until retirement age in return for their absolute loyalty to the company. This system played an important role during Japan's high economic growth period. In recent times, more employees are being laid off, making it increasingly necessary for workers to prepare for future job changes by acquiring special knowledge and skills.

年功序列 *nenko-joretsu*｜seniority ranking system

Nenko-joretsu is a seniority ranking system where promotions and pay are determined by the length of one's service to a company. This system played an important role during Japan's high economic growth period. Now, as Japan goes through economic restructuring, companies are putting more emphasis on merit-based promotion systems.

リストラ *risutora*｜restructuring

Risutora is the Japanese abbreviation for restructuring. Restructuring is when the organization of a company is changed. This usually means that some people will lose their jobs.

バブル経済とは、特定の資産の価値が異常なレベルまで上昇することです。1980年代後半に、日本では不動産価格と株価が劇的に値上がりしました。「バブルの崩壊」とはその価格の下落をいいます。

終身雇用は生涯にわたって雇用する制度です。従業員は企業への全面的な忠誠と引き換えに、定年までの雇用が保証されます。この制度は、高度経済成長期の日本で重要な役割を果たしました。近年、レイオフされる従業員が増加し、労働者にとって、特殊な技能や知識を得て将来の転職に備えることが、ますます必要になってきています。

年功序列は昇進と給与が勤続年数によって決められる制度です。日本経済の高度成長期には重要な役割を果たしましたが、経済の再編成が日本中で吹き荒れる現在では、実力主義が主流になりつつあります。

リストラとはリストラクチャリングを略した日本語です。リストラクチャリングとは、会社組織の変革期のことです。この語には通常、仕事を失う人が出るという意味が含まれています。

天下り *amakudari*

Amakudari is the practice of business organizations hiring retired high-level bureaucrats. The companies allegedly receive favors from the bureaucrats, or their departments, and in return they offer retiring bureaucrats private positions at high salaries. This practice has been strongly criticized, but it is still prevalent in various organizations. Reform of the civil-service system to stop *amakudari* has been a challenge for the government.

 **Related Key Words｜関連キーワード**

MP3
72

談合 *dango*｜bid-rigging

Dango refers to bid-rigging. Bid-rigging is an agreement where prospective bidders illegally consult with each other and agree to submit bids that have been prearranged among themselves. This practice is believed to be common in the construction industry where companies take turns being the "lowest" bidder.

ボーナス *bonasu*｜bonus

Bonasu is a lump sum of money periodically given to employees in addition to their monthly salaries. The amount of the bonus is based on the company's performance, and is usually given in June and in December.

春闘 *shunto*

Shunto is the "spring labor offensive." Many industry-based labor unions coordinate demands for wage increases and benefits in the spring.

天下りは退職した高級官僚を企業が雇用する慣行をいいます。企業は、官僚または その部署から便宜を受ける一方、見返りに退職した官僚個人に高額な報酬の地位を与えます。この慣行は強い批判を浴びていますが、いまだに多くの組織で広く行われています。公務員制度の改革による天下りの根絶が、政府の重大な課題となっています。

談合は不正競争入札のことです。談合は入札参加予定者同士が不法に相談し合い、関係者間であらかじめ取り決めた価格での入札に同意することです。建設業界では、この行為は一般的に行われているといわれ、各企業が順番に「最低」入札価格提示者になる事例があります。

ボーナスは、月々の給与に加えて、定期的に従業員に支給される一時金です。ボーナスの金額は、各企業の業績に基づいて決められ、通常6月と12月に支給されます。

春闘は「春に行われる労働闘争」のことです。産業別に結成された多くの労働組合が、春に賃上げや手当の要求を一斉に行います。

根回し　*nemawashi*

Nemawashi is a process that aims to gain consensus and avoid conflicts prior to formal decision making. In the process, the views and interests of all those involved are considered in order to hammer out a proposal that would likely be supported by everyone.

系列　*keiretsu*

Keiretsu are affiliated business enterprise groups. In general, the enterprises in the same *keiretsu* cooperate with each other, own equity in one another, and protect affiliates from mergers and acquisitions. The term also refers to the regroupings of former subsidiaries of corporate cliques that existed before the end of World War II.

ブラック企業　*burakku kigyo* | black company

Burakku kigyo, or black companies, originally referred to companies engaged in criminal activities, usually by having connections with organized crime. Today the term encompasses companies that exploit their employees. The victimized employees often include part-time workers, who are in turn called *burakku arubaito*, meaning black part-time workers.

Related Vocabulary | 関連語彙

- 就職活動：job hunting
- 失業率：unemployment rate
- 週休2日制：five-day workweek
- 残業：overtime
- 定年退職：mandatory retirement
- 早期退職：early retirement
- 公共投資：public investment
- 技術革新：technological innovation
- IT：information technology
- 株式市場：a stock market
- 強気筋市場：a bull market
- 弱気筋市場：a bear market
- 契約社員：a contract employee
- 派遣社員：a temporary employee / a temp
- 在宅勤務：telecommuting
- 公定歩合：official discount rate
- 国債：national bond

根回しは、正式な意思決定に先行してコンセンサスをはかり、意見の衝突を避けるという方法です。根回しの過程では、全員が支持する可能性の高い案を練り上げるために、関係者全員の意見や利害が検討されます。

系列は提携した企業グループです。一般に同じ系列の企業は互いに協力し合い、お互いの株式を保有し合うことで、系列内の企業を吸収合併から保護します。また系列という用語は、第二次世界大戦終結以前に存在した旧財閥系子会社が、企業グループを再編成することを指す場合もあります。

ブラック企業は、もともと、組織犯罪に関係した犯罪行為を行う企業を意味していました。今では、従業員を酷使する企業も意味しています。その犠牲となる従業員は非正規であることが多く、彼らはブラックアルバイトと呼ばれます。

■外資系会社：foreign-affiliated company
■退職金：retirement allowance
■人員削減：downsizing
■規制緩和：deregulation
■有給休暇：a paid holiday
■国民所得：national income
■国民総生産：gross national product (GNP)

■国内総生産：gross domestic product (GDP)
■外国人労働者：a foreign worker
■転勤：transfer
■（夫の）単身赴任：husband-only transfer

Beautiful, compact, and practical.

F : When I was back home, the newspapers and magazines were writing about the economic problems here in Japan. Is it really so bad?

J : A lot of companies have gone bankrupt, and a lot of people have lost their jobs. There are also a lot of people who are stuck in dead-end jobs simply because they couldn't find anything better.

F : But I see new buildings being built all over. And the stores are full of people. It's hard to believe that there's a problem.

J : Take my word for it, the department stores aren't as busy as they used to be. The stores that are full of people are probably discount stores.

F : Are things getting better?

J : I think so. The prices for many things have become lower, so that's good news for consumers. Japan is still a wealthy country with a lot of technological know-how. I'm an optimist, and I think Japan has a bright future.

F : I hope you're right.

J : Did you know that Japan was exporting the *kyo-sensu* way back in the 13th century?

F : Oh, you mean folding fans? They're so beautiful.

J : Beautifully designed, compact size, and practical. You can say that about many of Japan's products. And in the future I think Japan will continue to be a leader in robotics and high-speed trains like the maglev.

F : I saw a robot demonstration the other day. It was amazing, but I couldn't help wondering what they will be used for.

J : Hmm. I'm still wondering about that myself.

美しくて、小さくて、実用性があって

F：国に帰っている間に、新聞や雑誌が、日本の経済問題についていろいろ書いていたけど。それほど深刻な状況なの？

J：多くの企業が倒産し、失業者がたくさん出ているわ。それに多くの人たちが今より良い仕事を見つけきれなくて、将来性のない仕事から抜け出せないでいるの。

F：でも、あちこちで新しいビルが建設されているのを見かけるよ。商店はお客でいっぱいだし、問題があるように思えないけど。

J：デパートに前ほどはお客がいない、というのはたしかね。客でいっぱいの店というのは、きっとディスカウントストアよ。

F：状況は良くなってきているの？

J：そう思うけど。いろんな物の値段が下がってきているし、それは消費者にとっては良いことだわ。日本は相変わらず豊かな国で、技術のノウハウもたくさん持っているもの。私は楽観主義者だから、状況は良くなっていくと思っているわ。

F：そうなるといいね。

J：日本は13世紀にはもう京扇子を輸出していたことを知ってる？

F：ああ、折りたたみ式のファンのことか。とてもきれいだね。

J：デザインが美しく、コンパクトで、実用的よね。日本製品の多くについても同じことがいえるわ。それに将来的には、日本がロボット工学やリニアモーターカーなどの分野でリードし続けると思うわ。

F：先日、ロボットのデモを見たよ。驚きだったね。でもこの先、何に使うのかよくわからなかったな。

J：うーん。それについては、まだよくわからないわ。

be stuck in ～：～から抜け出せない	folding fan：扇子
dead-end：将来性のない	robotics：ロボット工学
take my word for it：信じてください	maglev：リニアモーターカー
optimist：楽観主義者	

 **Introduction** | 概説

家族が社会の最小の単位だとすれば、人間関係の基礎もそこで育まれるといえます。大家族が基本だった一昔前は、家族関係も当然、現代とは違っていました。

The Japanese are known for being a group-oriented people, and the family is naturally the most basic group unit. Traditionally, this meant an extended family with the eldest male at the head. The oldest son was usually the heir, which gave him a higher position as well as more responsibility in the family.

現代日本では、大家族ではなく、核家族が中心の社会となっています。特に家庭および社会における女性の地位の向上は、社会全体の変革をもたらしました。

In modern times, changing laws and a changing society have caused a distinctive trend toward more nuclear families. With husbands working long hours, their wives have taken over many of the household responsibilities—in effect decreasing the power of males in the household. For many women, the image of married life and motherhood is one of hard work and heavy responsibilities. Furthermore, a wealthier society, better education, and more job opportunities have given women opportunities that didn't exist before. This may be why the average age for marriage has increased, divorces are on the rise, and the birth rate remains low.

Not only has the average family size decreased, the number of single-person households now makes up over 35% of all household types.

　日本人は集団志向の国民として知られており、家族はたいてい1つのユニットとして、当然のものとして認識されています。伝統的にこれは、大家族において最年長の男性が主人であることを意味しました。長男が後継ぎとなるのが普通で、家族の中では、ほかのメンバーより責任も重い代わりに、特別扱いを受ける地位が約束されたのです。

a group-oriented people：
　集団志向的な国民

extended family：（親族も含む）大家族
heir：相続人

　現代になって、法律の改正や社会の変化によって、核家族化が大きな流れとなりました。夫は長時間働き、妻は家事の大部分の責任を引き受け、その結果、家庭内における男性の力は弱くなっていきました。多くの女性にとって、結婚生活および母親のイメージは、きつい仕事と重い責任を伴うものとなります。さらに、より豊かな社会、より良い教育、増えた就業機会は、以前は考えられなかったチャンスを女性に与えてきました。そのような理由もあって、結婚年齢は上がり、離婚が増加し、出生率は低いままです。

　世帯の平均構成員数が減少しただけでなく、単身世帯の数が今では全世帯の35パーセント以上を占めています。

distinctive：独特の、目立った

birth rate：出生率

子どもへの過度の期待は、教育の過熱につながります。子どもたちは塾通いや試験から強いストレスを受けているのです。

Of critical importance to a Japanese family is the education of the children. With an exam-oriented education system that can affect the entire future of a student, much time and money is devoted to giving children an advantage. Many children attend cram schools called *juku*, and they feel intense pressure to do well on examinations as well as to conform to society's expectations.

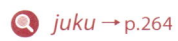 *juku* → p.264

そのような子どもたちが通う学校は、これまであまり見られなかった問題に悩まされています。いじめやひきこもりといった現象です。

The schools are facing some problems that were, until recently, very rare. There has been an increase in violence and **bullying**. Some victims of abuse have been killed or committed suicide. Another odd trend are the cases of *hikikomori*, which is when individuals isolate themselves by refusing to leave their home or room.

 bullying → p.264   *hikikomori* → p.264

日本の家庭で決定的に重要なのは子どもの教育です。試験によって生徒の将来が決まってしまうような受験教育システムのもとで、子どもが少しでも有利になるようにと多くの時間とお金が注がれます。たくさんの子どもたちが塾に通い、社会の期待に応えるため、試験で良い成績を取るために、大きなストレスを強いられています。

> conform to society's expectations：社会の期待に応える

　学校は、最近までほとんど見られなかった問題に直面しています。その一つは、暴力やいじめが増加していることです。いじめの犠牲者となって殺害されたり、自殺する生徒も出るほどです。また、自分の家や部屋から出ようとせずに人との接触を断ってしまう、ひきこもりと呼ばれる異常な事例も見られます。

> commit suicide：自殺する　　　　isolate *oneself*：自分を隔離する

学校の外に目を向けると少年犯罪の多さが目立ちます。なかには動機が見当たらない犯罪もあり、その原因についてさまざまな議論が行われています。

As for the behavior of the youth, the rates of juvenile crime, drug use, and teen pregnancy are lower in Japan than in other developed countries. Nevertheless, Japan has long prided itself on the nation's low crime rates, so there has been much hand-wringing over the fact that a large percentage of crime in Japan is committed by young people. Sometimes the crimes have had no motive, which further perplexes the older generations. There are a wide variety of explanations for the causes of juvenile crime. Some people suggest it was the rapid changes in the family. Others suggest that the poor economy and lack of opportunities for young people are breeding grounds for juvenile crime.

若者の素行を見ると、少年犯罪、覚醒剤の乱用、未成年の妊娠などは他の先進諸国より少ないのがわかります。それでも、かねてから犯罪率の低さを自負してきた日本としては、若者が引き起こす犯罪の割合が大きいという事実が大きな懸念です。なかには動機が全く見当たらない犯罪もあり、上の世代をさらに当惑させています。少年犯罪の原因についてはさまざまな意見があります。家族のあり方の急激な変化だと言う人もいれば、不景気や若者が将来に希望が持てないことなどが、少年犯罪の温床となっていると言う人もいます。

pride *oneself* on 〜：〜を自負する
hand-wringing：懸念

perplex：〜を当惑させる
breeding grounds for 〜：〜の温床

19

Family Issues

概説

塾 *juku* | cram school

Juku, sometimes called cram schools, are private schools that help Japanese students prepare for entrance examinations for junior and senior high school. Although *juku* have often been criticized for their emphasis on rote memorization, some progressive *juku* today are using a more creative approach in teaching. Over 50% of junior high school students attend *juku*.

いじめ *ijime* | bullying

Ijime is bullying. The bullies inflict emotional or physical abuse on those in weaker positions. In extreme cases, victims of bullying have committed suicide or been murdered. This has been a problem in some Japanese schools.

ひきこもり *hikikomori*

Hikikomori is the situation where individuals isolate themselves from society. This includes students refusing to go to school and adults refusing to go to work. *Hikikomori* is often caused by bullying or other abuse. In extreme cases the individual stays in his or her room and refuses contact with people.

 **Related Key Words** | 関連キーワード

MP3
76

援助交際 *enjo-kosai* | compensated dating

Enjo-kosai, sometimes called "compensated dating," is the situation where some high school girls have relations with adults in return for money. Those relations often involve prostitution. Although new laws have discouraged the practice, there is still concern that the use of smartphones has made it easier for the activity to remain hidden.

塾は、中学・高校入試のための受験準備の手助けをする私設学校です。塾は丸暗記を強調することから、しばしば批判の対象となってきましたが、今日の進歩的な塾には、より創造的な教育方法を採用しているところもあります。中学校では、半数を超える生徒が塾に通っています。

いじめは弱い立場の者を精神的、肉体的に攻撃して苦しめることです。最悪の場合、被害者が自殺してしまったり、殺されてしまうこともあります。このことは、一部の学校で問題になっています。

ひきこもりは、社会から自分で自分を隔離してしまうことをいいます。これには、学校に行かない子どもや、仕事に行かない大人も含まれます。ひきこもりは、いじめなどの虐待に原因があることもよくあります。極端なケースでは自分の部屋に閉じこもってしまい、人との接触を拒絶するようになってしまいます。

援助交際は、女子高生が金銭と引き換えに成人と交際をすることです。このような交際はしばしば売春行為を伴います。新しい法律ができて、援助交際を行いにくくはなったものの、スマホを使うことで、見えないところで援助交際が続けられているという懸念が残っています。

お受験　*ojuken*

Ojuken is the situation where pre-school children take entrance examinations for prestigious private kindergartens or elementary schools. Having children that attend such schools is a status symbol for some mothers. Attending such a school also makes it easier to enter prestigious junior and senior high schools.

浪人　*ronin*

Ronin originally referred to lordless warriors in the Edo Period. Today, however, the term also refers to young people who have failed the entrance examinations to universities and are studying for the next year's examinations.

Related Vocabulary | 関連語彙

- 幼児虐待：child abuse
- 育児放棄：child neglect
- 絵本：picture story book
- 英才教育：special education for the gifted
- とび入学：grade-skipping
- 教育改革：education reform
- 少年法：the Juvenile Law
- 少年非行：juvenile delinquency
- 少年犯罪：juvenile crime
- 家出：running away from home
- 家庭内暴力：domestic violence
- 離婚：divorce
- おしどり夫婦：a happily-married couple
- 介護保険：nursing care insurance
- 家事の分担：a division of household chores
- 別居：a marital separation

お受験は、就学前の子どもに、私立の一流幼稚園や一流小学校への入学試験を受けさせることです。そのような学校に子どもを入学させることが、ステータスシンボルだと思う母親もいます。また、そのような学校に通うことで、一流中学や一流高校への進学が楽になります。

浪人は、もともと江戸時代の主人を持たない侍のことを意味していました。しかし、今日では、大学入試に落ちて翌年の入試のために勉強をしている、若い人たちのこともいいます。

■出産休暇：maternity leave
■育児休暇：childcare leave
■核家族：a nuclear family
■老人ホーム：a nursing home
■児童相談所：a child counseling center
■寝たきり老人：bedridden elderly / invalid elderly
■育児ノイローゼ：infant-care neurosis

■帰国子女：children who have lived overseas / a returnee
■留学：study abroad
■義務教育：compulsory education
■生涯教育：lifelong education / continued education
■戸籍：official family registry
■住民票：residence certificate

Dialogue 1 | 対話

Japan can rely more on robots.

F : I keep hearing about the low birth rate in Japan. What's the deal with that?

J : People are marrying later and they're having fewer children. The birth rate has been very low for many years now. In fact, the population of Japan is declining.

F : Well, that's a good thing. Japan's too crowded.

J : There are good points and bad points. You see, there will be fewer workers, which of course means fewer taxpayers. At the same time, government expenses for things like health care are likely to increase because a larger portion of the population will be elderly. This will put a strain on the economy. It's likely the government will raise our taxes.

F : That doesn't sound good at all. Maybe Japan can rely more on robots.

J : Well, automation will certainly help and so will raising the retirement age. We also need to create a better environment for women who want to work and raise a family at the same time. Increasing the number of childcare facilities would be a big help.

F : But you also need to take care of the elderly. That must be a big problem.

J : You're right. Traditionally, the elderly were taken care of at home by their children. Now, with smaller families and more nuclear families, it seems we need to have alternatives. I think we need more nursing homes and senior citizen communities.

日本はもっとロボットを使えば

F：日本の出生率の低さについて何度も耳にするけど。いったいどういうことなの？

J：初婚年齢が高くなって、生まれる子どもの数が減ってしまったのさ。ここ何年もの間、出生率はとても低くなっているし、事実、日本の人口は減り始めているんだ。

F：それはいいことじゃない？　日本は人口が多すぎるのよ。

J：いい側面と悪い側面とがあるよ。つまり、働く人が減るということは、当然、納税者も減ることを意味するんだ。それと同時に、人口の多くが高齢化するため、医療関連などの政府支出も増加する可能性が高い。日本経済に与える悪影響は大きいんだ。政府は僕たちの税金を引き上げる可能性が高いね。

F：全然いいことじゃないわね。日本はもっとロボットを使えばいいのに。

J：そうだね。たしかにオートメーション化も効果的だね。定年を引き上げるのも効果的だ。それに、子育てしながら働きたいと思っている女性の環境を整備する必要があるね。保育所の数を増やすと、ずいぶん助かるはずだよ。

F：高齢者の介護も必要になるわね。これは大変な問題だわ。

J：そのとおり。昔からお年寄りの面倒は家で子どもたちが見ていたんだ。今は家族が少なくなって、核家族化しているから、ほかの選択肢が必要だよ。介護施設や、高齢者のためのコミュニティを増やす必要があると思うね。

19

Family Issues

対話

What's the deal with that?：
　それがどうかしたのですか。
you see：ほら

put a strain on 〜：〜を損なう
retirement age：定年

Dialogue 2 | 対話

What is a parasite single?

J : Have you heard about "parasite singles"?

F : No, but it sounds terrible. What is it?

J : Many young adults continue to live with their parents. Some people say they are immature and selfish.

F : What do you think?

J : I think it's okay as long as the parents are happy with the situation and the children do their fair share of the housework. And the ones that work have large disposable incomes. Restaurants, department stores, and travel agencies get a lot of business from these so-called parasite singles.

F : I keep hearing bad news about young people. It seems to be exaggerated.

J : You're right. The media tends to sensationalize issues involving juveniles. Nevertheless, there have been some very unusual crimes committed by juveniles in the past several years. Sometimes there doesn't seem to be any clear reason for the crime.

F : Is it because of drugs?

J : I don't think so. School and social pressures have been blamed. Parents have been blamed. Some people say that the kids are spoiled and too materialistic. I'm not sure what the cause is—I don't think anybody really knows.

「パラサイトシングル」 って何？

J：「パラサイトシングル」という言葉は聞いたことある？

F：いや、でもすごい言葉だね。いったいどういうことだい？

J：若い大人の多くがそのまま両親と一緒に住んでいる、ということ。そのような人たちは未成熟で、独善的だと言う人もいるわ。

F：君はどう思う？

J：両親がそれで満足していて、子どものほうもやるべき家事をちゃんとやっているのなら、問題ないと思うわ。それに、仕事をしていれば可処分所得がたくさん残ることになるし。レストランやデパート、旅行会社なんかは、パラサイトシングルと呼ばれる人たちを相手にいい商売ができるわね。

F：若い人たちについて、悪い話ばかり聞かされるよね。ちょっと誇張されすぎているように思うけど。

J：そのとおりよ。マスコミが若い人が起こした事件をセンセーショナルに取り上げすぎるのよ。それでも、ここ何年かの間に、これまでになかったような犯罪を青少年が引き起こすケースがあったわね。犯罪の動機が全くわからないような事件もあるように思えるわ。

F：それはドラッグのせいかい？

J：そうじゃないと思う。学校や社会が彼らを追い込んでいるとも、親のせいだともいわれているけど。子どもたちが甘やかされすぎていて、お金とか物ばかり大事にしすぎると指摘する人もいるの。でも、私には原因はよくわからない。誰も本当のところはわかってないと思うわ。

immature：未熟の
selfish：自己中心的な
fair share：それ相応の分量
disposable income：可処分所得
exaggerated：誇張されて

sensationalize：
　　～をセンセーショナルに取り上げる
juvenile：青少年
spoil：～を甘やかす
materialistic：物質主義の

Introduction | 概説

MP3
79

日本は今、さまざまな困難や課題に直面しています。日本にはそれらを乗り切る資質があるのでしょうか。

Like any country, Japan faces various difficulties and challenges as it experiences the many changes of the early 21st century. Although the mass media has been especially pessimistic about Japan's prospects, they seem to overlook many of the advantages Japan has.

少子高齢化や移民の少なさによって労働力不足が予期されます。しかし、見方を変えると、日本はまだ豊かな労働資源を持っています。

Japan's low birth rate and relatively small number of immigrants has resulted in a society that is aging rapidly. As Japan works to solve the problems associated with an aged society, other countries will likely look at the Japanese model to see what works, or what doesn't work. One such problem is the predicted labor shortage and resulting loss of tax revenue. But keep in mind that many young adults and women, especially mothers, are currently underemployed or not employed at all. Furthermore, many workers reaching retirement age are healthy enough to continue working for many years. These people represent a reserve force of Japanese workers.

近隣諸国との友好関係と核拡散問題も大きな課題です。対処の鍵は、互恵貿易と平和主義にあるようです。

Another challenge facing the country is to maintain peace and harmony with its neighbors, and to encourage a nuclear-free world.

　どの国にもいえることですが、日本は21世紀を迎えてすぐに起こった数々の変化を経て、さまざまな困難や課題に直面しています。マスコミは日本の行く末について特に悲観的ですが、日本が持つ数多くの有利な点を見落としているようにも思えます。

pessimistic：悲観的な	overlook：〜を見落とす

　日本の低い出生率や比較的少ない移民の数は、急速な高齢化をもたらしました。日本が高齢社会に関連する問題の解決に取り組む中、他国は、どの政策が効果的で、どの政策がそうでないかを見極めるためのモデルとして、日本に注目していくことでしょう。高齢社会がもたらす問題の一つは、労働力不足とそれに伴う税収の減少が予期されることです。しかし、多くの若者や女性、特に母親は、現在パートで働いているか無職であることを忘れてはなりません。加えて、定年に届く年齢層の労働者の多くが、この後何年も働き続けられるほど健康です。こういった人材は日本の予備の労働力といえます。

labor shortage：労働力不足	underemployed：常時雇用でない
tax revenue：税収	reserve：予備の

　日本が直面するもう一つの課題は、近隣諸国と平和的で友好的な関係を保ちつつ、核兵器の廃絶を世界に促すことです。第二次世界大戦終結から長い

Many years after the end of World War II, there still is lingering animosity among the countries of East Asia. Nevertheless, the amount of mutually beneficial trade between Japan and countries like South Korea and China makes it unlikely that tensions will escalate into armed conflict.

As for nuclear weapons, Japan has strongly spoken in favor of nuclear non-proliferation, yet more and more countries have joined the Nuclear Club. Japan, for its part, still embraces its postwar vow to remain a peaceful country.

ハイテク分野で主導権を握る日本。激しい国際競争にさらされ、人々の収入格差が広がっているものの、日本の社会は暴動などが起こることなく、安定しています。

Japan has long been recognized as a nation that exports a wide variety of high-quality products. In this sense, Japan has prospered from globalization since long before it became a buzzword. Japan continues to be a leader in many high tech fields like electronics, high-speed rail transportation, and robotics.

Nevertheless, the high growth period of the 60's and 70's is a distant memory. Strong competition in global markets has forced Japan to adjust. Many Japanese companies have shifted production to countries with lower wages. Job opportunities have shrunk, and many companies have increased the hiring of irregular workers who receive relatively low pay and can easily be dismissed. The result is a widening income gap between those with stable, full-time jobs and those who just get by. This trend is especially distressing for a society that places so much value on social harmony and equality. But what is notable is that these new challenges have not resulted in social unrest as they have in so many other countries. Japanese people are used to working hard and are known for their perseverance. The nation has survived adversity many times before.

年月が過ぎた現在、東アジア諸国にはいまだに反日感情が残っています。しかし一方で、韓国や中国といった国々と、日本の間に見られる互恵的な貿易額を考えると、国家間の緊張が武力衝突へと発展する可能性は低いでしょう。

　核兵器について言うと、日本はこれまで核不拡散を強く訴えてきましたが、核保有国の仲間入りをする国が増えているのが現状です。日本側としては、依然として戦後の平和主義への誓いを堅持しています。

animosity：反感、敵意
armed conflict：武力衝突

nuclear non-proliferation：核不拡散
the Nuclear Club：核保有諸国

　日本は長い間、さまざまな高品質の製品を輸出する国として認識されてきました。その意味では、日本はグローバリゼーションが流行語になるはるか以前から、グローバリゼーションの恩恵を受けて繁栄してきました。日本は今後も、電子機器、高速鉄道輸送、ロボット工学などのハイテク分野の多くで、世界のリーダーとして君臨し続けるでしょう。

　とは言っても、1960年代や70年代の高度経済成長は遠い昔の話です。国際市場における熾烈な競争に、日本は順応せざるを得なくなっています。多くの日本企業が労働コストの低い国に生産拠点を移しています。雇用機会は縮小し、企業の多くが賃金の低い解雇も簡単な非正規労働者を増やしました。その結果、安定した常勤の職に就いている人と、日々やりくりしている人の間の収入格差が広がりました。この傾向は、調和や平等を重視する社会にとって特に大きな悩みです。しかし、注目すべき点は、他国ではこれらの新しい問題が社会不安を引き起こすのに、日本ではそうなりません。日本人は、勤勉に慣れており、忍耐強いことで知られています。日本人は、これまでに幾度となく逆境を乗り越えてきました。

buzzword：流行語、専門語
distant memory：昔の思い出
get by：なんとかやっていく

place value on 〜：〜を重視する
perseverance：忍耐強い
adversity：逆境

世界中が直面する環境問題。限られた自然資源を有効活用してきた日本人は、この分野でもリーダーシップを発揮できそうです。

Another challenge for Japan and the rest of the world is dealing with climate change as well as other environmentally related problems. Again, Japan has certain advantages as the country faces these problems. A well-developed mass transit system means that many people do not need gasoline-burning automobiles. Furthermore, Japan is a leader in the development of automobiles that have alternative propulsion systems.

2011年に起こった東日本大震災の傷跡は深く、数多くの未解決問題が日本を待ち受けています。

Japan still faces significant challenges regarding the 2011 disaster in the Tohoku region. Many thousands of people who left the region have not been able to return, or do not want to return, for various reasons. The attempt to safely decommission the nuclear power plants is ongoing and will be extraordinarily difficult and expensive. Many tough choices have to be made. How should the county's energy policy change? To what extent should damaged coastal areas be rebuilt? How can the country protect itself from future disasters?

歴史を振り返ると、日本は数多くの大変動を知恵と知識で乗り越えてきました。今こそ、その経験を生かす時なのかもしれません。

In Japan's long history, the Japanese have faced many major political, societal, and economic upheavals. In response to these upheavals, the country adapted and changed, fully employing the country's accumulated wisdom and knowledge. Japan now faces enormous challenges—it will be necessary for the people to weather through the difficulties, believe in their strengths, and utilize their potential to the fullest.

日本、および他国のすべてが直面するもう一つの課題が、気候変動を含む環境関連の問題に対処することです。これらの問題に向き合う中、ここでも日本はある優位性を持っています。高度に発達した大量輸送システムのおかげで、ほとんどの日本人はガソリンを消費する自動車を使う必要がないのです。それに加え、日本は内燃機関に代わる推進システムを備えた自動車開発においてリーダー格なのです。

climate change：気候変動 ┊ propulsion system：推進システム

　日本はいまだに、東北地方で起こった2011年の大災害に関する重要課題に直面しています。被災地域を去った多くの人たちは、さまざまな理由から帰還できていませんし、帰還したくない人もいます。被災した原子力発電所を安全に廃炉へと導く作業は進行中ではあるものの、多大な困難と膨大な費用がかかることになります。日本のエネルギー政策をどのように変えるべきか、被災地の沿岸地域はどの程度まで再建すべきか、将来的な災害からどのようにして日本を守るのか、など、難しい選択も数多くあります。

decommission：（原子炉の）廃炉 ┊ ongoing：進行中で

　長い歴史の中で、日本は数多くの政治的、社会的、経済的な大変動に直面してきました。これらの大変動に対し、日本が蓄積してきた知恵や知識を駆使して、日本は順応し、変化してきました。日本は今、途方もない課題に直面しています。今後の日本人に必要なのは、日本人の強みを信じてこれらの困難を乗り切り、持てる潜在能力を最大限に発揮していくことなのです。

upheaval：大変動、激変 ┊ weather (through) 〜：〜を切り抜ける

 **Dialogue** | 対話

How's that for resilience!

F : I keep reading in the English language newspapers about all the problems in Japan. Do the Japanese newspapers say the same thing?

J : I'm afraid so. There seem to be a lot of challenges facing Japan right now. The national debt is too high, the population is aging, and the political system seems … what's the word—dysfunctional.

F : Yes, I was reading about the Japanese debt. I know it's huge, but it's mostly financed by Japanese institutions. You don't owe the money to some foreign entity.

J : That's a good point, but Japan is aging. It seems unfair to expect the younger generations to deal with this problem.

F : You know, where I come from, recessions are harsh. You might see long lines at the unemployment offices. You see vacant homes and shops. You see rising crime, and on one occasion a full-blown riot. Here in Japan I see building construction going on. I see lines, not at the unemployment office, but at the *pachinko* parlors and Tokyo Disneyland. I can't help but think that the problems are exaggerated.

J : I like your optimism. I just wish more Japanese would see it your way. But on the other hand, Japan has a history of quickly changing and adapting when it's faced with great adversity. Maybe these feelings of gloom will shake Japan to reinvent itself.

F : What do you mean?

この立ち直りの早さってどうよ！

F： 英字新聞を読んでいると日本が抱える問題があれこれいつも出ているね。日本の新聞も同じかい？

J： 残念ながらそうね。今、日本が直面している課題が山ほどあるように思えるわ。日本の負債はあまりに巨額だし、国民も高齢化してしまって、それに政治のシステムも……、何て言うんだったっけ、そう、機能不全に思えるの。

F： そうだね。日本の負債について書いている記事を読んだよ。たしかに負債額は大きいけど、債権者は日本の機関がほとんどだよ。外国の組織にお金を借りているわけではないし。

J： それは救いね。でも日本は高齢化しているわ。若い世代にこの問題の処理を求めるのは公平じゃないように思えるの。

F： 知っているかい？　僕の国では景気後退が深刻さ。職業安定所には長い行列ができている。家や店も空っぽ。犯罪も多くなっているし、ある時なんて本格的な暴動も起こったよ。ここ日本ではビル建設が進んでいるし、長い行列も、職業安定所じゃなくパチンコ店や東京ディズニーランドでしか見ないよ。どう考えても、問題が誇張されているようにしか思えないけどね。

J： その楽観主義、好きよ。もっと多くの日本人があなたみたいな物の見方をしたらと思うわ。でもその半面、日本は大きな逆境に直面したとき、すばやく変化して順応していく歴史があるの。今の暗澹（あんたん）たる気持ちが日本を大変革へと揺り動かすかもしれないわ。

F： どういう意味だい？

J : After Japan's isolation period, in the late 19th century, it came to realize that the industrialized powers in Europe and America were growing stronger and were a threat. In fact, parts of China, Southeast Asia, and South Asia had already been colonized. Japan quickly embarked on a program to modernize, and that we did! In fact, Japan defeated Russia in the **Russo-Japanese War** in 1905. It was the first time an Asian country had defeated a European power in modern times.

F : I hate to remind you that 40 years after that, Japan was at the wrong end of the stick.

J : Exactly, but after losing the **Pacific War**, Japan again rebounded and became an economic powerhouse. How's that for resilience!

F : Hmm, you sound like quite the optimist yourself.

J : 19世紀後半に日本の鎖国時代が終わって、ヨーロッパやアメリカの先進工業国の力がより強大になり、脅威となってきたことに日本は気づいたの。事実、中国の一部や東南アジア、南アジアの諸国はすでに植民地化されていたわ。日本は急速に近代化の計画へと乗り出し、それを実現したの。実際、1905年の日露戦争で日本がロシアを破って、現代史ではアジアの国がヨーロッパの列強を破った最初の例となったわ。

F : これを言うのは嫌だけど、その40年後、日本は完全に判断を誤っちゃうよね。

J : たしかに。でも太平洋戦争に負けた後、日本はまた盛り返して経済大国になったわ。この立ち直りの早さってどうよ！

F : ふーん。君もかなりの楽観主義者じゃないか。

---

resilience：復元力
debt：負債、借金
dysfunctional：機能不全の
institution：組織、団体
entity：組織、団体
recession：景気後退、不景気
full-blown：本格的な
optimism：楽観主義

shake 〜 to *do*：〜を揺り動かして*do*させる
reinvent *oneself*：立ち直る
embark on 〜：〜に乗り出す
at the wrong end of the stick：
　完全に判断を誤って
How's that for 〜：すごく〜ではないか
⇒How about 〜に近いが、主に直前に述べた事柄に言及して用いる。

Tokyo: Japan's Heartbeat
東京：日本の中枢

Greater Tokyo Area: An overview
首都圏：全体像

Size and Importance │ 規模と機能

MP3
81

　The Greater **Tokyo** Metropolitan area contains Japan's two largest urban areas—**Tokyo** and Yokohama. Over 35 million people live in this area—sometimes in very densely populated neighborhoods. Many of Japan's largest corporations and universities are located here, as are five professional baseball teams. The Greater **Tokyo** Metropolitan area has several of the world's largest train stations by passenger volume. And the list goes on!

　In many ways the greater **Tokyo** Metropolitan area is different from the rest of Japan. With this in mind, we'd like to introduce this area in more detail.

🔍 Tokyo → p.48

Tokyo Metropolis Overview │ 東京都概観

MP3
82

　Although many people think of **Tokyo** as a city, it is in fact one of the 47 prefectures of Japan. Officially called **Tokyo** Metropolis, it contains 26 cities in the less-populated western part and 23 special wards in the more populated eastern areas. These 23 wards have their own elected leader and council, and operate much like a city. The government now uses the term "city" in their official English translation.

　首都圏には、東京と横浜という、日本最大規模の2都市があります。首都圏には3,500万もの人が住んでおり、人口密度が極めて高い地域もあります。日本最大規模の企業や大学の多くが首都圏にあり、プロ野球チームも5つが同地域をホームグラウンドとしています。また、首都圏には乗降客数で世界最大級の駅が複数存在します。このように、その特徴は枚挙にいとまがありません！

　いろいろな意味で、首都圏は日本の他の地域と異なります。このことを念頭に置いて、首都圏をさらに詳しく説明していきましょう。

the Greater Tokyo Metropolitan area： 　首都圏	densely populated：人口密度が高い by passenger volume：利用客数において

　多くの人は、東京を「市」（city）と考えていますが、実のところ東京は、日本にある47都道府県（prefectures）の一つです。正式には東京都（Tokyo Metropolis）と称され、人口密度が低めの西部地域に26市、人口密度が高めの東部地域に23の特別区があります。東京23区は、区民による直接選挙で選ばれる区長と区議会を有しており、運営上は市に似ています。政府は今では、その正式英訳語として"city"＊を用いています。ともかく、東京都と

At any rate, the entity known as **Tokyo** Metropolis is the capital of Japan and also the location of the Imperial Palace.

Climate | 気候

Tokyo belongs to the North Temperate Zone, with a mild climate and four distinct seasons. In spring, the weather is mild, with cherry blossoms in bloom throughout the city. May is perhaps the most comfortable month in **Tokyo**, with mostly warm and clear weather. From June to mid-July, there is a rainy season, which occasionally brings heavy rains. This is when the hydrangeas bloom. When the rainy season ends, it gets hot and humid. Sometimes temperatures exceed 30 or even 35 degrees Celsius. The summer heat continues into September but usually ceases in late September.

In autumn, rainy days and fine days alternate, and the temperature gradually goes down, resulting in beautiful colored leaves throughout the city. As winter approaches, it is often clear—a great time to view Mt. Fuji. The air gets chilly and dry as the north winds become stronger. In January and February there is sometimes snow. By February plum blossoms bloom, and soon after the cherry blossom buds grow bigger. Tokyoites eagerly keep track of the cherry blossom front as it approaches the city from the south. The cycle is complete.

いう自治体は日本の首都であり、皇居の所在地でもあるわけです。

*例えば、新宿区は、Shinjuku City が正式英語名とされています。

think of *A* as *B*：AをBと見なす	council：会議、（ここでは）区議会
special ward：特別区	entity：存在、（ここでは）自治体

　東京は北温帯に属しており、気候も温暖で四季の区別がはっきりしています。春の天候は穏やかで、あちこちで桜が咲き乱れます。東京の5月は、暖かくて晴れの日も多く、おそらく最も過ごしやすい時期となります。6月から7月中旬にかけては雨季があり、時に、大雨に見舞われます。この季節はアジサイが満開になります。雨季が終わると、蒸し暑い季節となります。気温は時に30℃を超え、35℃を上回る場合さえあります。夏の暑さは9月に入っても続きますが、9月下旬にはだいたい収まります。

　秋には、雨の日と晴れの日が交互にやってきて、気温も次第に下がっていき、東京の至るところで美しい紅葉が見られるようになります。冬が近づくと、空気も澄んできて、富士山がよく見える時期になります。北風が強くなり、空気も冷たく乾燥するようになります。1月と2月にはときどき雪も降ります。2月には梅の花が咲き、間もなく桜のつぼみも大きくなります。南から近づいて来る桜前線を東京都民が熱心に見守る中、また新しい春がめぐってきます。

the Temperate Zone：温帯	bud：つぼみ
cease：終わる	Tokyoites：東京都民
alternate：交互に訪れる	keep track of ～：～の経過を追う

History | 歴史

Tokyo was called Edo in premodern times. Development of the Edo area started in the 11th century, and by the 16th century the area had become an important traffic hub. However, in the 17th century Edo was transformed. At the end of Japan's warring period, the new *shogun*, Tokugawa Ieyasu, established the Tokugawa Shogunate in Edo. Although **Kyoto** was still the official capital, Edo became the country's new political center. The Tokugawa *shoguns* would rule Japan from Edo for the next 265 years. This period is now called the **Edo Period**, and during that time Edo would become the largest city in the world.

During the **Edo Period** there were over 200 feudal lords, called *daimyo*, who controlled different areas of Japan. Early on the Tokugawa government established a way to control the *daimyo* and to assess the loyalty of the feudal lords. The *daimyo* were instructed to spend time in both Edo and their respective fiefs, typically spending alternate years in each place.

This policy was to have profound effects on Edo and the rest of Japan. Roads were built or improved throughout Japan in order to handle the large feudal processions. The *daimyo* built gardens and grand estates in Edo. Merchants, craftspeople, and commoners moved into Edo for jobs and business opportunities. Additional housing and infrastructure had to be built for the rapidly growing population.

Another policy that the ***Shogun*** government adopted was the isolation policy, or ***sakoku*** policy. With some exceptions, Japan was cut off from the rest of the world. This may have protected Japan early on when the Western powers first colonized parts of Asia. But as Europe and the United States industrialized, their power expanded, and they increasingly demanded that Japan end its isolation policy.

In the mid-19th century, the ***Shogun*** government reopened the country. A period of instability followed, leading to the collapse of the

　近代より前の東京は、江戸と呼ばれていました。江戸地域の開発は11世紀に始まりましたが、16世紀になるころには、江戸は交通の要衝になっていました。しかし、江戸が全貌を変えるのは17世紀です。戦国時代の終わりに、新しい将軍、徳川家康が江戸に幕府を開きました。日本の正規の首都は依然として京都でしたが、江戸は日本の政治の新たな中心地となりました。その後、徳川家の将軍が265年間にわたって、江戸を中心に日本を支配します。その期間は今では江戸時代と呼ばれ、江戸の町は世界最大の都市へと発展していきます。

　江戸時代には、大名と呼ばれる200以上の領主が日本を分割支配していました。江戸幕府は早い時期に、大名を統制し、彼らの忠誠を評価する制度を確立しました。大名は江戸と領地の両方に、通常は1年ずつ交互に住むように命じられたのです。

　この政策は、江戸と他の地域に大きな影響を与えることになります。長蛇の大名行列が移動できるように、日本中に街道が新設・整備されました。大名は江戸に庭園付きの大邸宅を築きました。商人や職人や庶民が仕事や商機を求めて江戸へ移住してきます。急増する人口に見合うように、新しく住宅やインフラの整備が必要になりました。

　幕府が施行したもう一つの政策は、鎖国でした。一部の例外を除き、日本は外国との関係を断ったのです。西洋列強がアジアの一角に最初に植民地を設けたころの早い時期であれば、鎖国政策によって日本を守ることができたかもしれません。しかし、ヨーロッパ諸国や米国は、産業革命を達成して勢力を拡大し、日本に鎖国政策を終えるよう、ますます圧力をかけるようになりました。

　19世紀中ごろ、幕府は閉じていた国の門戸を再び開きました。その後、動乱の時期が続き、江戸幕府は倒壊への道をたどることになりました。

　1868年、明治天皇を元首に戴く新政府が樹立されました。公式な首都は京都から江戸へ遷され、名称も「東の都」を意味する東京に改められたのです。徳川家が所有していたかつての江戸城は新政府に接収され、新たな皇居に指定されました。日本は急速な近代化・西洋化を経て、20世紀初期には、

Tokugawa Shogunate.

In 1868, a new government was established with the Emperor Meiji at its head. The official capital was moved from **Kyoto** to Edo. The name Edo was changed to **Tokyo**, meaning "eastern capital." The former Edo Castle, owned by the Tokugawa Clan, was confiscated by the new government and designated as the new Imperial Palace. Japan went through rapid modernization and Westernization. By the early 20th century, Japan had fully industrialized and was the most powerful nation in Asia.

In 1923, **Tokyo** was hit by the Great Kanto Earthquake, which resulted in devastation of much of **Tokyo**. Although the city was quickly rebuilt, the disaster continues to remind Tokyoites that a devastating earthquake may someday revisit the city.

In the 1930s, military ambition eventually led Japan to all-out war with China in 1937. By 1939, Japan had control over large areas of China but was not able to secure complete victory. Meanwhile, tensions with the United States escalated into the **Pacific War** in 1941. Despite early victories for Japan, the United States proved to be more resilient than expected. Eventually, the U.S. recaptured islands in the Pacific that allowed land-based aircraft to reach Japan. As the capital of Japan, **Tokyo** was naturally a prime target. The city was heavily bombed, and over 100,000 people lost their lives. The war ended in 1945.

The immediate postwar period was a time of hardship, but it was also a time of profound change for the country and for **Tokyo**. With change comes new opportunities. In the 1950s and 60s, Japan saw rapid economic growth. Tokyo Tower, which was completed in 1958, became a landmark of Japan's economic restoration. **Tokyo** hosted the Olympic Games in 1964 and has since continued to grow as a metropolis, continuing to play a key role in Japan's economy.

🔍 *shogun* → p.28   Kyoto → p.48   Edo Period → p.26
   sakoku → p.28   Pacific War → p.36

産業革命を完遂し、アジアで最強の国となりました。

1923 年、東京は関東大震災に襲われます。その結果、東京の多くが廃墟となりました。東京はすぐに復興しましたが、関東大震災は、破滅的な地震がまたいつか東京を襲うかもしれないという恐怖を都民に植え付けることになりました。

1930 年代になって、軍の野望はついに 1937 年の中国との全面戦争を引き起こしました。1939 年までの間に中国における日本の占領地は拡大しましたが、完全勝利を得ることはできませんでした。そんな中、米国との緊張関係は、1941 年に太平洋戦争へと発展しました。開戦初期は日本が勝利しましたが、米国は予想以上に立ち直りが早く、最終的には米国が太平洋の島々を奪還し、そこを基地として陸上飛行機を日本に飛ばせるようになりました。東京は日本の首都であったため、当然、格好の標的となりました。東京は激しい空襲にさらされ、10 万人以上が犠牲となったのです。戦争は 1945 年に終結しました。

戦後直後は苦しい時期でしたが、日本そして東京にとって、変革の時期でもありました。変化とともに新しい機会も訪れたのです。1950 年代と 60 年代には、日本は高度経済成長期を迎えました。1958 年に完成した東京タワーは、日本経済復興のランドマークともなりました。東京は、1964 年にオリンピック競技大会の開催国となり、以後、日本経済において中心的な役割を担いながら、大都市として発展し続けています。

premodern times：近代以前
traffic hub：交通の要衝
assess：〜を評価する
alternate years：隔年
profound：重大な、深い
feudal procession：大名行列
commoner：庶民
be cut off from 〜：〜から閉ざされる
instability：不安定

collapse：崩壊
clan：一族、一門
be confiscated by 〜：
　〜によって接収される
go through 〜：〜を経験する
all-out war：全面戦争
resilient：立ち直りの早い
hardship：苦悩

Transbortation｜交通

MP3 85

Public transportation is well-developed all over Japan, but nothing compares to **Tokyo**. If you open a train and subway map, you'll find that all the different color-coded lines look like a bowl of colored spaghetti. Just for reference, let's introduce the Yamanote Line. This line is circular and encompasses the central part of **Tokyo**. Numerous train and subway lines connect with the stations of the Yamanote Line. The **Tokyo** train and subway network is the preferred mode of travel for millions of workers, students, tourists, and anyone else needing to get around in the metropolis.

To make fare payment fast and efficient, rechargeable IC cards are available. A card will automatically deduct the fare when scanned over a reader at the ticket gate. Similar cards are available across Japan. Of course cash is still accepted. Another big time saver when using the **Tokyo** train and subway system is that there are dedicated websites and phone applications that can help you with times, transfer points, costs, and more.

S ightseeing Areas / Travel options for Tokyo
観光地／東京観光の選択肢

Historical Places｜史跡

MP3 86

When someone comes to central **Tokyo** for the first time, they may notice that the city is filled with Western-style concrete buildings and high rises. But due to the city's long history, there are many places of historical interest all across **Tokyo**. They include the massive stone walls and outer buildings of the Imperial Palace, former residences of feudal lords of the Edo days, and beautiful Japanese gardens such as

　日本はどこでも公共交通機関がよく発達していますが、東京は群を抜いています。電車や地下鉄の地図を広げると、すべて異なる色にぬり分けられた路線が、カラフルなスパゲッティのように広がっています。参考までに、山手線を紹介しましょう。山手線は環状線で、東京の中心部の周りを走っています。おびただしい数の電車や地下鉄の路線が、山手線の駅と接続されています。東京の列車・地下鉄網は、労働者、学生、旅行者を含め、都内を移動する必要がある数百万の人たちにとって、格好の交通手段となっています。

　運賃の支払いを迅速かつ効率よく行うために、チャージが可能なICカードを使うことができます。改札にある読み取り機にかざすと、カードが自動的に運賃を差し引きます。同類のカードが日本全国で発行されていますが、もちろん、現金も使用できます。東京の鉄道や地下鉄を使うときに、時間短縮に大いに役立つもう一つの手段が、専用のウェブサイトやスマホのアプリで、時刻表、接続駅、運賃その他を提示してくれます。

encompass：〜を取り囲む　　　　　　deduct：〜を差し引く
get around：あちこちに移動する　　　　dedicated：専用の
rechargeable：チャージ式の

　東京の中心部を初めて訪れる人は、この町が洋風建築物や高層ビルだらけであることに気がつくでしょう。しかし、東京の歴史は長いため、街中に数多くの史跡が遺っています。たとえば、皇居の重厚な石垣や外郭、江戸時代に建てられた大名の旧宅や、六義園・小石川後楽園といった美しい日本庭園などなど。また、興味深い寺や神社もあちこちにあります。有名なものでは、隅田川のほとりにある浅草寺、原宿駅近くにある明治神宮などが挙げられま

Rikugien and Koishikawa-Korakuen. There are also many interesting **temples** and **shrines** throughout the city, the more famous being Sensoji Temple along the Sumida River and Meiji Shrine located near Harajuku Station. Some Western-style structures built in the late 19th and early 20th centuries still stand grandly in the heart of **Tokyo**, including Nicolai Cathedral—a Greek Orthodox Church. And not so old, but still significant, is the beautifully designed Yoyogi National Gymnasium, one of the venues used for the 1964 Tokyo Olympic Games.

🔍 temples → p.144   shrines → p.144

Tokyo Bay and Rivers｜東京湾と河川

Several big rivers flow through the Kanto plain, where **Tokyo** lies, and they used to cause a lot of floods in the old days. In the **Edo Period**, the Tokugawa Shogunate, aiming to prevent floods and improve transportation, made significant improvements to the waterways of Edo. Rivers were rerouted and new channels were made. Edo became a city of water. The development of the waterfront also started in the **Edo Period**. Areas of Tokyo Bay were reclaimed to expand land areas, and the process continues in the modern era. Although reclaimed land was once used primarily for industrial purposes, today sightseeing spots like the Odaiba waterfront and the Tokyo Disney Resort also sit on reclaimed land.

The rivers and the Tokyo Bay waterfront continue to be an important part of **Tokyo**'s cityscape. There are many parks and walkways along the water. You can also use water buses to travel along the Sumida River and into Tokyo Bay. Commercial fishing and sport fishing are popular. Now the **Tokyo** government plans to improve the water transportation systems for sightseeing and as an alternative transportation means in times of disasters. **Tokyo** will never be Venice, but sometime in the future the city may once again be a city of water.

す。19世紀末から20世紀初期に建てられた西洋建築では、ギリシャ正教の大聖堂であるニコライ堂などがあり、東京の中心で今でも威容を誇っています。それほど古くはありませんが、重要な建築物として挙げられるのが、美しい設計の国立代々木競技場です。同競技場は、1964年の東京オリンピックの舞台の一つとなりました。

Greek Orthodox Church：ギリシャ正教会　｜　venue：開催地

　東京が位置する関東平野を貫いて何本もの大きな河川が流れており、昔は頻繁に洪水を引き起こしたものです。江戸時代に幕府は、洪水の防止と交通の整備を目指し、江戸の水路を徹底整備しました。河川の流路が変えられ、新たな水路が開かれ、江戸は水の都となったのです。ウォーターフロントの開発も江戸時代に始まりました。東京湾岸地域は陸地を拡大するために埋め立てられ、現代に至っても埋め立ては続けられています。かつて埋め立て地は主に産業用地として使われていましたが、今日では、お台場ウォーターフロントや東京ディズニーリゾートなどの観光地も埋め立て地にあります。

　河川と東京湾ウォーターフロントは、今でも東京の景観において重要な役割を果たしています。水辺には数多くの公園や散策路が設けられています。また、隅田川に沿って東京湾へと人を運ぶ水上バスを利用することもできます。漁業やスポーツフィッシングも盛んです。東京都は、観光および災害時の代替交通手段確保のために、水上交通網の整備を計画しています。ヴェニスとまではいかないでしょうが、近い将来、東京が再び水の都と呼ばれる日がくるかもしれません。

be reclaimed：埋め立てられる　｜　means：手段

Natural Areas │ 自然地域

Even in the heart of **Tokyo**, there are many parks and gardens where greenery flourishes—Shinjuku Gyoen National Garden, Hibiya Park, Ueno Park, Yoyogi Park, and so on. If you venture to the western part of **Tokyo**, you can find many areas of exceptional natural beauty. Mt. Takao and the Tama River area are just two examples of areas that have trekking routes and beautiful views. Both places can be easily reached by train.

And heading to the south, out through Tokyo Bay, we find another surprise. The Izu and Ogasawara Island chains are technically part of **Tokyo** Municipality. These volcanic islands extend far out into the Pacific Ocean. The Ogasawara Islands are about one thousand kilometers from **Tokyo** and feature a subtropical climate and abundant nature.

Shopping Areas │ ショッピング街

Tokyo is a city that provides shopping for almost any interest or taste or budget. For brand goods, the streets in Ginza and Shinjuku are lined with shops and department stores. Shibuya and Ikebukuro are versatile shopping areas, catering to a wide variety of needs and customers. Harajuku is a fashion mecca for young people, especially teenagers. In an area called Kappabashi there is a shopping area for amateur and professional cooks alike. High quality knives, traditional *noren* curtains, and plastic food items are all available. These days, many train stations comprise shopping malls, where a wide variety of food items are available. In the Tokyo Bay area, Odaiba is a popular destination. In addition to shopping malls, Odaiba has beautiful night scenery, a small beach, and some museums.

　東京の中心にでさえ、新宿御苑、日比谷公園、上野公園、代々木公園など、緑に恵まれた数多くの公園や庭園があります。東京の西部へ足を延ばすと、優れた自然景観を有する地が数多くあります。高尾山や多摩川地域はその好例で、トレッキングコースや絶景スポットがあり、いずれも電車で気軽にアクセスできます。

　一方、東京湾を出て南へ行くと、また別の自然景観が現れます。伊豆諸島と小笠原諸島は、行政区画上、東京都の一部です。これらの火山島は太平洋に長く南に伸びて連なっています。小笠原諸島は、東京から約千キロメートル離れており、亜熱帯気候と豊かな自然が特徴です。

venture to 〜：思い切って〜へ行く	municipality：自治体
exceptional：例外的な、並外れた	abundant：豊かな

　東京は、興味があるもの、お好みのもの、予算に合うものなど、どのようなショッピング願望もかなえてくれる街です。ブランド品なら、銀座や新宿の目抜き通りに店舗やデパートが立ち並んでいます。渋谷や池袋は、幅広いニーズや顧客に対応できる、万能のショッピングスポットです。原宿は若い人たち、特にティーンエイジャーに人気のファッションのメッカです。合羽橋と呼ばれる地域は、アマ・プロを問わず、料理好きの買い物天国です。高級包丁や昔ながらののれん、食品サンプルなど、なんでも売っています。最近では、多くの駅の構内に商店街が設けられており、さまざまな食べ物が売られています。東京湾岸地域では、お台場が人気のスポットです。ショッピングモールに加え、美しい夜景や小型のビーチなどがあり、博物館もいくつかあります。

versatile：万能の	comprise：〜を含む

The Olympic Games | オリンピック

Tokyo was the first Asian city to be awarded the Olympic Games. Scheduled to be held in 1940, the event was cancelled because the Second World War had begun. When the war ended in 1945, **Tokyo** and many other Japanese cities were heavily damaged. Those were some tough times, but the city eventually bounced back. In 1957 a **Tokyo** railway company had the world speed record for narrow gauge trains, which inspired Japanese engineers to go for bigger and faster trains. Business was booming, and confidence was building. Tokyo Tower, still an icon of the city, was completed in 1958. It was the tallest freestanding tower in the world. The next year, in 1959, the IOC awarded **Tokyo** the 1964 Olympic Games. What followed was an unprecedented building boom. On October 1, 1964 Japan opened its breakthrough high-speed rail line between **Tokyo** and Osaka—the bullet train. Nine days later, the opening ceremony for the 1964 Olympic Games was held on October 10.

　東京は、アジアの都市として最初のオリンピック開催地に選ばれました。1940年に開催される予定だった東京オリンピックは、第二次世界大戦が始まったために幻に終わりました。戦争が終わった1945年当時、東京を含め多くの日本の都市は大打撃を受けていました。大変な時期ではありましたが、東京はやがて立ち直ります。1957年に東京の鉄道会社が、狭軌列車としては世界最高速度を記録*し、日本の技師たちは、さらに大きくて速い列車の開発に着手しました。景気は良くなり、自信も醸成されていきます。今でも東京の象徴である東京タワーが1958年に完成し、世界で最も高い自立鉄塔となりました。翌年の1959年、世界オリンピック委員会は1964年のオリンピック開催地を東京に決定したのです。その後は、前代未聞の建設ブームが到来しました。1964年10月1日には、画期的な高速鉄道である新幹線が東京・大阪間で開通し、その9日後の10月10日に、1964年東京オリンピックの開会式が行われました。

*この車両は小田急3000形電車で、1957年に東海道線での高速走行試験において、時速145kmを出し、当時の狭軌鉄道における世界記録を樹立しました。

bounce back：立ち直る	icon：象徴的存在、アイコン
narrow gauge：	freestanding tower：自立鉄塔
狭軌の（鉄道のレールの間隔が標準軌間	unprecedented：前代未聞の
より狭い、ということ）	breakthrough：画期的な

Tokyo is Awesome!

J : Well, it seems like your stay in Japan is almost over. Did you enjoy your time here?

F : Yes, of course. I've had a lot of great experiences, but I feel like I've only cracked the surface. There are so many things to see and do.

J : Then you'll have to come back soon.

F : Exactly.

J : What part of your trip did you enjoy most?

F : Hmm, that's difficult. Of course I loved seeing the beautiful scenery in the countryside and the historic buildings in **Kyoto** and **Nara**. But I pretty much knew what to expect at those places from reading the travel guide. I think it was **Tokyo** that was most fascinating. It was like a new adventure every day.

J : What do you mean?

F : Well, sometimes it was the huge contrast between traditional culture and a modern big city. One minute I'm walking out of Shinjuku Station, the busiest train station in the world, and the next I'm in a beautiful garden with a tea house, stone lanterns, and a pond full of colorful carp.

J : I think you can find this kind of contrast in other cities like Osaka … or Rome.

F : That's true. But I also found it fascinating to walk thru the streets. There are so many different kinds of shops and people.

J : You mean Takeshita Street in Harajuku? The young people's hangout?

東京ってすごい！

J: 日本での滞在もそろそろ終わりのようだね。楽しめたかい？

F: もちろん。すばらしい体験がたくさんあったわ。でも、表面をなぞっただけって感じね。見ること、やることがあまりに多いんだもの。

J: では、また近いうちに日本に来ないとね。

F: おっしゃるとおり。

J: 旅で一番楽しかったのは何だい？

F: うーん、それは難しいわね。田舎の美しい風景や京都とか奈良の古い建物はもちろん良かったけど、ガイドブックを読んで見どころについてはかなり知っていたからね。やっぱり、一番魅力的だったのは東京だと思うわ。毎日が新しい冒険って感じ。

J: どういうこと？

F: 時折、伝統文化と近代都市の対照的な側面に遭遇したわ。世界一利用客が多い新宿駅を出たと思ったら、すぐに美しい庭園に着いたの。茶室や石灯籠や色とりどりの鯉がいる池があったわ。

J: そういう対照的な側面なら、大阪でも、または、ローマでも見かけるはずだよ。

F: それはそうだわ。でも、通りを歩いているだけでも魅力的だと思ったの。ほんとにいろんなお店や人たちばかりで。

J: 原宿の竹下通りとかかい？　あの若者のたまり場の？

F : That's a really unusual place. The shops are interesting, but I enjoyed people-watching the most. I was really surprised by the gothic-lolita fashion. But there are many interesting places in **Tokyo**, and they all have a different vibe. The Odaiba area was a lot of fun, but so was the Ameyoko area near Ueno Station. I also had fun strolling thru the old-town area around Sensoji Temple.

J : I'm glad to hear you enjoyed yourself. But I have to ask you—is there anything that troubled you during your trip? Maybe the rush hour trains?

F : The rush hour train was just another adventure. It helped me understand how you Tokyoites live. But, I have to be honest—I wouldn't want to ride a rush hour train every day like you do.

J : I'm used to it. So, do you have any complaints at all?

F : You know, I love Japanese food. And there are so many restaurants around, small and large. And the fresh seafood—it's to die for!

J : Are you trying to avoid my question?

F : No, not at all. My complaint is that it was so hard to read the menus. I felt like a child because I had to point at a picture or rely on a Japanese friend like you to help me understand the menu.

J : Ah, yes, I see your point. With tourists to Japan increasing, restaurant managers should consider getting their menus translated into other languages.

F : That would make life easier. But I have to admit, those plastic food displays they put in the front windows of restaurants—that is so awesome.

F： あれってほんとに独特な場所ね。お店も面白いけど、人を見るのが一番楽しめたわ。ゴシック風のロリータファッションには本当にびっくり。でも、東京には面白い場所がたくさんあって、それぞれの雰囲気がまた違うのよ。お台場も楽しかったけど、上野駅の近くのアメ横も良かったわね。浅草寺近辺の古い町並みを歩くのも楽しかったわ。

J： 楽しめたみたいでうれしいよ。でも聞きたことがあるんだ。旅の途中で何か困ったことはなかったかい？　たとえば、ラッシュアワーの電車とか？

F： ラッシュアワーの電車もまた一つの冒険よ。東京都民がどんな生活をしてるかわかったから。でもね、正直言って、あなたみたいに毎日ラッシュアワーの電車に乗るのはごめんだわ。

J： 僕は慣れちゃってるからね。それで、何も不平はないのかい？

F： ほら、私って日本食が好きでしょ。レストランがすごく多くて、大きいのやら小さいのやら。それに新鮮な魚介類ね。とてもすてき。

J： 僕の質問をはぐらかしてるの？

F： 全然。私の不平っていうのは、そのメニューが読めなかったことよ。写真を指し示したり、あなたのような日本人の友達に手伝ってもらったりして、まるで子どもになった気分だったわ。

J： そうだな、その気持ちはわかるよ。日本に来る観光客が増えているから、レストランの経営側もメニューをいろんな言語に訳すことを考えたほうがいいな。

F： それだと日本にいるのも楽になるわね。でも、正直、レストランのショーウィンドーに飾られているプラスチックの食品サンプル、あれはすごいわ。

---

awesome：すごい、最高の
crack the surface：
　　外殻を割る（中身に達していないという意味）
one minute ... and the next 〜：
　　…かと思えば〜（次から次に、というニュアンス）

thru：〜を抜けて（＝through）
hangout：たまり場
vibe：雰囲気（＝vibration）
stroll through 〜：〜をぶらつく、散歩する
to die for：非常にすばらしい

本書に登場するすべてのキーワード、関連キーワードの参照ページ一覧です。

著者紹介

江口 裕之 (Eguchi Hiroyuki)

1957年、長崎県生まれ。CEL 英語ソリューションズ最高教育責任者、通訳案内士（英語）、日本文化研究家。国立北九州高専化学工学科卒業後、プロのミュージシャンとして東京を本拠地に全国で演奏活動を展開。その後、通訳・翻訳家および通訳案内士として活躍。2001年1月、東京に英語学校のCEL英語ソリューションズを設立。2009〜13年、NHK Eテレ語学番組「トラッドジャパン」講師。2017年4〜6月NHKラジオ語学番組「短期集中！3か月英会話」講師。著書に『日本まるごと英単語帳』（NHK出版）、『英語で伝えたい ふつうの日本』（DHC）、音楽CDに『My Good Ol' Songs』（Athor Harmonics / Radio Days）など。

ダニエル・ドゥーマス (Daniel Dumas)

アメリカ合衆国出身、カリフォルニア州立大学卒業。1981年に初来日。1991年に日本に移住して以来、一貫して英語教育に携わる。英会話学校、高校、専門学校など、さまざまな教育現場での豊富な教師経験を持つ。2001年1月、CEL英語ソリューションズ設立と同時に参画。現在、チーフ・インストラクターとして、通訳案内士国家試験対策や英検1級試験対策の英語指導に尽力。英語、日本文化、そして異文化コミュニケーションの指導に専心している。

CEL英語ソリューションズ　http://www.cel-eigo.com/

英語で語る日本事情2020 ［音声ダウンロード版］

2025年3月5日　初版発行

著　者	江口裕之／ダニエル・ドゥーマス	
	©Eguchi Hiroyuki & Daniel Dumas, 2017	
発行者	伊藤秀樹	
発行所	株式会社 ジャパンタイムズ出版	
	〒102-0082 東京都千代田区一番町2-2 一番町第二TGビル2F	
	ウェブサイト　https://jtpublishing.co.jp/	
印刷所	日経印刷株式会社	

本書の内容に関するお問い合わせは、上記ウェブサイトまたは郵便でお受けいたします。
定価はカバーに表示してあります。

万一、乱丁落丁のある場合は、送料当社負担でお取り替えいたします。
（株）ジャパンタイムズ出版・出版営業部あてにお送りください。

Printed in Japan　ISBN978-4-7890-1914-9